FORCED FEDERALISM

AMERICAN INDIAN LAW AND POLICY SERIES
Lindsay G. Robertson, General Editor

Forced Federalism
Contemporary Challenges to Indigenous Nationhood

Jeff Corntassel and Richard C. Witmer

Foreword by Lindsay G. Robertson

UNIVERSITY OF OKLAHOMA PRESS : NORMAN

Library of Congress Cataloging-in-Publication Data

Corntassel, Jeff, 1966–
    Forced federalism : contemporary challenges to indigenous nation-
hood / Jeff Corntassel and Richard C. Witmer ; foreword by Lindsay G.
Robertson.
        p.   cm. — (American Indian law and policy series ; v. 3)
    Includes bibliographical references and index.
    ISBN 978-0-8061-4191-6 (paper)
    1. Indians of North America—Politics and government. 2. Indians
of North America—Government relations. 3. Indians of North America—
Legal status, laws, etc. 4. State government—United States. 5. Local
government—United States. 6. Self-determination, National—United
States. 7. United States—Politics and government. 8. United States—
Race relations. 9. United States—Social Policy. I. Witmer, Richard C.,
1966– II. Title.
    E98.T77.C67 2008
    323.1197—dc22

                                                            2007032084

Forced Federalism: Contemporary Challenges to Indigenous Nationhood is
Volume 3 in the American Indian Law and Policy Series.

The paper in this book meets the guidelines for permanence and durability of the Committee on Production Guidelines for Book Longevity
of the Council on Library Resources. ∞

To Jeff's grandmother
Floris "Bacca" Roberts
and grandfather
Robert J. Corntassel

Contents

Figures and Tables

FIGURES

TABLES

Series Editor's Foreword

Lindsay G. Robertson

Federal Indian policy has been marked by fluctuation. In the early days of the Republic, the federal government sought to remove eastern tribes to the West. When European-Americans began moving west, the policy objective switched to elimination of tribal governments and assimilation of indigenous peoples. The New Deal brought renewed support for indigenous self-governance, a move reversed in the 1950s when Congress again set about assimilating indigenous peoples, this time by terminating the federal-tribal relationship. In the 1970s the U.S. government repudiated termination, and a new era of federal support for indigenous self-governance began. According to conventional wisdom, this modern era of self-determination continues today.

Jeff Corntassel and Richard Witmer II offer a different view. Noting the increasing prevalence of negotiation between tribes and states, often undertaken at federal direction, the authors suggest that the federal policy of self-determination has been replaced by a policy of forced federalism, which compels indigenous polities to participate in the federal order at a subnational level. This, they argue, poses an underappreciated threat to indigenous nationhood. Their thesis is both thought-provoking and unique, and they raise questions important to the continuing dialogue about indigenous rights. Their assessment comes at an apt historical moment. At the very time the United Nations General Assembly adopted the Declaration on the Rights of Indigenous Peoples, a document internationalizing indigenous rights,

Corntassel and Witmer contend indigenous polities in the United States are being federalized.

The University of Oklahoma Press and I are pleased to offer *Forced Federalism* as the third title in the American Indian Law and Policy Series.

Preface

This book is the culmination of more than ten years of speaking with indigenous leaders, conducting surveys of indigenous governments across the country since 1994, and researching the complexities of the forced federalism era (1988–present). Robert Morin first used the term "forced federalism" at a Western Social Sciences Association conference in 1995. At this same conference, we presented our findings on American Indian support of political office seekers from the 1994 election, and the forced federalism project was born. Since that time, we have tried to come to grips with the implications of the forced federalism policy era and its significance for indigenous nations as they confront new challenges with state policymakers. This book is an attempt to navigate the political and economic terrain that is rapidly changing because of policy shifts initiated by the federal devolution of powers to state governments and changing public perceptions of indigenous peoples. Before proceeding, however, it is important to make some terminological distinctions.

Beginning with the colonial construct of "indios" since Columbus's ill-fated attempt at ethnography, the terminological discourse surrounding the first peoples in the Americas has become exceedingly complex. When asked for a favored term to describe the indigenous nations of North America, we usually reply that it is better to make reference to a specific nation's preferred community designation since none of the terms attempting to blend all indigenous people into a single category are adequate. Some researchers and indigenous peoples make a case for preferring certain terms, such as "Native American," over others, such as "tribe." However, as Cherokee sociologist Matthew Snipp notes, the term "Native American" is imprecise in that it "includes Hawaiian natives and the descendants of immigrants from all nations, along with American Indians, Eskimos and Aleuts."[1] This term is also imprecise for referring to indigenous peoples only within the United States, as the Americas denote the entire western hemisphere. Joane Nagel also points out the problems with using "tribe" to designate indigenous nations, as this term is almost exclusively applied to non-European, nonwhite groups.[2]

Indigenous peoples in the United States tend to favor "American Indian," as it is the predominant term used in many treaties, congressional statutes, and executive agreements. In fact, we started this project using "American Indian" when making reference to indigenous peoples, given its widespread use in Native communities and scholarship. However, we have begun to realize that the ways we speak about one another as first peoples need to be decolonized. We will use the terms "indigenous" and "Native" interchangeably in this book to refer to the descendants of the original inhabitants of the United States. While the these terms are already widely used by indigenous and non-indigenous scholars, neither of them adequately describes the approximately 4.1 million indigenous peoples within the United States or the approximately 370 million indigenous peoples worldwide. Whenever possible we will refer to indigenous nations by their preferred community designations but understand that group members may self-identify using broader terms, such as "Native" or "indigenous," to place their identities in a wider context.

In describing how contemporary U.S. and state policies affect indigenous nations during the forced federalism era, it is important to begin by defining federalism. Federalism generally describes dynamic, constitutionally based, intergovernmental relationships between a federal government and its constituent entities, such as states in the United States.[3] The structures and processes of federal systems consist of evolving power sharing arrangements between two or more governmental units, whereby each possesses a degree of autonomy, legitimacy, and constitutional linkages within the overall system. However, since indigenous nations existed well before the formation of the U.S. government, their powers of self-determination are not derived from federal or state constitutions. Well before "new federalism" policies, which precipitated a widespread transfer of federal powers to state governments during the 1970s and 1980s, indigenous nations had held a political status higher than that of states. In fact, the federal trust relationship, which is an exclusive federal government to indigenous government relationship based on prior treaties, direct consultation with Congress on indigenous affairs, federal statutory obligations, and court decisions, was historically constructed to protect indigenous nations from state encroachment. Therefore, newly (d)evolving federal arrangements since the passage of the U.S. Indian Gaming and Regulatory Act (IGRA) of 1988 force indigenous leaders to negotiate with state governments for policy jurisdiction regarding governance, taxation, economic development, hunting and fishing on Native homelands, and so on. It is this reshaping of U.S. federalism from the 1990s to the present day that we examine in this book to better understand how indigenous governments are responding to these new challenges to their nationhood.

Because of the widespread confusion over the use of the term "sovereignty," which is often used to describe indigenous inherent political, economic, and cultural powers at both the collective and individual levels, we instead use the terms "nationhood" and "self-determination." As eminent Lakota scholar Vine Deloria, Jr., points out, U.S. policymakers generally ascribe a political-legal definition to sovereignty: "The conflict over Indian sovereignty today originates in part because of the misconception held by the non-Indians with respect to social institutions and nationality and the adoption of that misconception by Indian political leaders, in some cases, as a means of communicating with and influencing the larger social and political institutions."[4] President George W. Bush's recent attempt to define sovereignty illustrates the lack of clarity that this term holds with policymakers and its emptiness as a political-legal framework:

Q: What do you think tribal sovereignty means in the 21st century, and how do we resolve conflicts between tribes and the Federal and the State governments?

The President: Tribal sovereignty means that: It's sovereign. You're a—you've been given sovereignty, and you're viewed as a sovereign entity. And therefore, the relationship between the Federal Government and tribes is one between sovereign entities.[5]

Legally speaking, sovereignty denotes a country's absolute political authority over populations within its borders. Given the Western orientation of this term, "sovereignty" is increasingly an inadequate term to describe the goals and aspirations of indigenous nations. As Kanien' kehaka (Mohawk) scholar Taiaiake Alfred points out, "Sovereignty is an exclusionary concept rooted in an adversarial and coercive Western notion of power. . . . [S]o long as sovereignty remains a goal of indigenous politics, therefore, Native communities will occupy a dependent and reactionary position relative to the state."[6]

In contrast to Western, state-centered notions of sovereignty, traditional conceptions of indigenous nationhood emphasize that "there is no absolute authority, no coercive enforcement of decisions, no hierarchy, and no separate ruling entity."[7] "Nationhood" is a more appropriate term to describe indigenous peoples, community relationships and governance, and, therefore, it will be used throughout the book. Closely related to the principles of nationhood described by Alfred is the notion of peoplehood. According to recent research undertaken by Cherokee/Creek scholar Tom Holm, peoplehood consists of four interlocking concepts: sacred history, ceremonial cycles, language, and ancestral homelands. A peoplehood model is predicated on a view of identity that is both dynamic and interconnected: "No single element of the model is more or less important than the others."[8] Subsequent research demonstrates the potential for using peoplehood/nationhood when discussing indigenous community building:

> It follows that for many indigenous communities, peoplehood, as we are describing it, is seen as an aspiration rather than a recognized present reality. As [Robert K.] Thomas states, "Among some enduring peoples the very absence of, or the losing of, one of these important four symbols can, in itself, become a strong symbol of peoplehood." This somewhat counter-intuitive response to cultural loss further illustrates the adaptive nature and contextual relevance of peoplehood to particular indigenous communities. This also reinforced our view that the peoplehood concept is a flexible and dynamic alternative to static political and legal definitional approaches to indigenous identities.[9]

Nationhood, therefore, is deemed a more inclusive and accurate concept than sovereignty and stresses the political and cultural relationships indigenous peoples maintain with their homelands, relatives, clans, and so on through their languages, ceremonial practices, and sacred histories, which are all intertwined.

Finally, we should point out that this book is not a legal analysis of the forced federalism era. Other scholars, such as David Wilkins, Vine Deloria, Jr., Clifford Lytle, and Charles Wilkinson, have already written extensive legal analyses of indigenous political and cultural struggles within the U.S. political system.[10] Departing from a strictly legal approach, this book examines the political mobilization of indigenous nations from the 1990s through the present day as they encounter new challenges to community governance and self-determination at the state and federal levels of policymaking.

Although some of the material in this book is deliberately provocative, it is not intended to second guess indigenous leaders who have made or are making daily decisions affecting the futures of their nations. This work attempts to provide deeper insights into the current political terrain and to promote further discussions regarding the degree to which indigenous peoples should participate in the U.S. political system, as well as long-term strategies for regenerating indigenous nationhood. The forced federalism era represents a fundamental shift away from the exclusive federal trust relationship between indigenous nations and the U.S. federal government. For this reason, it is important to fully understand the implications of this policy shift for Native communities and state decision makers. When writing about ongoing indigenous-state conflicts, we strike a balance by pointing out several potential areas for cooperation between indigenous nations and state policymakers. For indigenous peoples in the United States this is a critical time in our history, and the stakes are high—contemporary challenges to indigenous nationhood are more subtle than previous policy eras but are ultimately just as deadly.

Acknowledgments

As a Tsalagi (Cherokee Nation) who also happens to be trained in political science and indigenous policy, I begin by honoring my ancestors and relatives in Georgia, Tennessee, Oklahoma, Washington, California, and Alaska. This book has been a difficult journey, and I recognize the sacrifices made by my family members and friends so that I could complete this work. Namely, I could not have done this without the love and support of my wife, Laura Parisi, and the incredible editing and advice that she lent to this project. Additionally, I thank my parents, Gary and Jean, and brother, Brian, for all their encouragement and for sending me mounds of newspaper clippings and even visiting the First Nation Recycling Company in California to provide me with information for this project. *Wado* as well to my in-laws, Joyce and Bill, for keeping me apprised of indigenous politics in Oklahoma. My Aunt Ruth has also been vigilant in keeping me updated with the indigenous politics in northern California, while Terry Abrams, A.J., Theresa, and Colin Maneen kept me up to the minute on news from Tonawanda Seneca and Native politics in the Northeast.

This project could not have been carried out without the cooperation and participation of 168 indigenous nations from across the United States (for a full listing, see appendix A) responding to the forced federalism surveys in 1994, 1996, 1998, and 2000. In exchange for taking the time to fill out the surveys, all the data for these surveys has been shared with these participating nations (through regular mail updates and webpage access) to assist in their future decisions to regenerate indigenous nationhood during the forced federalism era. Additionally, I thank the following four people for taking time from their busy schedules to be interviewed for this book: Randy Noka, first councilmember for the Narragansett Nation; Russ Lehman, managing director of the First Americans Education Project in Washington; Chief Chad "Corntassel" Smith, principal chief of the Cherokee Nation; and Brad Carson, Cherokee citizen and former U.S. Representative (Second Congressional District of Oklahoma) as well as 2004 U.S. Senate candidate (Oklahoma). Brad is now director of business opportunities for Cherokee Nation business.

Initial funding for the forced federalism surveys was provided by a grant from the Social and Behavioral Sciences Research Institute (SBSRI) at the University of Arizona. Thanks to Nancy Henkle at SBSRI for all of her help in getting this project off the ground. I also thank David Wilkins and Maggie Murdock for their early support and feedback on the project. Taking graduate seminars in indigenous policy at the University of Arizona with David Wilkins and Tom Holm inspired me to pursue this area of research.

Several colleagues and friends have been invaluable in providing feedback, support, and inspiration for this project, and I wish to thank them for taking their time and energy to educate me (I take full responsibility for any inaccuracies that might remain): Taiaiake Alfred, Doug Borer, Dave Colnic, Sam Cook, Leon Corntassel, Jim Davis, Harry Dyer, Earnie Frost, Susan Grogan, Michele Hale, Lenora Scraper Hamilton, Karen Hult, Leroy Little Bear, Ilja Luciak, Tim Luke, Dan McCool, Anne McCulloch, Devon Mihesuah, Paula Mohan, Robert Morin, Joane Nagel, Monica Nuvamsa, Sharon O'Brien, Cornel Pewewardy, Richard Rich, Steve Russell, Benny Smith, Dovie Thomason, Charles Walcott, and J. Cedric Woods.

I thank Rick Witmer for his contributions. Rick coded and ran the 1994, 1996, and 1998 survey data and wrote up preliminary results for chapters 4 and 5. A special thanks also goes to research assistant Carina Diller for coding the 2000 survey data and updating the results; her extensive editing of chapters 4 and 5 is also greatly appreciated. Thanks also to George Davis for his assistance with the 1996 surveys as well as L. Jeanne Kaufmann at the National Conference of State Legislatures for her tremendous assistance in providing data on current state legislation. I could not have completed this project without the patience and assistance of the Indigenous Governance (IGOV) staff; I thank Taiaiake Alfred, program director, for his excellent editing suggestions, as well as Susanne Thiessen, Lisa Hallgren, and Vanessa Watts for working with my hectic writing schedule. Thanks also to Indigenous Governance Program masters' students Janice Makokis, Angela Polifroni, Shalene Jobin, and Kirsten Mikkelsen, who provided thoughtful and insightful comments on earlier drafts of this work.

I am especially grateful to the three anonymous reviewers of this manuscript provided by the University of Oklahoma Press for their careful reading of the text and for providing constructive feedback that greatly assisted in making this a better book.

Finally, thanks to the staff at the University of Oklahoma Press: Kim Wiar, for originally supporting the proposal, along with the invaluable assistance of editors Alessandra Jacobi Tamulevich, Jean Hurtado, and John Drayton.

Wado (Thank you)

Jeff Corntassel

Rick Witmer wishes to acknowledge David Wilkins and Clifford Lytle, whose guidance and encouragement during graduate school at the University of Arizona helped foster an interest in American Indian politics and policy. Colleagues Fred Boehmke, at the University of Iowa and Glenn Phelps at Northern Arizona University provided valuable input and advice, while NAU graduate students Aaron Mason and John Wilmer provided important research assistance on the surveys and intergovernmental agreements. A special thanks to my parents, Richard and Doris Witmer, and sister, Beth Ann Murphy, who were helpful in hosting and facilitating a number of our earlier meetings on the project during summer and winter breaks. And finally, thanks to my wife, Erika, whose help was immeasurable.

Rick would also like to acknowledge Jeff's work as first author. In some projects ordering is a matter of alphabetical convenience; in this case it reflects Jeff's efforts in taking the lead on the project.

Richard C. Witmer

FORCED FEDERALISM

CHAPTER ONE

Contemporary Challenges to Indigenous Nationhood

They [indigenous governments] owe no allegiance to the States, and receive from them no protection. Because of the local ill feeling, the people of the States where they [indigenous peoples] are found are often their deadliest enemies.

United States v. Kagama, 1886

Articles of compact between the original States and the people and States in the said territory . . . forever remain unalterable, unless by common consent, to wit: . . . Article 3 . . . The utmost good faith shall always be observed towards the Indians; their lands and property shall never be taken from them without their consent; and, in their property, rights, and liberty, they shall never be invaded or disturbed, unless in just and lawful wars authorized by Congress; but laws founded in justice and humanity, shall from time to time be made for preventing wrongs being done to them, and for preserving peace and friendship with them.

Northwest Ordinance of 1787

The Navajo Nation is the largest of the 562 federally recognized indigenous nations in the United States, but without the prominent white sign along the highway welcoming motorists to the Navajo (Diné) reservation, few people driving through northern Arizona would notice that they had crossed a nation's borders.[1] Fewer still might realize that they have entered another time zone. The Navajo Nation operates on Pacific standard time, not mountain standard, which is the time all other Arizona residents use.[2]

3

Control over the application of time zones is just one subtle form of governance that indigenous nations exercise within their own communities and homelands today. More substantively, indigenous nations have their own languages, cultural practices, sacred histories, citizenship requirements, judicial systems, and governmental bodies that provide the basis for indigenous nationhood. As nations that existed long before the formation of the United States, indigenous peoples of Turtle Island have historically transcended all state jurisdictional claims in matters pertaining to their homelands and communities.[3] In fact, indigenous nations have always held a political status higher than that of state governments.

However, the "utmost good faith" has not been practiced by state policymakers, as they have repeatedly challenged the territorial and governance jurisdictions of indigenous nations since the passage of the Indian Gaming and Regulatory Act (IGRA) in 1988. Anthropologist Kate Spilde refers to the post-IGRA phenomenon as one of "rich Indian racism," where false images related to indigenous gaming are created and propagated by governmental and media entities.[4] These stereotypes motivate and enable state policymakers to deny indigenous nationhood and self-determination in two interrelated ways: (1) "by insisting tribes prove that they still need sovereign rights to be self-sufficient" and (2) "by invoking the notion that gaming tribes are less 'authentically' Indian, diminishing their claims to political independence."[5]

Consequently, rich Indian racism places indigenous peoples in a precarious position, where they constantly have to justify their existence both in terms of the legitimacy of their self-determination powers and proof of the "authenticity" of their identities.[6] First, policymakers invoking rich Indian racist attitudes contend that indigenous peoples do not *need* what they used to. According to this logic, gaming has magically provided indigenous nations with a surplus of economic wealth, which should be heavily regulated and taxed by state governments. It follows from this reasoning that treaty-based rights, such as hunting and fishing, and homeland claims are no longer considered necessary for the survival of these entrepreneurial indigenous nations.

Second, rich Indian racist attitudes invoked by state policymakers require indigenous peoples to demonstrate that they *deserve* self-determination and a distinct nationhood status. This assumption falsely claims that someone is a "real" indigenous person only if he or she is considered a victim of failed policies, historical circumstances, and so on. During the post-IGRA era, rich Indian racism has led to increased regulation by state and local policymakers as they attempt to place limits on indigenous casinos and other forms of self-determination through the negotiation of indigenous-state compacts. It is evident from this new stereotype of indigenous peoples that the biggest challenges facing indigenous communities today are those of representation and governance. As former principal chief of the Cherokee Nation Wilma Mankiller argues, "Perception is as much of a threat as anti-sovereignty legislation. We have to regain control of our image."[7]

Managing the politics of perception is one of the major struggles for indigenous peoples today as they confront the realities of a new era in indigenous policy, which we refer to as forced federalism (1988–present). The forced federalism era differs markedly from the previous self-determination era, which entailed providing indigenous nations with greater administrative control over the contracting of education, health care, and other services on their homelands. As a result of IGRA in 1988 and the subsequent transfer of federal powers to state governments, indigenous nations have now been *forced* into dangerous political and legal relationships with state governments that challenge their cultures and nationhood status. This rapid devolution of federal powers to state governments in the area of indigenous policy undermines the once exclusive federal government–to–indigenous government relationship based on 379 prior treaties, direct consultation with Congress on indigenous affairs, federal statutory obligations, and court decisions.

Therefore, given the devolution of federal powers to states, indigenous nations have become more vulnerable to the jurisdictional claims of local governing bodies, such as state and municipal policymakers. Invoking rich Indian images, these local governing agencies are more likely to exercise their newly created jurisdictional claims to impose new regulatory policies targeting indigenous nations (i.e., taxation, revenue sharing, etc.) in ways that benefit them economically and politically.

Thus far, researchers examining indigenous-state interactions have predominantly relied on regional case studies, policy overviews, and legal analysis.[8] This book is the only one of its kind to systematically investigate the effects of forced federalism on indigenous nations using case studies of indigenous-state conflicts, interviews with indigenous leaders (Randy Noka of the Narragansett Nation, Chief Chad Smith of the Cherokee Nation, Brad Carson of the Cherokee Nation), findings from surveys of indigenous leaders between 1994 and 2000, opinion polls conducted with indigenous and non-indigenous people, and data from the National Governors' Association (NGA) annual meetings, the National Conference of State Legislatures (NCLS), and the Center for Responsive Politics.[9] The purpose of this research is to examine the changing intergovernmental relationships between indigenous nations and local, state, and federal governments in the United States since 1988 and to uncover how socially constructed images of indigenous peoples have a major influence on policymaking both historically (discussed later in this chapter) and in this current era of intergovernmental relations.

Stereotypes of rich Indians are motivating state governors and other state decision makers to impose new regulation and jurisdictional claims on indigenous nations. In response, indigenous nations are mobilizing politically and economically to reframe the politics of perception on their own terms. Contemporary indigenous leaders are confronting rich Indian racism by utilizing new diplomatic strategies and forms of political mobilization, but widespread involvement in U.S. elections carries serious risks. As Oren Lyons, faithkeeper of the Onondaga Nation, states, "If a nation feels like a nation, acts like a nation, then you will be a nation."[10] Amid threats to indigenous nationhood, Lyons's words challenge indigenous communities and leaders to act like nations, not like interest groups, stakeholders, or smaller versions of U.S. bureaucracies.

The findings of this book provide an in-depth look at indigenous political mobilization strategies and the increasing regulatory oversight of state actors, such as governors and legislators, in indigenous policy during the 1990s and into the twenty-first century. However, the question remains whether indigenous nations are seeking political and economic solutions at the state government level at the expense of local, community-based solutions. Ultimately, this book contends, the long-term solutions to confronting rich Indian racism do not arise from emulating the political behavior of other U.S. citizens; rather, the strength of indigenous nations comes from protecting indigenous homelands and regenerating their cultural and political forms of governance. There is an urgent need to confront rich

Indian racism and regain control of indigenous images as indigenous peoples face new kinds of challenges in this turbulent policy era.

As a result of the reshaping of indigenous-state relations, several state officials have begun to treat indigenous peoples as "merely part of the service population or as local interest group[s]" rather than as nations.[11] For example, in 2001 Texas attorney general John Cornyn waged a legal battle against the Tigua (Ysleta del Sur Pueblo) and Alabama-Coushatta nations to stop their gaming operations. Cornyn ultimately succeeded in shutting down both Tigua and Alabama-Coushatta gaming operations in 2002 and even persuaded U.S. district judge John Hannah to reduce indigenous nations' political status to the equivalent of "voluntary associations" such as sororities or fraternities.[12]

Shortly after the Tigua and Alabama-Coushatta casino closures, the Tiguas then paid $4.2 million to lobbyists to try to get Congress to intervene to reopen their casino. However, the lobbyists that the Tiguas hired, Jack Abramoff and Michael Scanlon, were the same ones previously hired by religious activist Ralph Reed to help the state of Texas conduct a massive media campaign to shut the Tigua casino down in 2002.[13] In an e-mail to Reed on February 11, 2002, Abramoff wrote, "I wish those moronic Tiguas were smarter in their political contributions. I'd love us to get our mitts on that moolah!! Oh well, stupid folks get wiped out."[14]

Ten days after the Tigua casino closure, Abramoff wrote to a Tigua government official stating that he would get Republican leaders in Congress to rectify the "gross indignity perpetuated by the Texas state authorities."[15] Abramoff and Scanlon opportunistically (and illegally) worked both sides of the Tigua closure to their financial advantage but ultimately failed to get the Tigua casino reopened. In the meantime, Abramoff and Scanlon still collected the $4.2 million paid to them by the Tigua Nation. The Tiguas also contributed over $250,000 to congressional campaigns between 2002 and 2004 based on Abramoff's recommendations.

As the Tigua Nation example demonstrates, indigenous peoples are confronting a new era of rich Indian racism that has led to unprecedented attacks on their nationhood. The campaign to close the Tigua casino and the reduction of indigenous nations' political status in Texas to voluntary associations illustrate how the self-determining authority of the Tiguas and other indigenous nations has been challenged by state policymakers invoking rich Indian images. However, conflicts over how indigenous peoples are represented and treated by policymakers and the general public have been prevalent throughout indigenous historical contacts with the United States.[16]

HISTORICAL IMAGES AND POLICY OUTOMES

In his seminal work *The White Man's Indian,* historian Robert Berkhofer documents how invented images of indigenous peoples have influenced policymaking from the colonial era to the present: "Whether one looks to the history of the relationships between White claims and native lands, between White political sovereignty and Indian governments, between White commerce and native economics, or between White philanthropy and Red welfare, one finds the same fundamental imagery serving both as moral and intellectual justification for White policies and as explanation for their failure or successes. The primary premise of that imagery is the deficiency of the Indian as compared to the White."[17]

Among these images and social constructions of indigenous peoples, the legal fiction of the "Doctrine of Discovery" is probably the most notorious example of a colonial stereotype used to establish official policy. This fifteenth-century legal and theological doctrine asserted that if a European country encountered a territory occupied by indigenous people, the original title of the land rightfully belonged to the newly arriving, "civilized" European settlers by way of "discovery." According to this colonial construct, Native people were deemed "infidels" or "heathens" and "presumed to lack the rational capacity necessary to assume an equal status or to exercise equal rights under the West's medievally derived colonizing law."[18] The legal fiction of Doctrine of Discovery eventually found its way to the U.S. Supreme Court in 1823, when Chief Justice John Marshall delivered the opinion of the court in the *Johnson v. McIntosh* case:

> However extravagant the pretension of converting the discovery of an inhabited country into conquest may appear; if the principle has been asserted in the first instance, and afterwards sustained; if a country has been acquired and held under it; if the property of the great mass of the community originates in

it, it becomes the law of the land, and cannot be questioned. So, too, with respect to the concomitant principle, that the Indian inhabitants are to be considered merely as occupants, to be protected, indeed, while in peace, in the possession of their lands, but to be deemed incapable of transferring the absolute title to others.[19]

In this unanimous opinion, Marshall basically argued that even if a faulty logic was applied to Native peoples during the initial "discovery," the mere fact that this practice was sustained and later led to the formation of the United States makes it the unquestioned "law of the land." Invented images of indigenous peoples as "uncivilized" or "occupants" are not the least bit benign when considering the long-term policy implications. Such legal fictions and myths quickly become embedded in political institutions and have been perpetuated by successive generations.

Some stereotypes, such as the "noble savage," came into prominence during first contact with colonial powers, and others, such as the "child-like Native" and the "rich Indian" are more recent inventions.[20] Table 1.1 illustrates the distinct U.S. policy shifts since the 1770s and dominant images and social constructions of indigenous peoples during each period. For example, during the push for assimilation during the 1870s, the political status of Native peoples was predominantly as wards in need of protection. Stereotypical images of indigenous peoples as "childlike" and "vanishing" are common in newspaper accounts and policy dictates of the time.[21]

Amid an accelerated push for Native assimilation, Congress passed the General Allotment Act, also known as the Dawes Act, in 1887. Despite extensive efforts by the "Five Civilized Tribes" to lobby members of Congress to reverse the allotment policy, the Allotment Act was eventually amended in 1891, 1906, and 1910, until it applied to almost every indigenous nation in the country.[22] Believing that collectively held land was an obstacle to the "civilization" of Native peoples, the act broke up reservations and distributed plots of land to individual indigenous people. As described by the commissioner of Indian affairs in 1886, "The common field is the seat of barbarism, the separate farm [is] the door to civilization."[23] According to the allotment policy, Native "heads of households" were to receive 160 acres of land, while those under eighteen received 40 acres. After

TABLE 1.1
Historical Phases and Images of Indigenous Policy, 1770s–Present

	Policy	Major laws	Political status/image
1770s–1820s	International sovereign diplomacy	1787 Northwest Ordinance	Noble savages
1830s–1850s	Removal	1830 Indian Removal Act treaties	Domestic dependent nations, blood-thirsty savages, warlike
1850s–1870s	Reservation	Reservation treaties	Wards in need of protection, blood-thirsty savages, childlike
1870s–1930s	Assimilation	1871 End of treaty making 1885 Major crimes act 1887 Allotment Act (Dawes Act)	Wards in need of protection, vanishing, childlike
1930s–1950s	Indigenous self-rule	1934 Indian Reorganization Act (Wheeler-Howard Act)	Quasi-sovereigns, noble savages
1950s–1960s	Termination (assimilation)	1953 Resolution 108 1953 Public Law 280	Termination of quasi-sovereign status, noble savages, patriots
1960s–1988	Self-determination	1968 Indian Civil Rights Act 1975 Indian Self-Determination Act 1978 Indian Child Welfare Act 1978 Indian Religious Freedom Act	Domestic dependent nations, quasi-sovereigns, militant protestors, spirit guides, environmental stewards
1988–present	Forced federalism	1988 Indian Gaming Regulatory Act 1988 Tribal Self-Governance Act 2000 Indian Economic Development and Contract Encouragement Act	Domestic dependent nations, quasi-sovereigns, rich Indians, interest groups

SOURCES: Modified from Cornell, *Return of the Native*, 14; Coward, *Newspaper Indian*; O'Brien, *American Indian Tribal Governments*, 258; Weston, *Native Americans in the News*; Wilkins, *American Indian Politics*, 105, 231–35.

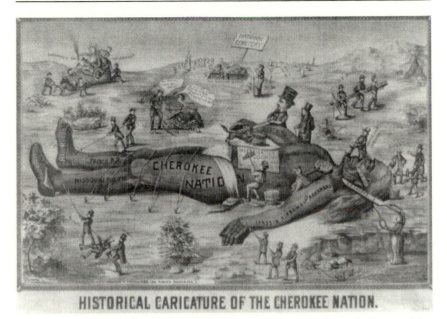

Figure 1.1. Historical Caricature of the Cherokee Nation, 1886. Courtesy of the Library of Congress.

the individual allotments were parceled out, the leftover, or "surplus," Native homelands were sold to the highest bidder. By 1934 Native land holdings were reduced by 90 million acres, down from 138 million in 1887 to 48 million in 1934 because of rampant land speculation and fraud.[24]

An 1886 "Historical Caricature of the Cherokee Nation" demonstrates the multiple pressures and interests acting to partition indigenous nations during this time (see figure 1.1). One can readily see the symbolism of the Cherokee Nation tied to the ground, which was allegorical to the Lilliputian lands of *Gulliver's Travels*. In this caricature, the U.S. courts are cutting the hair of the Native in their efforts to "civilize," as missionaries bore into the skull of the Cherokee to proselytize. The "body" of the Cherokee Nation is partitioned by railroads at the feet, while the arms, which represent lands in Alabama and Arkansas, are being sawed off by state policymakers. "Uncle Sam" sits on the bridge of the Cherokee Nation's nose with the title of "Coroner" to make this depiction of the "vanishing Native" complete. Such a vivid image of an indigenous nation being divided by multiple loyalties and interests is just as relevant today as it was in 1886.

Another caricature drawn by Thomas Nast in 1880 demonstrates a prevailing image of indigenous peoples as childlike during this period (see figure 1.2). According to the caption, granting the right to vote to indigenous people is deemed "the cheapest and quickest way of civilizing them." As Natives appear awestruck and mystified by the ballot box, the secretary of the interior casually introduces them to "the Ballot, the Great Protector of the Age." At the top of the cartoon, caricatures of African Americans, Scots, and Irish are depicted with the caption "Civilized by the ballot box." Clearly, these images of indigenous peoples reflect the stereotypical childlike Native of the allotment era and depict the urgency on the part of Congress, missionaries, land speculators, and other interested parties to assimilate Native peoples into the U.S. system.

The appointment of long-time indigenous advocate John Collier as commissioner of Indian affairs in 1933 signaled a new policy shift toward reinstating indigenous governments. Collier's vision of a "Red Atlantis" and perceptions of indigenous peoples as noble savages replaced previous images of indigenous peoples as childlike and vanishing. Consequently, after several consultations with indigenous nations around the country, the Indian Reorganization Act (IRA, also known as the Wheeler-Howard bill) was passed by Congress in 1934 to counter the previous allotment policies.[25] Serving as further justification for Collier's vision of a "Red Atlantis," the press during this time often used "idealized imagery of Native Americans as possessing characteristics superior to those of whites."[26]

Public perceptions of indigenous peoples shifted quickly with the impending threat of World War II. The federal government's attention and resources were quickly being diverted away from Native communities. Indigenous people also volunteered to serve in World War II at a high rate, which left communities without key personnel and leadership. By 1945 Collier had resigned, and President Harry Truman's administration rejected many of Collier's indigenous policies and programs. The dominant image of the 1940s and 1950s was the patriotic warrior, another variation of the noble savage. As journalism professor Mary Ann Weston points out, "In World War II, Indians were portrayed as patriotic warriors who were eager to fight to defend the country that had brought them to the brink of physical and cultural extinction. Article after article repeated and embellished the image of innate warriors and scouts who were instinctively superior fighters."[27]

Figure 1.2. Cartoon of Indigenous Voters, by Thomas Nast, 1880

Invented images of Native peoples as super-patriotic and loyal motivated Congress to abandon its trust relationship with indigenous nations in an effort to promote assimilation. Beginning with House Concurrent Resolution 108 in 1953, federal services to over 109 indigenous nations and bands were effectively terminated by legislation that eliminated special Native programs and, in most cases, resulted in the sale of reservation lands.[28]

A clear break from the termination era occurred when President Lyndon B. Johnson articulated a new direction for federal policy in his March 6, 1968, speech titled "Special Message to the Congress on the Problems of the American Indian: The Forgotten American." He proposed a new goal for Native programs "that ends the old debate about 'termination' of Indian programs and stresses self-determination; a goal that erases old attitudes of paternalism and promotes partnership self-help." Invoking images of indigenous peoples as victims of previous U.S. policies, Johnson spoke of indigenous peoples as being a "a symbol of the drama and excitement of the earliest America. But for two centuries, he has been an alien in his own land." While President Richard Nixon is often credited with the new federal emphasis on indigenous self-determination, this policy shift was really initiated by his predecessor, President Johnson. When Nixon took office in 1969, he quickly established indigenous peoples as a central part of his policy agenda for self-determination.

As a reflection of Nixon's new emphasis on indigenous policy, Senate Bill 1017 (PL 93-638), titled "The Indian Self-Determination and Educational Assistance Act," passed on January 4, 1975. The act itself was vaguely worded and sought to "provide for the full participation of Indian tribes in programs and services conducted by the Federal government." Essentially the legislation facilitated the direct contracting of indigenous nations with the federal government, under the auspices of the Department of the Interior, for health and educational services. Native peoples who were still wary of yet another government termination policy, referred to it as the "Self-Termination Act." By 1988 the Self-Governance Act, which was a derivation of the 1975 Self-Determination Act, allowed twenty-two participating indigenous governments to bypass the bureaucratically challenged Bureau of Indian Affairs (BIA) and contract directly with the federal government for health care and education services.

Prevalent media images of indigenous peoples as militants during this time provide some context for the policy shift. Direct confrontations between Native peoples and the U.S. government over treaty rights and self-determination became increasingly common during the 1960s and 1970s, beginning with the fish-ins in the 1960s and culminating with the seventy-one-day occupation of Wounded Knee by the American Indian Movement (AIM) in 1973. During this time, U.S. newspapers frequently used terms such as "militants" and "insurgents" to describe the protest actions of indigenous peoples. Timothy Baylor studied NBC's news coverage of AIM from 1968 to 1979 and found that the network depicted AIM's goals as militant or as another indigenous stereotype 98 percent of the time. Key motivations for AIM's actions, such as promoting treaty rights or civil rights, were rarely discussed in the NBC coverage. The most common image in the network's coverage of AIM was that of the militant with a focus on "violence and the breakdown of law and order."[29]

Besides the angry militant image, public perceptions of Natives as environmentalists were also widespread. Indigenous peoples were often portrayed as "the unspoiled children of nature who held the key to salvation of decadent white society by their closeness to the natural world and communal institutions."[30] Coupled with social constructions of Native peoples as environmental stewards was the imagery of the spiritual Native person holding ancient and exotic powers. Policy reflected these well-known perceptions and stereotypes, and the American Indian Religious Freedom Act was passed in 1978.

Juxtaposed with the rhetoric of self-determination under Nixon, emphasis shifted in the 1980s to economic development. Perceptions of indigenous peoples as potential entrepreneurs were widespread under President Ronald Reagan's administration, which emphasized "trickle-down" economic theory: "Without sound reservation economies, the concept of self-government has little meaning. In the past, despite good intentions, the federal government has been one of the major obstacles to economic progress."[31]

Signaling another change in U.S. policy, in a 1983 speech President Reagan referred to indigenous nations and states as equal partners in obtaining funding through block grants and building local autonomy. This was a cornerstone of Reagan's "new federalism," which was his attempt to return policy power to the states and local governments, reversing the accumulation of power at the federal level since the New Deal in the 1930s. However, this policy shift had unforeseen layers of complexity, as it compelled indigenous nations to negotiate with states as equals and therefore undermined their once exclusive relationship with the federal government during eras of removal in the 1830s and termination in the 1950s. Self-determination policies of the 1970s and 1980s now gave way to forced federalism and increased indigenous-state interactions during the 1990s driven by contemporary images of indigenous peoples as rich Indians and interest groups.

THE FORCED FEDERALISM ERA, 1988–PRESENT

Historical patterns suggest that every twenty years or so a new U.S. policy shift emerges that attempts to eliminate indigenous nations altogether or to assimilate Native peoples into the U.S. system. The latest U.S. policy shift is no different. Over the past twenty years, the relationship between indigenous governments and the U.S. government has undergone a fundamental transformation. The 1970s and 1980s were regarded as the self-determination era in which the approximately 562 indigenous nations were given greater control over the administration of education, health care, and other services. The forced federalism era began in 1988 with the passage of IGRA and the further institutionalization of an indigenous-state compact system, which is designed to enable states and indigenous governments to draw up and ratify agreements that "provide for the application of civil, criminal, and regulatory laws of either entity over Indians and non-Indians as the parties may see fit to agree."[32]

In compact negotiations since 1988, states have largely ignored historic, treaty-based relationships that indigenous nations have had with the federal government. As Kate Spilde explains, "Federal policy, as well as public opinion, is often deliberately ahistorical."[33] For example, when originally seeking statehood, territories with indigenous nations situated inside their borders formally recognized the elevated status of indigenous nations. Twelve western territories hosting more than 80 percent of Native peoples in the United States were required by the federal government to include "Indian disclaimer clauses" in their constitutions, legally precluding them from asserting jurisdictional control on indigenous nation homelands.[34] Since that time, states have actively violated these Indian disclaimer clauses and have disregarded the federal trust relationship. As with previous policy eras, such as removal in the 1830s and termination during the 1950s, the federal government has once again off-loaded its trust responsibilities to state governments.

The once exclusive federal trust relationship, which comprises 379 ratified treaties as well as executive agreements, direct consultation with Congress on Indian affairs, federal statutory obligations, and court decisions, guarantees direct indigenous government–to–federal government relations. This historic trust relationship now appears to be fundamentally challenged again by state governments as they have received more jurisdictional powers from the federal government, including the institutionalization of an indigenous-state compact system. The passage of IGRA in 1988 emphasized indigenous-state compacts as the way to formalize gaming agreements with state policymakers, and, consequently, state governors and officials are asserting more dominance over indigenous nations within their state boundaries.

Since 1988 the federal government has compelled or coerced indigenous nations to negotiate away their powers of governance and jurisdiction of their homelands relating to taxation, gaming, hunting and fishing rights, homeland security, and so on vis-à-vis indigenous-state compacts with state governments that have historically shown animosity toward them. This contemporary devolution process, which transfers federal powers to state and local governments, has been labeled "new federalism" but is just the latest attempt by the federal government to off-load their trust responsibilities to indigenous peoples onto state and local governments. Tensions over the division of federal and state powers surfaced in the 1830s with two Supreme Court cases filed by the Cherokee Nation. In an 1831 case, *Cherokee Nation v. Georgia*, Chief Justice Marshall referred to Native people as "domestic dependent nations" whose relationship to the United States was "that of a ward to a guardian." While not considered international sovereigns under this case holding, indigenous people were found to posses some degree of self-determination in governing themselves. Marshall further expounded on indigenous-state relationships in *Worcestor v. Georgia* (1832): "The Cherokee Nation, then, is a distinct community, occupying its own territory, with boundaries accurately described, and which the citizens of Georgia have no right to enter, but with the assent of the Cherokees themselves, or in conformity with treaties and with the acts of congress. The whole intercourse between the United States and this nation is by our constitution and laws, vested in the government of the United States."

In response to Marshall's *Worcestor* ruling, President Andrew Jackson is alleged to have said, "John Marshall has made his decision: now let him enforce it," setting the stage for the forced removal of indigenous peoples from their homelands.[35] Beginning with the 1830s removal era, which privileged states' rights over those of indigenous nations, over fifty indigenous nations were forcibly relocated from their homelands.

By the 1950s another federal relocation program was enacted through termination legislation, which denied recognition and federal services for over 109 indigenous nations and bands, often resulting in the transfer of federal responsibilities and services to state governments. Through the withdrawal of federal services and enactment of urban training programs, the ultimate goal of termination policies was to destroy indigenous nations through the desegregation of Indian communities and the integration of Indians with the rest of society.[36] In legislation that laid the groundwork for the forced federalism era, Public Law 280, which was passed in 1953, gave five states (California, Minnesota, Nebraska, Oregon, and Wisconsin) full criminal and some civil jurisdiction over indigenous nations and provided the legal basis for other states to assert this same jurisdictional power. Consequently, states were granted rights that the federal government previously reserved on a government-to-government basis with indigenous nations.

The transfer of federal powers to state governments accelerated with the passage of IGRA in 1988. Since 1988 state and local governments have begun to assert jurisdictional claims over indigenous nations in seven distinct areas relating to indigenous governance

> 1. *Criminal jurisdiction and policing:* States are attempting to extend their jurisdiction for criminal matters under Public Law 280.[37] Natives and state and local governments are engaged in ongoing disputes regarding law enforcement and punishment for indigenous and non-indigenous persons committing crimes on indigenous homelands.

2. *Hunting and fishing rights:* Despite guarantee of hunting and fishing rights by prior treaties and constructive agreements, indigenous peoples are being challenged by states in the name of conservation and environmental protection. Additionally, some state governments, such as Montana and South Dakota, are asserting that indigenous peoples are subject to the same hunting and fishing regulations as non-indigenous people despite the existence of indigenous treaties that guarantee their hunting and fishing rights.

3. *Self governance:* State legislators and members of state executive branches increasingly claim jurisdictional control over issues of indigenous governance, such as water rights and policy decisions, such as the Yakima ban on alcohol in Washington. State intrusion into areas once reserved exclusively for the indigenous governments has been growing.

4. *Taxation and economic development:* Efforts are being made by state and local governments to raise revenue by taxing transactions—namely, gaming—on indigenous land. This has been especially problematic regarding alleged state rights to tax indigenous-owned businesses selling motor fuels and tobacco products and has led to highly publicized indigenous nation–state disputes in New York and Rhode Island.

5. *Child-protection and welfare:* States have initiated efforts to amend the Indian Child Welfare Act (ICWA) of 1978, which provides indigenous nations with authority to determine the indigenous citizenship of their children. State efforts to reform ICWA undermine indigenous nationhood by imposing state governmental standards of "Indianness" and by proposing to adopt "objective" measures of cultural ties.[38]

6. *Gaming:* Indigenous gaming is a growing and controversial area in which indigenous-state compacts provide state governments with opportunities to limit and tax indigenous casino profits.[39] Intractable disputes over the renewal of gaming compacts have occurred between state governors and indigenous nations in California, Arizona, and New Mexico.

7. *Homeland security:* The Homeland Security Act of 2002, passed in response to the attacks of September 11, 2001, channels all funding assistance through state governments and places indigenous nations in the same classification as cities when

determining funding priorities and violates the exclusive federal
government–to–indigenous government relationship.

While federalism scholars tend to agree that the Nixon administration initiated the devolution of federal policymaking power to states
and local governments (a process intensified under the Reagan
administration), researchers to date have failed to determine specifically how forced federalism affects indigenous nations.[40] Policy
scholars from the Harvard Project on American Indian Economic
Development, such as Stephen Cornell and Jonathan Taylor, contend
that delegation of powers to state governments alone is not dangerous
to indigenous sovereignty and actually has the potential to "significantly boost tribal self-rule."[41] At the same time, a 1998 report published
by the American Indian Policy Center, a nonprofit indigenous think-
tank in Minnesota, concludes that "states are leading the attack on
tribal sovereignty" in the areas of taxation, criminal jurisdiction, and
diminished reservation boundaries.[42] While research undertaken by
the American Indian Policy Center seems to confirm some of the
new challenges to indigenous self-determination since 1988, subsequent
research by Cornell and Taylor reflects how theory has not kept
pace with reality regarding contemporary indigenous policymaking
and political mobilization.

How, then, are indigenous nations responding to state challenges
to their nationhood in an era of forced federalism? In a 1989 examination of the effects of federal policy on indigenous nations, Native
political researcher Emma Gross outlined two possible scenarios for
indigenous nations in the United States: either the BIA and other
federal agencies will control Indian tribal activities or indigenous peoples
will make the most of educational and entrepreneurial activities and
devote their resources to developing their economies and to extending
their influence in the local and national political arenas.[43]

Based on the survey responses and the case studies discussed in
chapter 4, it is clear that the latter situation is now coming into
effect. However, Gross did not account for the domination of indigenous affairs by state and local governments in her model. Given
the changing relationships between indigenous nations and states,
other scholars contend that "tribes and the states essentially have
two choices: they can litigate or they can cooperate."[44] But such a

narrow perspective overlooks other forms of indigenous cultural and political self-determination. Based on the research in this book, indigenous nations have pursued far more than just two available options. Various forms of economic development (including, but not limited to, gaming) on indigenous homelands have expanded opportunities for indigenous political mobilization since 1988, and a number of political strategies have been used by indigenous nations during the 1990s and into the twenty-first century to counter increased state encroachment on indigenous governance and homeland autonomy.

While general analyses of indigenous responses to the challenges of forced federalism are insightful, it is also useful to examine how specific indigenous communities have responded to the increased interactions with state governments. One such example of contemporary indigenous nation–state conflicts is the Narragansett Nation (Rhode Island), who saw their plans to open a casino blocked by U.S. senator John Chaffee's rider to a 1996 Omnibus Appropriations Act. According to the Chaffee provision passed by Congress, the eighteen-hundred-acre Narragansett reservation lands were subject to state and *not* federal law as specified under the terms of the 1978 Rhode Island Indian Claims Settlement Act. While this bill seemed to contradict federal oversight of indigenous gaming outlined by IGRA, the U.S. Court of Appeals decided against the Narragansett claims by upholding the legality of the 1996 Omnibus Appropriations Act. Randy Noka, first councilmember for the twenty-eight-hundred-member Narragansett Nation, points out that the court's ruling singled out the Narragansetts as "the only tribe out of this whole nation of 562 tribes, the only tribe, that has had their rights taken away like that."[45]

As a result of the Court of Appeals ruling, the Narragansett Nation was subjected to Rhode Island state jurisdiction regarding any future casino gaming proposals on reservation lands. When they attempted to put a casino referendum before the voters both locally and statewide, the Rhode Island House Finance Committee voted down legislation that would have put a Narragansett casino referendum on the 2000 ballot.[46] Furthermore, Governor Don Carcieri of Rhode Island has refused to approve continued funding for a Narragansett housing project on federal lands, citing fears that the Narragansett Nation might build a casino on this land if the financing were approved.[47] As Noka points out, "It's not just gaming, certainly. We're at war about our self-determination, about exercising the rights of a nation that we have under federal law."[48]

Despite Governor Carcieri's continued opposition to a Narragansett casino in Rhode Island, the Narragansett Nation has sought backing from Harrah's Entertainment for a proposed $1 billion casino in West Warwick, Rhode Island. After several years of lobbying to get a referendum to the voters on casino gaming, the Narragansetts have been prevented from putting forward a statewide ballot during the 2004 and 2005 election cycles. However, this changed in 2006 when a ballot measure (listed as "Question 1" on the ballot) was put forward to voters that would amend the Rhode Island constitution to permit a privately owned and privately operated resort casino to be regulated and taxed by the state.

In their advertising campaigns leading up to the November 7, 2006, election, Harrah's Entertainment spent $5 million on public relations efforts (polls, consultants, donations to community groups, etc.) to gain Rhode Island voter approval, while the Narragansetts stressed the need for gaming to provide housing and jobs for their nation. Opponents to the gaming initiative also led high-profile campaigns. A Rhode Island organization called Save Our State (SOS) spent over $2 million on ad campaigns against the proposed casino and played on voter fears of casino corruption, increased traffic, and decreased profits for local businesses. On its website, SOS even questioned the Narragansett role in the casino operation by claiming that "Harrah's says it will 'partner' with the Narragansett Indians to operate a casino in West Warwick. But 95% of the profits will go to Las Vegas and the Narragansett Tribe will have no management or operational role in the casino."[49] The two other casinos in Rhode Island, Lincoln Park and Newport Grand, also campaigned strongly against the proposed gaming facility along with Governor Carcieri. The governor continued to oppose a Harrah's/Narragansett casino on the grounds that nothing would prevent Harrah's and the Narragansetts from paying a "substantially lower tax rate" to the state of Rhode Island.[50] Such thinking exemplifies a rich Indian racism mentality that was evident throughout the campaign.

On November 7, 2006, Question 1 was defeated by a wide margin, with of 63 percent of Rhode Islanders voting against the casino and only 37 percent voting for the measure.[51] Immediately following the

2006 election, Narragansett chief sachem Matthew Thomas vowed to continue lobbying Congress to remove the 1996 Chafee amendment, which prevents the Narragansetts from operating a casino on their own homelands under IGRA.[52]

As the Narragansett casino example shows, indigenous nations today face a high risk when putting their powers of governance and self-determination up for a popular vote. While such a referendum strategy has been successfully used by indigenous nations in Arizona (1996) and California (1998 and 2000), this strategy failed in Maine when the Passamaquoddy and Penobscot nations lost a 2003 referendum by a nearly two-to-one margin to run casinos—even with the condition that part of the revenue would be used for state education and municipal revenue sharing.[53]

The Narragansett example also demonstrates that the transition to the forced federalism era represents a fundamental shift in government-to-government relations for indigenous nations. During the forced federalism era, relationships between indigenous nations and state and local governments are decidedly more contentious when economic development issues such as gaming are being negotiated. Policymakers invoking rich Indian images are increasingly likely to set strategies that regulate indigenous nations and diminish indigenous self-determination and governance capacities.

In their comprehensive analysis of indigenous sovereignty and federal law, Lumbee scholar David Wilkins and Creek/Cherokee scholar K. Tsianina Lomawaima highlight the potential for conflict as federalism has been redefined: "The current reshaping of federalism to strengthen the states, and weaken the federal government and tribes, is occurring despite the fact that tribal sovereignty does not derive from state or federal constitutions, and despite the fact that tribal sovereignty is inherent and originates from within the collective will of each Indian community."[54] With every addition of political actors and complexity to the policymaking process, the ability of indigenous nations to represent themselves on their own terms is being compromised.

Yet not all indigenous-state interactions during the contemporary era have been conflictual. Although increased interaction between indigenous nations and states has led to conflict in some areas, such as gaming and taxation, where indigenous nations tend to be viewed by states as competitors for jobs and income, it has led to

cooperation in other areas where indigenous nations and states
seemingly have mutual interests, such as natural resource management. In Oregon, for example, under the governor's direction, state
agency officials meet regularly with indigenous nations throughout
the year to discuss areas of potential conflict as well as hold annual
summits between federal, indigenous and state governments to discuss
potential policies.[55] Other cooperative efforts include the Commission on State-Tribal Relations (CSTR), which was founded in 1977
to "stabilize state-tribal relations and de-escalate conflicts."[56]

CONFRONTING RICH INDIAN RACISM AND THE POLITICS OF PERCEPTION

Rich Indian stereotypes serve to undermine indigenous identities and
self-determination claims, and managing the politics of perception
becomes a never-ending task for indigenous nations. It can often
distract leaders from focusing on the real roots of their power: protection of homelands, revitalizing indigenous languages, engaging
in ceremonial life, and reminding others of their sacred histories. As
an alternative to bureaucratic structures and decision making institutions, indigenous governance is an ongoing process of honoring and
renewing individual and community relationships and responsibilities.
These principles of indigenous nationhood are best exemplified by
the Tsalagi (Cherokee) concept of *Gadugi* (other nations have their
own indigenous words for similar values), which entails "a built-in
spirit of community camaraderie. This means that whatever issues or
concerns arising in collective living have to be addressed in a unitary
way and that no one is left alone to climb out of a life endeavor; it
reflects a collective community base."[57] Policies driven by rich Indian
racism directly challenge the unity of indigenous nations and the
community principles of *Gadugi*.

The politics of perception have played out in a number of ways,
ranging from media stereotypes of indigenous peoples to systemic
racism in policymaking institutions. According to an *Indian Country
Today* poll of 450 indigenous community leaders and scholars in the
United States, 76 percent of the respondents claimed that there is a
"growing anti-Indian sentiment in the country."[58] When asked "What
do you believe is the primary cause of anti-Indian sentiment?" those

responding overwhelmingly cited that at the root of the current anti-indigenous backlash were "media stereotypes" (45 percent), followed by "U.S. government" (33 percent) and "systemic racism" (22 percent). As the polls results demonstrate, contemporary challenges to indigenous nationhood originate from a number of sources. Survey respondent Suze L'fox (Delaware) explains further: "There are several things I hear repeatedly: Indians don't pay taxes (then take my tax bill please!), I bet you wish you were (enter name of tribe with a casino), and Indians don't have to work or worry about anything because . . . . (enter federal handouts, casinos, oil—how about Native American art?) . . . Therefore, I think anti-Indian sentiment basically comes from lack of education, publicity about tribes with casinos, and just plain stupidity."[59]

Rich Indian racism is not just confined to policymakers. Citizen groups such as SOS in Rhode Island have formed to oppose and question the identities of indigenous peoples and their self-determining authority as First Nations. Evoking the memories of the states' rights debates during President Andrew Jackson's administration, which ultimately led to the forced removal of some fifty indigenous nations from their ancestral homelands in the 1830s, an anti-indigenous backlash is gaining momentum among non-indigenous reservation landholders and businesspersons across the United States. Claiming to be victims of taxation without representation, these "new terminators" are the latest version of an older movement portraying indigenous nations as "separatist, discriminatory, and even racist."[60] Groups such as One Nation (Oklahoma) and the Upstate Citizens for Equality (New York) advocate the complete abrogation of indigenous treaty rights and termination of the federal trust relationship under the guise of equality: "Federal policy is driving Americans apart by fueling divisiveness between tribal governments and their neighbors. It has become obvious that tax and regulatory inequities favor the tribes and threaten to thwart economic development efforts across our nation."[61]

While challenges to indigenous governance have become more commonplace by groups invoking rich Indian images as well as the federal courts during the 1990s, state governments also draw on this form of public support to justify their expanded jurisdictional oversight of indigenous nations. Alliances of convenience between citizen groups promoting an anti-indigenous agenda, and state policymakers seeking to capitalize politically on rich Indian images pose formidable new challenges to indigenous nations and peoples.

When responding to rich Indian racism, indigenous nations run the risk of seeking only political or economic solutions to challenges that also require the strong cultural and spiritual foundations of *Gadugi*. Casinos and other forms of economic development being promoted on indigenous homelands tend to have a strong gravitational pull that, despite the best of intentions, can distract leaders from the true powers of indigenous nations. Lobbying activities of indigenous nations reflect the changing community priorities as tax exemptions and compact negotiations slowly displace education, language programs, and health care as priorities.

In response to increasing threats of state and local jurisdictional encroachment within their homelands, indigenous nations are mobilizing politically to meet challenges to their governance capabilities and are rearticulating their self-determination in local, regional, and global forums. Is the prophetic warning issued by the U.S. Supreme Court in the case *United States v. Kagama* (1886) regarding states as the "deadliest enemies" of indigenous nations as relevant today as it was in the late nineteenth century? Or are indigenous and state governments today partners in the "utmost good faith," as the Northwest Ordinance mandated in 1787? The following chapters discuss how and why indigenous peoples have mobilized to meet contemporary challenges to their nationhood and self-determination.

CHAPTER TWO

Current Social Constructions of Indigenous Peoples

Whole nations have melted away in our presence like balls of snow before the sun, and have scarcely left their names behind, except as imperfectly recorded by their enemies and destroyers.

Cherokee war chief Dragging Canoe speaking to the treaty delegation at Sycamore Shoals, March 15, 1775

Distorted images of indigenous people are pervasive in the United States. One can readily see Natives depicted on products ranging from butter to chewing tobacco. These are not harmless depictions. Manufactured images of the bloodthirsty savage, the noble savage, the childlike Indian, the spirit guide, the militant protestor, and, now, the rich Indian that reduce indigenous peoples to one-dimensional stereotypes have become embedded in U.S. educational and governmental policymaking institutions.[1] By presenting indigenous peoples as subhuman caricatures, such contrived images deny true indigenous existences and the daily realities of contemporary Native peoples. To make matters worse, as a rich Indian racism model suggests, these stereotypes have been and continue to be used to inform policymaking decisions in terms of denying the "authenticity" of indigenous peoples and challenging the self-determining authority of indigenous nations.

This chapter takes an in-depth look at common social constructions, policy tools, and rationales that decision makers have employed when making indigenous policy during the forced federalism era and how social constructions have changed since the passage of the Indian Gaming Regulatory Act (IGRA) in 1988. Using a social constructions framework developed by political scientists Anne Schneider and Helen Ingram, the following sections describe how socially constructed images (e.g., militant, emerging contender, dependent) are applied to indigenous peoples during the policymaking process, add theoretical depth to the rich Indian racism model, provide additional insights into the complexities of decision making by state and federal policymakers, and expose existing power relations between policymaking elites and indigenous communities.[2]

GAMBLING ON NATIVE HOMELANDS

The passage of IGRA ushered in a new emphasis on states' rights. One year earlier in the 1987 case *California v. Cabazon Band of Mission Indians* (480 U.S. 202), the U.S. Supreme Court concluded that if gaming was lawful elsewhere in California, the state was precluded from asserting jurisdiction over similar gaming operations on Native homelands.

As a response to the lack of state oversight in the Cabazon case, IGRA compelled indigenous governments to negotiate compacts with state governments before beginning casino-style, or class III, gaming operations on Native homelands by establishing three classes of gaming:

> Class I gaming consists of "social games [played] solely for prizes of minimal value or traditional forms of indigenous gaming engaged in by individuals as part of, or in connection with, native ceremonies or celebrations."
>
> Class II gaming includes bingo, games similar to bingo, a select group of listed games played at the same location as bingo, and certain nonbanking card games. This form of gaming falls within the jurisdiction of indigenous nations but is subject to oversight by the National Indian Gaming Commission.
>
> Class III gaming covers "all forms of gaming that are not class I gaming or class II gaming." Class III gaming is lawful on Native lands only if conducted in conformance with an indigenous-state compact.[3]

Three criteria must be satisfied before class III gaming can take place: (1) the state in which the indigenous territory is located must permit similar gaming activities for any group, (2) the indigenous nation must pass its own resolution authorizing gaming activities, and (3) all gaming activities must be conducted in conformity with a compact negotiated by the indigenous nation and the state. According to the provisions of IGRA, net revenues from indigenous gaming facilities can only be used toward one of the following five areas: to fund tribal government operations or programs, to provide for the general welfare of the Indian tribe and its members, to promote tribal economic development, to donate to charitable organizations, or to help fund operations of local government agencies.

Conflicts have arisen as indigenous nations and states often have different ideas about the type and volume of gaming that should be permissible on Native homelands. In addition, some state governments have used IGRA to demand gaming proceeds as the price of negotiating a compact, which violates the exclusive federal trust relationship and the original policy dictates of IGRA: "Nothing in this section shall be interpreted as conferring upon a State or any of its political subdivisions authority to impose any tax, fee, charge, or other assessment upon an Indian tribe or upon any other person or entity authorized by an Indian tribe to engage in a class III activity. No State may refuse to enter into the negotiations described in paragraph (3)(A) based upon the lack of authority in such State, or its political subdivisions, to impose such a tax, fee, charge, or other assessment." State governors in Arizona, California, and Minnesota have conveniently ignored this policy when negotiating indigenous-state compacts. Consequently, the compacting system has made indigenous-state interactions more litigious and contentious.

As of this writing, there are 224 indigenous governments engaged in class II or class III gaming operations (330 total casinos), and they have negotiated a total of 255 indigenous-state compacts in twenty-eight states. Indigenous gaming revenue from 2004 was $16.7 billion, or approximately 22 percent of the total for the entire U.S. gaming industry.[4] The forty-three largest casinos, which represent only 5.5 percent of the overall reservation population, generated 64 percent of the total gaming revenues ($10.7 billion) in 2004. In contrast, the ten lowest-earning casinos, representing 42 percent of the overall reservation population, earned just 1 percent of all casino revenue.[5] Clearly, not all 224 indigenous nations operating casinos are getting wealthy. Furthermore, according to a 1998 Native Americans in Philanthropy study, even if gaming revenues were distributed equally to all indigenous peoples in the United States, the amount distributed, $3,000 per person, would not be enough to raise the indigenous per capita income of $4,500 to the current U.S. average of $14,400.[6]

Despite persistent images of rich Indians, most indigenous nations running casinos are breaking even. Some have even lost money, as evidenced by the closure of the Lummi Casino (Washington) in 1997 due to competition with gaming facilities in Canada.[7] Other indigenous nations have closed their casinos because of declining profits: the La Jolla Band of Luiseño Indians (California) closed their small slot arcade casino in 2005, the Crow Nation (Montana) shut down the Little Bighorn Casino in 2000 (it has since reopened), and the Hualapais (Arizona) closed their casino in 1995 after only seven months of operations (they have since opened a $30 million skywalk over the edge of the Grand Canyon). Still other indigenous nations had their casinos shut down by state government actions, such as the previously discussed court-ordered closures of the Tigua's Speaking Rock Casino and the Alabama-Coushatta Casino in Texas in 2002.

While only 40 percent of all federally recognized indigenous nations engage in casino gaming, indigenous peoples are increasingly being grouped into socially constructed categories as rich Indians in the U.S. political arena.[8] The following section examines how these stereotypical images are directly affecting indigenous nations.

CURRENT SOCIAL CONSTRUCTIONS OF INDIGENOUS PEOPLES

Social constructions of "target populations" (i.e., communities, such as indigenous nations, earmarked to be the main recipients of particular policy outcomes, whether rewards or punishments) refer to "the values and meanings associated with events, persons, groups, regions, countries, or any other objective or subjective situation."[9] Social constructions emerge from a number of sources either from within the target group or from the general public and sometimes can become "so ingrained most people accept them as real and as the only interpretation they can imagine."[10] While some socially constructed images, such as depictions of criminals as deviants, remain fairly constant over time, others, such as those applied to indigenous nations, are continually debated and manipulated.[11] These socially constructed images greatly influence the policy process when government decision makers characterize target populations as being either "undeserving" or "deserving" beneficiaries of policy outcomes.

Rich Indian social constructions are often perpetuated by media images, such as a 2002 *Time* magazine special report on indigenous gaming that inaccurately stresses the wealth and political influence of all indigenous nations who run casinos, characterizing it as "out of control." The illustration used to introduce an article titled "Playing the Political Slots" depicts a slot machine adorned with profiles of the stereotypical noble savage while massive amounts of money fly out of the bottom of the machine. Written on the base of the slot machine are the following words: "Jackpot! Winners: Casinos! Politicians! Losers: Taxpayers!"[12] While this article is not alone in conveying stereotypical images of rich Indians, it serves as an example of how distorted images of indigenous people and community strategies for economic development are constructed and reinforced.[13]

Images of rich Indians are now an easily recognizable feature of U.S. popular culture. Despite the fact that indigenous nations engage in several other forms of economic development (eco-tourism, motor fuels, tobacco sales, etc.), the general public appears fixated on the existence and success of indigenous gaming operations. Whether in an episode of *The Simpsons* television show depicting a Native casino on a remote island or *The Family Circus* cartoon in which one of the two young boys playing "Cowboys and Indians" pretends to be an Indian casino owner (see figure 2.1), the image of the rich Indian is all too common.[14]

The imagery of the rich Indian is also a regular feature in contemporary political campaigns and movements. Most notably, Arnold Schwarzenegger's 2003 gubernatorial election campaign in California stressed, "It's time for them [indigenous nations] to pay their fair share." The following is a script from one of Schwarzenegger's television ads:

A slot machine labeled "California Indian Casinos" appears on-screen, then the camera pans down as the slots stop on

THE FAMILY CIRCUS   By Bil Keane

4-20

©2002 Bil Keane, Inc.
Dist. by King Features Synd.
www.familycircus.com

JEFF
and
BIL KEANE

"... And I'll be an Indian. With a casino."

Figure 2.1. *The Family Circus* cartoon, by Bill Keane, 2002

"$120,000,000" and the words "Paid for by Californians for Schwarzenegger" appear. Schwarzenegger's voice is heard saying: "Indian casino tribes play money politics in Sacramento: $120 million in the last five years." Then Schwarzenegger, in a beige sport coat and white shirt with no tie, appears on-screen and speaks directly into the camera: "Their casinos make billions, yet they pay no taxes and virtually nothing to the state. Other states require revenue from Indian gaming, but not us. It's time for them to pay their fair share. All the other major candidates take their money and pander to them. I don't play that game. Give me your vote and I guarantee you things will change.[15]

The ad falsely indicates that all indigenous peoples are getting rich at the expense of California taxpayers. Consistent with a rich Indian racist model, the message was loud and clear: as emerging contenders on the political scene, the "unfair" activities of rich indigenous nations with casinos needed to be heavily taxed and regulated by state government officials. This idea resonated well with California voters, as Governor Schwarzenegger won the 2003 recall election over Grey Davis with 48 percent of the vote. Rich Indian images invoked during Schwarzenegger's campaign were instrumental in his new policy agenda as governor. Shortly after taking office, Governor Schwarzenegger renegotiated five indigenous nation–state compacts that force these indigenous nations to collectively contribute to an unprecedented $1 billion bond fund for the state and pay approximately $150 million a year in taxes to the state until the compacts expire in 2030.

Popular stereotypes of indigenous peoples today are increasingly shaped by policymakers. Indigenous people are ever more likely to be portrayed as rich, emerging contenders with "special rights" in state and federal politics (see figure 2.2). As socially constructed views of rich Indians with "special rights" become more prevalent among state governors and legislators, one would expect to see more regulatory policies targeting Native peoples as a result. According to Schneider and Ingram, "Social constructions become central to the strategies of public officials, especially those who are in elected or highly visible positions where they are expected to pay attention to public preferences, because people care intensely not only about what they receive from government, but what others are receiving as well, and why."[16]

Figure 2.2 demonstrates how contemporary indigenous nations might fit into a social constructions model based on widespread public perceptions of indigenous social conditions, federal legal status, strategies for achieving self-determination, and available resource base. The figure outlines several aspects of socially constructed Native images based on perceptions of a target population's relative power (stronger versus weaker) and how these targeted groups are perceived within society (either as deserving or undeserving). Having little or no grounding in reality, the three categories of indigenous nations

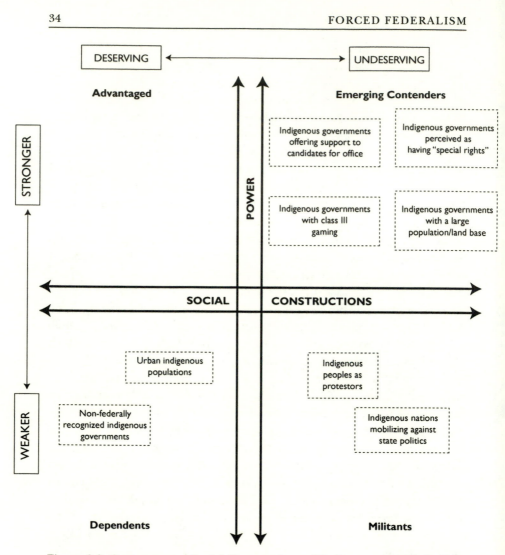

Figure 2.2. Contemporary Social Constructions of Indigenous People in U.S. Policy Contexts

in figure 2.2—"emerging contenders" (used interchangeably with the rich Indian image), "militants," and "dependents"—are invoked by policy elites to simplify the policymaking process, manipulate power, and appeal to their constituents. These categorizations are driven by the perceptions of the policymakers, the demands of their Native and non-Native constituents, and multiple other cultural and political contexts.

Not surprisingly, indigenous peoples are often treated as rich Indians or emerging contenders by state policymakers. According to this category, indigenous peoples are regarded as increasingly powerful entities and are often characterized as "undeserving" in terms of their political and economic power. A standard policymaking response is to extensively regulate them through taxation and revenue sharing to capitalize on their status as "undeserving" and to keep their power in check.

The socially constructed categories for indigenous nations may overlap according to the issue that they are pursuing and the ways in which they choose to exercise their powers. For example, as discussed in chapter 1, the Narragansett Nation was targeted by rich Indian racism when they expressed a desire to open a casino in Rhode Island. However, as we will see later in this chapter, the Narragansetts were portrayed as militants when they defended their right to operate a tax-free smoke shop on Narragansett territory.

Only five years after the indigenous right to vote was granted in Arizona, the Arizona Commission of Indian Affairs was established in 1953 to "consider and study conditions among the Indians residing within the state." Since that time, indigenous nations in Arizona have become much more active in state and federal affairs. For example, the very first American Indian Voters Convention was held in Phoenix, Arizona, in 1996 and was attended by more than five hundred people from all twenty-one federally recognized indigenous nations in Arizona. During the forced federalism era, indigenous peoples in Arizona and more generally are more likely regarded as rich, emerging contenders in the political arena, and this often leads to conflicts with state actors.

A 1992 conflict over gaming in Arizona demonstrates how social constructions of indigenous peoples can alternate between images of militants and emerging contenders.[19] This clash began when Arizona governor Fife Symington refused to consider the negotiation of indigenous-state gaming compacts. Governor Symington also claimed that five indigenous nations running casinos in Arizona were not legally allowed to operate according to IGRA policy and threatened to confiscate their slot machines. Early on the morning of May 12, 1992, five different indigenous communities were raided by the agents from the Federal Bureau of Investigation intent on seizing all their slot machines. After setting up SWAT teams on the roof of the

Fort McDowell Casino, federal agents loaded 349 gaming machines onto moving vans. Responding immediately to this encroachment onto their territory, citizens of Fort McDowell Yavapai Nation mobilized to set up a roadblock. Using all available quarry trucks nearby as well as pieces of heavy machinery, a blockade of the casino's access road was set up, and federal agents were stopped from removing the gaming machines from the community.[20] This intense standoff lasted for several hours until indigenous leaders, such as Yavapai Nation president Clinton Pattea, and Governor Symington agreed to a "cooling off" period.[21] All 349 of the gaming machines were destroyed three weeks later.[22]

Policymakers often respond to perceived militants negatively, with punishment or selective enforcement of policies. In this case, the perceived militancy of the Fort McDowell citizens raised their profile as emerging contenders with federal and state government officials. By February of 1993 a federal mediator, former Arizona Supreme Court justice Frank X. Gordon, sided with three of Arizona's indigenous nations by asserting that the governor could not unilaterally limit the number of slot machines operating in indigenous communities. In response to the mediator's decision, Symington called a special session of the state legislature to enact a bill that would criminally prohibit class III gaming in Arizona while leaving the state lottery and pari-mutuel betting at horse and dog tracks untouched. The conflict subsided when Secretary of the Interior Bruce Babbitt proposed a compromise position, linking the allocation of slot machines to the population size of particular indigenous communities; by April 1994 sixteen indigenous nations had entered into compacts with the state of Arizona.[23]

As this example illustrates, rich Indian and emerging contender images lead to heavier regulation measures by state policymakers. In this case, the indigenous-state compacts were designed to limit the scope and type of gaming operations. According to Schneider and Ingram's research, policy benefits offered to emerging contenders tend to be more symbolic, hollow, and deceptive. While the sixteen indigenous-state compacts negotiated in 1994 were praised publicly as an alternative to litigation, negotiations only delayed future indigenous-state conflicts. In May 1995 Governor Symington took a stand against indigenous gaming once again by refusing to negotiate any further indigenous-state compacts.[24]

Another example of a militant social construction involves the Narragansett Nation (discussed in chapter 1). On July 12, 2003, after several meetings where Rhode Island governor Don Carcieri voiced his objections, the Narragansetts opened a tax-free smoke shop on their homelands. Two days later, twenty-four state troopers with a search warrant raided the Narragansett Smoke Shop. The state troopers met with determined resistance as some were wrestled to the ground by Narragansetts protecting their shop and territory. When the dust cleared, eight people were taken to the hospital with injuries, and eight Narragansetts were arrested, including Chief Sachem Matthew Thomas.[25] The state maintained that the Narragansett Smoke Shop violated the Rhode Island Claims Settlement of 1978, which specifies that indigenous lands are subject to state jurisdiction. Judge William Smith of the federal district court later ruled that the July 14, 2003, raid by state troopers violated neither federal law nor the tribes sovereign rights. In May 2006, the First Circuit U.S. Court of Appeals affirmed the earlier district court ruling and held that the "state officers were authorized to execute the warrant against the Tribe and to arrest tribal members incident to the enforcement of the State's civil and criminal laws."[26] The majority opinion of the court went on to assert that "the Tribe abandoned any right to an autonomous enclave, submitting itself to state law as a quid pro quo for obtaining the land that it cherished."[27]

Such a legal outcome is predictable based on a social constructions model of rich Indians. While the Narragansett Nation never ceded away their self-determining authority under the Rhode Island Claims Settlement of 1978, the court's language ("abandoned any right to an autonomous enclave") is another example of legal fiction that reinforces state policymakers' claims of jurisdictional oversight of the Narragansett Nation. State and federal authorities used the 2003 raid to challenge Narragansett self-determination and treaty rights by enacting punitive policies designed to expand the state's jurisdictional scope of the Rhode Island Claims Settlement of 1978. As Circuit Judge Torruella wrote in his dissenting opinion, "There should be no question but that the State's actions directed against the Tribe constituted a clear and egregious violation of its tribal sovereignty."[28]

Newspaper accounts of the police raid on the Narragansett Smoke Shop alternated between describing it as a "scuffle," "protest," "resistance," and "melee." While standard imagery of the "militant" was not as prominent in the write-ups, newspaper pictures tell a different story. The *New York Times* ran a picture showing two Narragansetts shoving a police officer, while the coverage from a Native-run Internet news organization based on the Winnebago Reservation, Indianz.com, showed pictures of troopers pinning Narragansett men and women on the ground; in one picture, a Narragansett man was hand-cuffed and face down on the ground with a police German shepherd lunging at him.[29] While Narragansetts were initially portrayed as militants by Governor Carcieri and the mainstream news coverage, subsequent reports highlighted the unjust nature of the raid and the overreaction by state troopers.

Even with strong, positive public reaction to this event, this support for Narragansett peoples did not translate into political capital when their casino proposal was voted down by a wide margin in 2006. Rich Indian images were invoked to undermine the self-determining authority of the Narragansett Nation with respect to gaming. With increasing state regulation of indigenous nations and the framing of indigenous nations as emerging contenders, policy responses to the Narragansetts and other Native nations throughout the United States have been what a social constructions model would predict: hollow and deceptive.

Another example involves portrayals of non-federally recognized indigenous nations as both dependents and emerging contenders. There are over two hundred non-federally recognized indigenous nations throughout the United States, including the Houma Nation (Louisiana), the Nipmuc Nation (Massachusetts), the Duwamish Indian Nation (Washington), the Lumbee Nation (North Carolina), and the eight state-recognized indigenous nations in Virginia.[30] As one of the indigenous nations in Virginia, the Monacan Nation has its roots in Siouan-speaking peoples, with over fourteen hundred Monacan citizens living in Amherst County, Virginia, today.[31] While Monacans might be categorized as dependent by some state policymakers in Virginia when described as a non-federally recognized indigenous nation, this all depends on the political context and one's frame of reference. For example, the Monacan Nation has lobbied members of Congress for federal recognition, secured the repatriation of ancestral remains from state museums, purchased 120 acres of the original Johns' Settlement on Bear Mountain, and encouraged people to vote for political candidates friendly to their efforts.[32] As anthropologist

Sam Cook observes, "the Monacans do compose a formidable voting bloc, and candidates for state, local and national office frequently request a special audience with the tribe near election time."[33] The political activities of the Monacans and other non-federally recognized indigenous nations in the southeastern United States bear this out. Based on a survey of a small number of non-federally recognized indigenous nations taken in 1998, 57 percent of those indigenous nations responding claimed that state government officials paid "some" or "a good deal of" attention to what their community was thinking before setting policies affecting them. In addition, 71 percent of the respondents claimed that the federal government paid no attention to their concerns. In other words, indigenous leaders of non-federally recognized indigenous nations believe that states and local governments were more responsive to their needs than the federal government.[34]

In terms of perceived effect of their political actions, five indigenous nations responding to the survey (71 percent) believe that their nation had "little influence on election outcomes." Only one nation responding believed that their nation had "no influence on election outcomes," while the other respondent believed that their nation had a "good deal of influence on election outcomes." When asked which issues motivated them to vote, issue positions of political candidates and membership in their nation were identified as the key factors. Overall, the survey results demonstrate that non-federally recognized indigenous nations are politically active and defy widespread prevailing social constructions of politically inactive nations dependent on state and local programs.

However, without the benefits of federal recognition, which would enable Monacans and other Virginia indigenous nations to strengthen their communities with increased federal protections for religious freedom (1978 American Indian Religious Freedom Act) and child welfare (1978 Indian Child Welfare Act), along with eligibility for federal assistance in the areas of education and health care (1975 Self-Determination and Educational Assistance Act, 1988 Self-Governance Project), housing programs through HUD, and so on, the Monacan Nation has limited resources to influence state policymaking agendas.

With regards to the Monacan example, the specter of the rich Indian also affects those seeking federal recognition. Former Virginia governor James Gilmore and U.S. Representative Frank Wolf have repeatedly asserted that Virginia indigenous nations are essentially seeking federal recognition to open casinos. Despite the hypocrisy of such a claim, especially given the commonwealth of Virginia's strong attachment to proceeds from the lottery since 1987 and legalized betting on horse races, Virginia indigenous nations, including the Monacan Nation, have never expressed a desire to establish casinos. As Cook explains, "the Monacans have consistently asserted that although they have no intentions of establishing a casino if they receive federal recognition, they would regard it as their sovereign right if they chose to do so."[35] In fact, if any desire to run gaming establishments existed, Virginia indigenous nations could have opened high stakes bingo parlors beginning in the 1970s. Bingo parlors are major sources of revenue for indigenous nations around the country and allowable as class II gaming under federal and state law. As Monacan chief Kenneth Branham states, "If we were interested in any form of gambling, very simply, we could have bingo parlors right now."[36]

Therefore, despite being viewed as dependents by some policymakers when seeking state funding or requesting ancestral remains housed in state museums, the Monacans and other indigenous nations may also be arbitrarily portrayed as emerging contenders with special rights when pursuing federal recognition.[37] The Monacan example exhibits the manipulation of rich Indian social constructions by policy elites, often based solely on the political considerations of elected officials seeking power. Such state regulatory oversight undermines the self-determining authority of indigenous nations by exploiting public and private fears over imagined indigenous nation economic development initiatives.

A similar incidence of rich Indian racism occurred in Arkansas in November 2005. Arkansas state legislators rejected a proposal to grant state recognition to indigenous nations, fearing that state recognition would somehow lead to the opening of indigenous-run casinos in their state. Apparently, a State Department of Finance and Administration official warned legislators that state recognition of Indian tribes and groups could hasten federal recognition, which could open the door to Indian casinos and smoke shops on tribal land without the state's consent.[38] Despite the inaccuracy of the state official's claim, false perceptions of indigenous peoples often trump the complex realities in policy decision making circles in a forced federalism context.

Policymakers treat indigenous peoples considered dependent as being powerless, helpless, needy, and, ultimately, private sector's responsibility.[39] While generally viewed as populations deserving benefits, dependent groups are by and large regarded with pity and deemed unable to act on their own behalf to change their powerless situation. Consequently, socially constructed dependents are heavily regulated by complex, governmental oversight regarding eligibility requirements for nation-building programs (i.e., federal recognition). While public officials want to appear sympathetic, they do not see any political advantage to directing resources toward the interests of those who lack political clout. This inaccurate perception of powerlessness is most pronounced for urban indigenous peoples and for non-federally recognized indigenous nations.

Social constructions of rich Indians have converged with images of indigenous peoples as emerging contenders. Public and policymaker perceptions of victimhood or dependence tend to be sympathetic but paternalistic; any attempt to break free of this stereotype places one into an emerging contender category and is regarded as potentially threatening to non-Native interests. When that happens, the prevailing public and policymaking approach shifts from pity to hostility. Anthropologist Kate Spilde's findings on rich Indian racism suggest that indigenous nations are caught in a trap of constantly defending both their nationhood and self-determination claims. When indigenous peoples do assert their powers of self-determination, they are often treated as emerging contenders by policymakers who attempt to tax or regulate them. Such circular and ethnocentric reasoning is difficult to counter in an era where state governments often frame the politics of perception and indigenous peoples are forced into a defensive position of responding to these distorted perceptions.

Invented images of Natives as casino rich or as aspiring casino entrepreneurs limit the ability of indigenous nations to act in the best interests of their communities. A prime example of an emerging contender where the dynamics of rich Indian racism are in full force is the Mashantucket Pequot Tribe in Connecticut, which runs the most profitable casino in the world: Foxwoods Resort Casino. During the 2002 election year, the Pequots donated a total of $410,825 to political candidates in the form of political action committees (PACs), soft money donations, and individual donations.[40] Yet these political contributions pale in comparison to their donations to the National

Museum of the American Indian ($10 million), Mystic Aquarium ($5 million), the 1995 Special Olympics World Games in Connecticut ($2 million), as well as other indigenous nations, such as the Oglala Nation (South Dakota) and Red Coat Chippewa (Minnesota) for school supplies.[41] Moreover, 25 percent of the annual profits from the Foxwoods Resort Casino's operation of slot machines go to the state of Connecticut.

Federally recognized by an act of Congress in 1983, the Mashantucket Pequot Nation initially opened a high-stakes bingo hall on their reservation in 1986. In the late 1980s when the Pequots requested the state of Connecticut to enter into negotiations for a casino, the state refused. Consequently, the secretary of the interior approved the Pequot casino without slot machines through publication in the Federal Register as "federal procedures" under the dictates of IGRA. To this day, there is no official compact between the state of Connecticut and the Mashantucket Pequots; all gaming on the reservation is governed by the Department of Interior IGRA federal procedures, which hold Pequot gaming rights in perpetuity (versus most indigenous-state compacts that are renegotiated every ten to twenty years).[42] However, even with this IGRA precedent, slot machines were still not allowable in the Foxwoods Resort Casino when it opened its doors for business in 1992.

By 1993 Governor Lowell Weicker, acting on behalf of the state of Connecticut, which was experiencing a budget crisis at the time, negotiated a memorandum of understanding (MOU) with the Mashantucket Pequots. This MOU granted the Pequots exclusive rights to run slot machines in the state in return for 25 percent of the annual profits from these machines going to the state of Connecticut.[43] The agreement was modified in 1994 to permit the Mohegan Nation to operate slot machines in Connecticut while also requiring the Mohegans to also contribute 25 percent of their annual slot machine profits to the state. Currently, the state of Connecticut draws approximately $350–400 million per year from the Pequot and Mohegan casinos.[44]

Consistent with Spilde's predictions that images of rich Indians often lead to challenges regarding "authenticity," the approximately eight hundred citizens of the Pequot Nation have had their identities and genealogies challenged by news reporters, corporate leaders, and politicians. For example, when testifying before the Senate Committee on Indian Affairs in 1992, casino mogul Donald Trump stated, "Now [the Pequots] don't look like real Indians to me, and they don't look like real Indians to other Indians."[45] Trump has since distanced himself from this statement after taking over the management of Trump 29, the Twenty-Nine Palms Band of Mission Indians' casino in California. He also contributed $9,192,807 to the Paucatuck Eastern Pequots in Connecticut to assist in their quest for federal recognition, which is now the subject of a lawsuit.[46]

The most blatant effort to challenge the legitimacy of Pequot identity, however, was a 2001 book titled *Without Reservation: How a Controversial Indian Tribe Rose to Power and Built the World's Largest Casino*, written by lawyer and investigative journalist Jeff Benedict. Amid contradictory reports and questionable anecdotal information, Benedict concludes that "the real Pequot tribe has been non-existent for years."[47] Interestingly, Benedict is now the president of the Connecticut Alliance against Casino Expansion, which was formed in 2002 to prevent future indigenous casinos from opening in Connecticut and to reform the federal recognition process of indigenous nations.[48]

Based on a social constructions approach, rich Indians, or emerging contenders, such as the Pequots, who opened the Foxwoods Casino in 1992, are often differentiated from historically advantaged groups, such as business executives and scientists, in that the former "have traditionally been disliked and discriminated against."[49] While policymakers tend to promise capacity-building measures to overcome the historical legacies of colonialism and racism toward Native peoples, the actual policy "almost never offers any actual redress of grievances for those it was intended to protect."[50] This is where rich Indian racism leads to increased state regulation and taxation by policymakers. For Pequots and other rich Indians or emerging contenders, policy burdens tend to be hidden or disguised by indigenous-state compact agreements, which set regulations on particular types of gaming, such as slot machines. Subtle regulatory controls found in tribal-state gaming compacts can often mask new state jurisdictional claims, such as Governor Arnold Schwarzenegger's renegotiation of five indigenous-state compacts, which allow the state of California a greater "regulatory power over the tribes in areas of tort law, mitigation, the environment and state inspection of machines."[51]

Another example of a rich Indian racist mentality is the amended 2000 tribal-state gaming compact between the Sisseton-Wahpeton Sioux Tribe and the state of South Dakota (see appendix B for a copy of the entire compact). Their gaming compact includes the following article under "General Provisions": "11.10. The Tribe hereto agrees that none of the funds generated by the gaming conducted under this compact shall be used by the tribe or its agents to influence the outcome of any local, state or federal elections conducted within the state of South Dakota." Unfortunately, limits on political contributions that were first applied to the Sisseton-Wahpeton Sioux indigenous-state compact have subsequently been extended to the other indigenous nations running casinos in South Dakota. Elsie Meeks (Oglala Lakota), who has run for state office in South Dakota, argues that this agreement "compromises tribal influence and voter involvement in a state where few tribal politicians have made their way into state seats."[52] Such a rich Indian racist measure is designed to limit the potential influence of Native peoples in state policymaking.

A final example of rich Indian racism and social constructions approach to policymaking took place in Minnesota. In 2004 Minnesota governor Tim Pawlenty proposed a gaming revenue sharing plan requiring indigenous nations operating casinos to pay the state $350 million per year for exclusive gaming rights.[53] If indigenous nations were to refuse his revenue-sharing plan, Governor Pawlenty threatened to open up the rest of Minnesota to corporate casinos to compete with the existing eighteen indigenous-run casinos for their profits. Not only was the governor's tactic a form of extortion against perceived rich Indians in Minnesota, but it violated IGRA policy, which specifically prohibits states from imposing "any tax, fee, charge, or other assessment upon an Indian tribe or upon any other person or entity authorized by an Indian tribe to engage in a class III activity."

Governor Pawlenty aggressively promoted his plan through television commercials and radio ads, claiming that his revenue sharing plan was a "better deal for all Minnesotans." Only two indigenous leaders (out of eleven indigenous nations who operate the eighteen casinos in Minnesota) actually met with the governor to discuss his proposed plan, and others banded together to vehemently reject his proposal. In a letter to Governor Pawlenty, Chairman Stanley Crooks of the Shakopee Mdewankanton Sioux (Dakota) Nation challenged the governor's revenue sharing plan: "There is not reasonable justification for you to demand, or otherwise expect, tribal governments in Minnesota to share any of their gaming revenues with state government. . . . Tribal gaming revenues are for tribal governments and Indian people to use in an effort to address historically dire conditions on Indian reservations. Such conditions persist today in most of Indian Country."[54] Pawlenty used the State of the State Address to respond to the indigenous leaders rejecting his revenue sharing proposal and to frame the issue as one of rich Indians unfairly withholding casino profits from all Minnesotans: "In my address last year, I spoke on the issue of gaming. My preference then is my preference now: To keep gaming within its existing contours, but to explore a better deal for all Minnesotans. My hope was that tribes with large casino gaming interests would make a fair payment to the state in exchange for being granted a monopoly and other benefits. It appears they're not interested in such an agreement."[55]

In sum, all these examples are consistent with Schneider and Ingram's findings that rich Indians or emerging contenders experience deceptive signals from policymakers and that policies deemed beneficial to this target population are often illogical and empty.[56] As the Pequots, the Sisseton-Wahpeton Sioux, and the Shakopee Mdewankanton Sioux examples demonstrate, the social constructions of rich Indians and emerging contenders are apt to be more negative than positive. The resulting state policy emphasis is placed on regulation of existing activity versus enacting true nation-building or capacity-building policy tools.

With the prevalence of rich Indian image since 1988, indigenous nations tend to be regarded as emerging contenders because of the proliferation of indigenous gaming (330 indigenous gaming facilities run by 196 Native nations throughout the United States)—even if they have no casino. In fact, most indigenous nations in the United States that run casinos are only breaking even with casino profits. Unfortunately, when they are labeled or conceived of as emerging contenders, indigenous nations tend to be treated by state policymakers as interest groups rather than as nations. This is an extension of the rich Indian racism model, which serves to deny indigenous identities while exerting more powers, such as taxation and regulation, over the day-to-day operations of indigenous governments.

Since state governors are the main actors who negotiate indigenous-state gaming compacts, how do the rich Indian and emerging contender images play into indigenous policy since the passage of IGRA in 1988? If indigenous nations are increasingly viewed as emerging contenders, one would expect a greater emphasis on regulatory and deceptive policies (versus policies designed for capacity building or community strengthening) from state governors and legislators. The following section examines policies from the National Governor's Association (NGA) annual meetings and state legislation from the National Conference of State Legislature (NCSL) to demonstrate how Natives have been increasingly regarded as emerging contenders in their states since the passage of IGRA in 1988.

REGULATORY AND NATION-BUILDING POLICIES

Which specific policy tools are used by state governors when dealing with rich Indians or emerging contenders? As Schneider and Ingram point out in their research on policy making contexts, the use of particular policy tools will affect certain desired political outcomes. In their extensive research they determined the five main means of formulating policy to be authority tools, inducements and sanctions, capacity-building tools, hortatory tools, and learning tools.[57] For example, policies making use of authority tools do not necessarily rely on the threat of sanctions or punishment to achieve the desired result. Instead, there is an underlying expectation that people will do what they are told without question because it is considered the right thing to do. Within an indigenous policy context, this type of thinking is indicative of paternalism reflective of colonial policymaking. Given that several colonial images, mentalities, and methods remain embedded in the institutional structures of the U.S. government, such as the Bureau of Indian Affairs, the authority policy tool continues to influence indigenous policymaking. Psychiatrist and revolutionary writer Frantz Fanon describes how this process of colonialism is an ongoing dialectic: "Colonialism is not satisfied merely with holding a people in its grip and emptying the native's brain of all form and content. By a kind of perverted logic, it turns to the past of the oppressed people, and distorts, disfigures, and destroys it. This work of devaluing pre-colonial history takes on a dialectical significance today."[58]

Another example of a policy framework, hortatory tools, relies on the use of symbols and values to motivate the general public.[59] Hortatory tools most closely relate to symbolic public recognition (versus the more substantial policies such as federal recognition), such as the annual celebration of Native Heritage Month. Along the same lines, while hortatory learning tools are useful for encouraging policy-makers and targets to resolve problems, they often are directed toward beginning a process of discovery rather than actually taking action toward any specific goal.[60] Given the pressing needs of indigenous communities in the areas of health care, education, counseling, economic livelihood, employment, and so on, the luxury of time for "discovery" is often not afforded to indigenous peoples whose main goal is survival.

Inducements as policy tools encourage ostensibly voluntary actions based on tangible payoffs, whereas sanctions are harsh punishments for failing to abide by certain policies. Yet both inducements and sanctions are forms of coercion (some more subtle than others). In that sense, they emphasize the regulatory powers wielded by policy-makers as more of a top-down, hierarchical approach as opposed to a community-building approach. This type of regulatory or coercive policy is most often used by policymakers viewing emerging contenders as either a threat or a competitor to their economic or political well-being.

Capacity-building is a strategy for Native communities seeking more access to education, technical assistance, and knowledge necessary to take positive actions to benefit an entire community. In contrast to regulatory policies that are designed to limit indigenous self-determining authority, capacity-building policies are intended to strengthen communities by enhancing their powers of self-determination.[61] This tool comes the closest to describing indigenous nation-building strategies. It also promotes decolonization or eradicating harmful institutional legacies, including the elimination of stereotypes promoted by colonial powers, such as childlike Indians as well as rich Indians. Therefore, the term used in this research that is the equivalent to "capacity building" is "nation building," which is a more appropriate description of indigenous self-determination goals and strategies.

In the following analysis of the National Governors' Association (NGA) meetings and the National Conference of State Legislature (NCSL) findings, the policies enacted are examined for their level of coercive and regulatory content versus community-based or nation-building tools. Indigenous nations as emerging contenders have found their way onto the policymaking agendas of the NGA as well as state legislatures on a scale not witnessed before the forced federalism era.

Before 1988 there was little mention of indigenous nations at the NGA annual proceedings. By 1993, however, indigenous nations were prominent on the NGA agenda as subjects of state regulatory oversight. Over the course of twenty years of NGA policymaking activity, there was a clear transition among state governors from nation-building policies of the 1980s to more regulation-driven indigenous policies during the 1990s.

As President Reagan promoted his philosophy of "new federalism" in the early 1980s, concern over state policy jurisdiction over indigenous affairs was first raised during the 1985 NGA meeting, resulting in a policy statement on the continuation of historical federal responsibilities. Interestingly, the governors criticize federal spending that reduced health, education, nutrition, and economic welfare services to "needy citizens," including indigenous nations, during the 1980s.[62] Further reductions in federal services were deemed allowable only if "time be allowed for sorting out of responsibilities among federal, state, and local governments."[63] There was uncertainty over how governors should proceed with regards to traditional federal jurisdictional spheres, and the NGA was attempting to provide some policy framework for sharing the distribution of these services. The only other mention of indigenous peoples during the 1980s is in 1988 with an NGA policy on enhancing educational programs for "at risk" populations, such as "residents of Indian reservations."[64]

Of the four times that indigenous people are mentioned at the NGA proceedings between 1980 and 1988, two are devoted to nation-building policies in education and employment. The other two aforementioned NGA policies are regulatory in nature and designed to clarify state jurisdictional claims with respect to Native water policy and cuts in federal services to indigenous nations. Between 1980 and 1988, state governors appear concerned about their role in indigenous policy but do not assert any claims of jurisdictional control over forms of economic development. It would be reasonable to say that indigenous nations were largely regarded as "dependent" by governors involved in these 1980–88 proceedings, given the language used and policies being promoted. By 1990, however, this perception began to shift to an emerging contender social construction, which coincides with the passage of IGRA in 1988.

In a revelation during the 1990 meetings, the NGA Executive Committee identified a "trend toward the erosion of state authority"

and much of the NGA agenda focused on "restoring the constitutional balance."[65] By 1993 indigenous gaming reached the NGA
agenda, which is not surprising given the high profile 1992 showdown
between Governor Symington and five indigenous nations in Arizona.
Given a widespread belief that state governors are "expected to
negotiate Indian gaming compacts that would be in conflict with
the laws of their states and beyond the requirements of IGRA," the
NGA adopted three recommendations to guide future indigenous-
state interactions:

> 1. "A state is not obligated to negotiate a compact to allow a
> tribe to operate any and all forms of Class III gaming simply
> because a state allows one form of Class III gaming."
> 2. "Mere inability to agree upon a compact should not indi-
> cate bad faith by either party."
> 3. "There must be clarification of the ability of a state to bar
> gaming on property taken into trust subsequent to the effective
> date of the Indian Gaming Regulatory Act."[66]

The 1993 NGA recommendations were designed to give states
the upper hand when negotiating gaming compacts by expanding
their authority and jurisdictional control over indigenous nations.
The NGA concern over "bad faith" highlights an unwillingness to let
indigenous-state compact disputes to be decided in favor of indigenous
nations and also represents a blatant effort to avoid mediation by
the U.S. secretary of the interior. Overall, the tone of these 1993
policy positions is a paternalistic assertion of states' rights and signi-
fies a deeper shift in thinking about indigenous nations—a transition from regarding them as dependents to that of competitors or
emerging contenders.

The trend toward more regulatory NGA approaches to indigenous
policy during the 1990s continued at the 1996 NGA meeting, when
governors sought clarification on indigenous-state environmental relations. In a policy position paper titled "Environmental Priorities and
Unfunded Mandates," governors called on Congress to set standards
for indigenous management of environmental resources. At the core
of this jurisdictional dispute was the notion that decisions about
natural resources and environmental issues may have significant
implications, economic and otherwise, beyond tribal boundaries.[67]

Debates over jurisdictional boundary disputes on Native homelands intensified during the 1996 meeting when the U.S. Supreme Court ruling in *Seminole Tribe of Florida v. Florida* was discussed. NGA attendees believed that the court reinforced state sovereignty with the ruling on the case.[68] Seeking relief from direct intervention by the secretary of the interior in indigenous-state gaming compacting, the NGA outlined an agenda to strengthen states' rights relative to indigenous nations: "Governors firmly believe that it is an inappropriate breach of state sovereignty for the federal government to compel states to negotiate tribal operation of gambling activities that are not otherwise permitted by state law."[69]

The role of states in providing health services to Native peoples was also the subject of a policy debate during the 1996 NGA session. Attendees claimed that "states do not have treaty-based trust responsibilities to provide health care to Native American peoples" and therefore were not required to "subsidize the U.S. government trust responsibility."[70] Coming to grips with a changing indigenous-state relationship, state governors attempted to delineate their roles in indigenous policy decisions and emphasize regulatory rather than nation-building policy tools in their efforts. The regulatory policy approach taken by state governors between 1988 and 2003 is consistent with the policy tools one would predict for indigenous peoples who have been socially constructed as emerging contenders.

By 1999 the NGA attendees recognized that in a "new economy" with more federal powers devolving to states, any removal of Native trust lands from the state and local tax rolls would have a significant effect.[71] Concerns were so widespread that NGA executive director Raymond Scheppach drafted a letter on October 14, 1999, to Secretary of the Interior Bruce Babbitt regarding the trust land conversion issue. Scheppach's letter contends that the "legislative history of the Indian Reorganization Act (IRA) is not accurately reflected in these proposed legislations" and that "the awarding of trust land status to property can have serious consequences on non-Indian communities." In questioning the objectivity of the Department of Interior and bypassing the once exclusive federal trust relationship, Scheppach demands that "states and affected local communities should be given a voice in this process," as "information from tribes may be inaccurate."[72] The language in the letter portrays indigenous nations as having some sort of unfair advantage without any reference to their preconstitutional, self-determining status as nations. Instead, they are portrayed as threatening to the well-being of non-indigenous communities as emerging economic competitors (i.e., rich Indians).

At the 2000 NGA meeting, governors declared that the "new economy" would require a "new framework and new models of governance on how to regulate, tax, and deliver government services and investments."[73] The issue of indigenous gaming was again featured in the discussions as governors expressed their opinion that "Congressional establishment of minimum regulatory standards should not preempt stricter state laws, nor should it prevent states from negotiating with tribal governments for more stringent regulatory standards as part of a tribal/state compact."[74] Of particular concern was the congressional proposal for changing the procedures for taking land into trust for indigenous nations. Governors at the 2000 NGA communicated anxiety over being excluded from the process of trust land conversion and proposed that "no trust land acquisition for gambling purposes pursuant either to federal statute or administrative purposes should be possible without a Governor's concurrence."[75]

The official NGA policy on the role of states, the federal government, and Indian tribal governments with respect to Indian gaming and other economic issues became effective in 2003 after undergoing some revisions. In this updated policy statement, NGA specifies its "traditional role of states as regulators of gambling," asserting that "it is an inappropriate breach of state sovereignty . . . for the federal government to compel states to negotiate tribal operation of gambling activities that are not available to others in the state."[76] Rather than acknowledge the self-determination of indigenous nations, the NGA chooses to regard them on par with "others in the state." This 2003 NGA policy position was designed to increase regulatory control over indigenous nations, who are regarded as rich, emerging contenders. With subheadings such as "The Scope of Gaming," "Regulatory Oversight," and "Unauthorized Tribal Gaming Activities," the NGA asserts jurisdiction in areas never intended by IGRA.

The NGA policy position that best exhibits changing intergovernmental relations is section 6.3, "The Governors' Role in Congressional and Other Federal Decision-Making," in which the NGA challenges the federal trust relationship with indigenous nations by asserting, "Tribal recognition through any federal administrative procedure should require the concurrence of the Governor(s) of the state(s) in which the tribe and/or the proposed land is located."[77] The once exclusive indigenous government–to–federal government relationship based on prior treaties, direct consultation with Congress on indigenous affairs, federal statutory obligations, and court decisions is openly contested by section 6.3. The resulting regulatory oversight that state governors presume to possess is based on a legal fiction developed in response to an emerging contenders social construction.

Much has changed since 1988. Based on the NGA proceedings, governors have steadily increased their jurisdiction over indigenous nations in the areas of taxation, health service, environmental protection, and gaming. As hypothesized earlier, with the onset of forced federalism in 1988, regulatory rather than nation-building policies have become more prevalent with regards to NGA focus on Native peoples. As long as states assert jurisdictional primacy over indigenous nations in areas of economic development, these two actors will remain at odds over the scope and domain of their rights as citizens.

Overall, regulatory rather than nation-building policies targeting indigenous nations have become more prevalent since 1993. Consequently, the jurisdictional domains between states and indigenous nations remains contentious despite the large number of indigenous-state compacts negotiated since 1988. Rather than being recognized as self-determining nations whose power supersedes state authority, the NGA evidence demonstrates that states view Native peoples as emerging contenders similar to other interest groups to be regulated and burdened by coercive policies, in line with the predicted outcomes of a social constructions model.

To gain a comprehensive view of legislative policies targeting Native peoples, all enacted state legislation addressing indigenous economic development (including all enacted gaming and taxation legislation targeting indigenous nations) and environmental policy (i.e., water rights, hunting and fishing rights, land and resource management, etc.) throughout the United States between 1994 and 2003 were examined. Detailed legislative reports from the National Conference of State Legislatures (NCSL) offer clues as to whether the enacted state legislation was primarily regulatory and coercive as a policy tool or whether it was community empowering by enhancing the capacity of indigenous nations. Table 2.1 shows the general trends in state policy-making that warrant further discussion. In state policies relating to indigenous economic development, regulatory policies greatly

TABLE 2.1
Policy Tools Used in State Legislation Relating to
Indigenous Nations, 1994–2003

	Economic development legislation		Environmental legislation	
	Regulatory no. (%)	Nation-buiding no. (%)	Regulatory no. (%)	Nation-building no. (%)
1994	19 (70)	8 (30)	1 (10)	9 (90)
1995	15 (63)	9 (37)	0	2 (100)
1998	28 (93)	2 (7)	3 (75)	1 (25)
1999	49 (96)	2 (4)	17 (45)	21 (55)
2000	36 (88)	5 (12)	20 (48)	22 (52)
2001	16 (53)	14 (47)	5 (38)	8 (62)
2002	6 (55)	5 (45)	1 (25)	3 (75)
2003	14 (78)	4 (22)	6 (55)	5 (45)

SOURCES: For 1994 data, Kimberly A. Moin, "1994 State Legislation on Native American Issues," National Conference of State Legislatures; for 1995 data, National Conference of State Legislatures, "1995 State Legislation on Native American Issues"; for 1998–2003 data, State Legislation Database on Native American Issues, National Conference on State Legislatures, http://www.ncsl.org/orpgrams/esnr/statetribal.cfm (accessed September 1, 2004).

NOTE: Missing years (1996–97) are due to budget shortfalls at NCSL in collecting the data.

outnumber nation-building efforts, often by a margin greater than ten to one. The exception appears to be 2001, when regulatory policies only slightly surpassed nation-building policies.

One example of nation-building economic development legislation in 2001 was House Bill 104/LD in Maine, which stated that "a federally recognized Indian tribe that operates high-stakes bingo is operating in the tribe's governmental capacity and is not subject to taxation."[78] In contrast, Louisiana Senate Resolution 136 had more of a regulatory focus; that legislation "urges and requests the secretary of the Department of the Interior to consider the will of the people regarding indigenous casino gaming and the significant effects gaming activity has on the surrounding communities before it authorizes the use of native lands for the purpose of conducting Class III gaming in certain parishes in the state."[79] These two policy tools have different goals when it comes to indigenous gaming. The bill from Maine clarifies an indigenous nation's tax-exempt status, while the resolution from Louisiana seeks additional oversight on indigenous casino development.

Overall, however, there is a clear trend toward increased regulation of all forms of indigenous economic development, whether motor fuels taxation or Native businesses operating on the reservation. This is most apparent in state legislatures around the country during the years 1998–2000. Based on the sheer volume of regulatory policies passed that target Native peoples (see table 2.1), state policymakers appear to regard indigenous nations as economic competitors for state revenue and are responding to them as emerging contenders.

Juxtaposed with economic development state legislation, environmental policies enacted between 1994 and 2003 were more likely to emphasize indigenous nation-building tools. Nation-building policies were most prominent in environmental areas such as wolf recovery, hunting and fishing freely on Native land, and water rights compacts. Overall, the data bears out a trend toward greater indigenous-state cooperation, as sociologist Erich Steinman points out: "Tribes' demonstration of their growing governmental capacity in natural-resources protection and other spheres also gave increasing credibility to their claims that they should be treated as peer-like governments and built additional trust with state-agency officials substantively concerned about their respective regulatory domains."[80]

A prime example of a regulatory policy enacted in 1999 was New Mexico Senate Bill 737, which established a process for the negotiation and approval for gaming compacts between the state and indigenous nations and required legislative ratification of all compacts. A more extreme case of regulatory policy is Oklahoma Senate Bill 1410 (2002), which established a moratorium on state-tribal compacts apportioning surface water or groundwater or implementing the exportation of certain water outside the state. A 2003 example of nation-building legislation is Washington Senate Resolution 8667, which "urges the Congress to allow the conveyance of approximately 20,000 acres of National Forest lands in the area of the Icicle River to the Colville Confederated Tribes, to be managed for the benefit of the Wenatchi people."[82] Another model of nation-building strategy, Oregon Senate Bill 961 (2001), allows for up to five hundred pounds of Department of Fish and Wildlife surplus salmon to be given to Burns Paiute Tribe for "historical, traditional, and cultural salmon ceremonies."[83]

Environmental, land management, and natural resource issues appear to be the areas most likely to generate indigenous-state cooperation and nation-building policies. A 2001 nationwide Zogby poll also provides some support for this contention, as 53 percent of those responding "trust Tribal governments to protect the environment at and near the reservations."[84] It follows that rather than being viewed as a zero-sum issue, environmental resources are more likely to be perceived by state policy makers as shared and, therefore, are less contentious than Native economic development initiatives.

SOME INITIAL CONCLUSIONS

The legislative data in table 2.1 coupled with the proceedings from the NGA conferences demonstrate that battlelines have been drawn around economic development issues. Social constructions of indigenous nations as emerging contenders appear to drive much of the policymaking at the state level. More encouraging are the larger number of nation-building policies in the area of environmental legislation, suggesting that these issues are not viewed by state policymakers to be as threatening to state budgets as gaming. This could be in part because of the ability of indigenous peoples themselves to draw on another historical image, the environmental steward, to provide political clout in certain contexts. As anthropologist Paul Nadasdy explains, "The image of the ecologically noble Indian is an extremely compelling one, appealing to sympathetic audiences around the world. By invoking the image, environmentalists and indigenous people alike tap into the image's rhetorical power, enabling them in some instances to galvanize broad—even worldwide—support for particular local struggles."[85]

The image of the environmental steward is generally perceived as deserving and beneficial to the public interest, which may lead to more nation-building legislation when it comes to environmental issues. However, the environmental steward image has its downsides. Certain environmental issues, such as indigenous water use, have been historically contentious and will only become more conflictual in the future given water scarcity and state attempts to control access to this resource.[86] In addition, the environmental steward image constricts indigenous peoples to Euroamerican standards of land protection and conservation that often run counter to their own belief systems and governance.[87]

The once exclusive federal trust relationship, which comprises 379 ratified treaties as well as executive agreements, direct consultation with Congress on indigenous affairs, federal statutory obligations, and court decisions, has been repeatedly challenged by states during the 1990s and into the twenty-first century. The off-loading of federal powers to state governments has made indigenous nations much more vulnerable to the jurisdictional claims of local governing bodies, such as state and municipal policymakers. As the findings suggest, state actors, such as governors and legislators, are now more likely to assert jurisdictional claims over indigenous nations to benefit themselves politically and economically. State actors have undertaken this challenge to indigenous self-determining authority primarily through the formulation of new regulatory policies that tax indigenous gaming and other forms of economic development, and specifically target nations they consider rich Indians perceived as having special rights.

CHAPTER THREE

Managing the Politics of Perception

If we don't frame the issues, someone else will frame the issues for us.

Wilma Mankiller, former principal chief
of the Cherokee Nation, 2005

The previous two chapters have documented how rich Indian images have been increasingly used by state and local policymakers to challenge the self-determining authority of indigenous nations. This chapter shifts the focus from policymaking at the state level to indigenous mobilization at the individual and community levels to examine how indigenous peoples are responding to rich Indian racism. How have indigenous nations mobilized politically, both historically and in the contemporary forced federalism era, to frame the politics of perception on their own terms? And who is framing the issues when indigenous peoples vote and lobby within the U.S. political system?

Political mobilization can occur in several forms, such as voting in elections, forming coalitions to lobby or providing resources for office holders and candidates, protesting or carrying out other acts of contention, targeting state or corporate entities through warrior societies, and so on. These are just some of the strategies that indigenous nations have used during the forced federalism era. However, when choosing whether or not to participate within the U.S. political system, indigenous peoples face a fundamental dilemma: does indigenous participation in U.S. politics compromise their self-determining authority and nationhood status, or is it an essential tool for reframing the politics of perception? As Lumbee scholar David Wilkins asks, "For if tribal governments and their multi-layered citizens are so actively engaged in non-Indian politics, can tribes still legitimately assert that they are in fact extra-constitutional sovereigns whose treaty and trust based rights originally affirmed their distinctive and independent sovereignty?"[1]

Of course, it is up to each individual and nation to adopt strategies that best serve their communities. However, it is useful to explore some of the trade-offs involved for those choosing to participate within the U.S. political system and how previous generations of indigenous leaders have addressed similar dilemmas when dealing with U.S. governmental officials. A brief historical examination of indigenous diplomatic strategies uncovers some important insights regarding the management of the politics of perception.

INDIGENOUS DIPLOMACIES

Before the formation of the United States, indigenous nations on Turtle Island engaged with colonial powers by sending delegations to global destinations to foster new alliances.[2] During the colonial era and formative stages of the U.S. government, these diplomatic missions were formalized into treaties of trade, peace, and friendship. Between 1776 and 1871, over 379 treaties were ratified between indigenous nations and the U.S. government that continue to form the basis of the indigenous government–to–federal government relationship.

Treaties, such as the 1785 Treaty of Hopewell between the Cherokee Nation and the U.S. government (see appendix C for the full text of the treaty), stressed the self-determining authority of indigenous nations on their own homelands, as evidenced by article 5: "If any citizen of the United States, or other person not being an Indian, shall attempt to settle on any of the lands westward or southward of the said boundary which are hereby allotted to the Indians for their hunting grounds, or having already settled and will not remove from the same within six months after the ratification of this treaty, such person shall forfeit the protection of the United States, and the Indians may punish him or not as they please."

Besides recognizing the ability of indigenous nations to punish those who encroached onto their territories, it was also common practice during this time to issue passports to travel to indigenous territories. For example, the Ordinance of 1786 for the "regulation and management of Indian affairs" required that superintendents issue passports to those visiting indigenous territories along with licenses for all traders seeking to operate within indigenous homelands.[3] As Vine Deloria, Jr., and David Wilkins state, "The whole thrust of the ordinance was to establish rules for American citizens, not for Indians or Indian tribes."[4]

In 1871 Congress passed a bill with a rider attached that prohibited future treaty making between the U.S. government and indigenous nations. Even though federal negotiators did not use the language of treaties after 1871, the U.S. Congress ratified over seventy indigenous-U.S. agreements between 1873 and 1911.[5] In addition, indigenous nations negotiated approximately thirty-five treaties of peace and friendship (often resolution of boundary disputes, permission to live on a nation's territory, etc.) with other indigenous nations between 1781 and 1902.[6] Inter-indigenous treaty making entailed forming sacred compacts involving entire communities and exemplified the self-determining authority of indigenous nations by allowing them to represent themselves on their own terms.

Besides establishing formal treaty relationships that continue to this day, indigenous peoples often engaged in other less formal diplomatic exchanges. As historian Herman Viola contends, gift giving was a key part of indigenous diplomacies, and "what they most appreciated were certain ceremonial gifts that denoted authority."[7] Medals, flags, uniforms, gorgets, pipe tomahawks, and weapons (mainly guns and swords) were exchanged to recognize indigenous leaders and pay tribute to their authority. Of these gifts, peace medals came to represent the most important symbols of alliances and were an essential part of indigenous diplomacies from first contact with European colonial powers (British, Spanish, French) until the U.S. Civil War.

The U.S. government began issuing its own peace medals in 1789, and each medal bore the likeness of the current president. On the reverse side, peace medals usually depicted a scene of clasped hands, denoting friendship.[8] Over time, however, the U.S. government considered receipt of peace medals by indigenous nations as a sign of submission to the U.S. government and not merely as a symbolic gesture of goodwill. Rather than portraying scenes of peace and friendship, the peace medals of the 1850s were decorated with symbols of assimilation, complete with imagery of the "noble savage" and "bloodthirsty savage." Peace medals issued during the administration of President Buchanan (1857–61), for example, depicted a pastoral scene with an Indian in a headdress plowing a field and children playing. Figures of two other Indians surround the center image; one of them holds a knife in his right hand and the scalp of the other in his left.[9] Buchanan's medal conveyed a clear message: choose either warfare or assimilation. The imagery of the Buchanan peace medal suggested that the paths of "civilization" (i.e., farming, Christianity) were inevitable and represented the only viable future for indigenous peoples. According to the narrow dichotomy presented on the medal, without Western "civilization," the "bloodthirsty savage" would continue to promote war among the people. Indigenous nations confronted Buchanan's politics of perception through continued diplomatic missions, whether to Washington, D.C., or elsewhere, to convey the strength and complexities of their self-determining authority.

Concerned with avoiding warfare with indigenous nations during the nineteenth century, U.S. government officials often invited indigenous delegations to Washington, D.C., to pacify "potentially militant Indians."[10] In fact, this diplomatic tactic was considered "a relatively inexpensive and effective method of introducing the Indian leadership to the resources and power of the United States."[11] According to the commissioner of Indian affairs, who was justifying his invitation to the Winnebago delegation of 1828, "This mode of conquering these people is merciful, and it is cheap, in comparison to what a war with them would cost, to say nothing of the loss of human life."[12] Besides being considered an inexpensive form of diplomacy, delegations were also intended to showcase the benefits of white civilization.[13]

Much like the message on President Buchanan's peace medals, indigenous delegations to Washington, D.C., carried a two-pronged strategy: to demonstrate U.S. power and to promote assimilation into the U.S. system. However, these delegations did not deter indigenous peoples from pursuing other strategies of protecting their homelands and asserting their self-determination through tactics such as lobbying. Furthermore, indigenous lobbying was not simply a political act. It held both spiritual and political significance. Robert Yellowtail's account of the 1917 Crow delegation, which was protesting the opening of their territory to settlement by homesteaders, illustrates the ceremonial aspects of indigenous lobbying:

The night before the final Senate hearing the old war chiefs with the delegation opened a sacred medicine bundle that they had brought to Washington. The medicine in the bundle was so powerful that it had made thirteen Crows into chiefs. In order to make the medicine work properly, however, the incense of buffalo chips was required. The chiefs asked Yellowtail and several other young men to visit the National Zoo and collect enough chips for a "medicine making" ceremony. Upon their return, the entire delegation assembled in a large dormitory room in their quarters at the National Hotel. The chiefs sat in a semicircle on the floor with the medicine bundle and their war regalia spread out before them. The other delegates watched silently as the chiefs burned the buffalo chips, sweet grass, and other ingredients over wood coals taken from the kitchen stove. . . . The next day the attempted appropriation of their land was soundly defeated.[14]

The lobbying tactics that indigenous delegations would use to convey their messages were innovative and effective. Indigenous leaders would often remind U.S. officials of their treaty obligations by bringing peace medals and other forms of treaty documentation to delegate meetings to jog officials' memories of these sacred compacts. As another example, Cherokee lobbyists would send members of Congress copies of the Cherokee Nation's newspaper, the *Cherokee Advocate*, and mail them greeting cards that contained key quotes from ratified treaties.[15]

The priority of indigenous lobbyists during the 1870s and 1880s was fairly straightforward: to protect their community against further encroachment, whether by the U.S. government, state governments, or citizens. The Cherokee, Chickasaw, Choctaw, Muskogee Confederation (Creeks), and Seminole nations intensely lobbied members of Congress in the 1880s to reverse allotment policies.[16] While these five nations managed to stave off the effects of allotment for a short time, by 1897 their unity was destroyed. At the same time, Congress passed a series of bills that whittled away their land rights.[17]

Indigenous nations have lobbied since the formation of the U.S. government, but the priorities have changed. Non-indigenous lobbying firms are now hired to promote indigenous issues in Congress, and large monetary contributions are made to U.S. political candidates and party organizations. The creation of the Cherokee Nation Washington Office (CNWO) in 2001, for example, demonstrates the new complexities of lobbying since the passage of IGRA. The mission of the CNWO is to connect "Cherokee Nation stakeholders to National, Regional and Local organizations, such as the National Congress of American Indians, the National Indian Health Board, the National Indian Education Association, the National Indian Gaming Association, the National Indian Business Association, etc."[18]

Another critical difference marking lobbying during the forced federalism era is that it does not solely occur in Washington, D.C. Given the powers that state and municipal governments assert over indigenous affairs, indigenous lobbying is just as likely to occur in the state capital or a local municipality as in Washington.

Besides lobbying, high profile examples of indigenous political mobilization in the 1950s, 1960s and 1970s, included protest activity, fish-ins, the 1969 occupation of Alcatraz Island, and the AIM siege at Wounded Knee in 1973. These and similar indigenous political actions have brought indigenous issues to the forefront of U.S. politics and reshaped indigenous-state relations. As active participants in the political arena, Native peoples have increased their visibility and influence at the federal, state, and local levels of governance in ways previously unimagined.

Voting in U.S. elections is one political strategy that indigenous peoples have increasingly pursued. The next section examines why and how indigenous peoples have voted in U.S. elections and supported candidates for office during the 1990s and into the twenty-first century.

INDIGENOUS PEOPLES AND U.S. ELECTIONS

The question of whether indigenous people should vote in U.S. elections has multiple layers given existing colonial legacies and the status of indigenous communities as treaty-based nations who existed before the formation of the United States. The Seneca, Akwesasne Mohawk, and Onondaga peoples, for example, contend that their nationhood would be undermined by widespread participation in external elections. In a 1998 speech Chief Irving Powless, Jr., of the Mohawk Nation questioned the legitimacy of the 1924 General Indian Citizenship Act: "The Haudenosaunee [also know as the Iroquois Confederacy] have never accepted this law. We do not consider ourselves as citizens of the United States."[19] As Kanien'kehaka (Mohawk) scholar Taiaiake Alfred points out, "as Iroquois people, we do not participate in the white man's government system because we are Rotinohshonni, not Canadian."[20]

In Canada the Kahnawake Mohawk Nation has been described as an election-free zone since 1960, when Ottawa first granted indigenous peoples the right to vote. As the grand chief of Kahnawake, Mike Delisle, Jr., describes it, "It's not a matter of not being interested in the issues—we are interested, because we ourselves are one of the issues in Canadian politics. We just don't consider ourselves part of the Canadian electorate, because we don't consider ourselves Canadian citizens."[21] According to an editorial in the *Eastern Door*, Kahnawake's newspaper, federal elections "place us in submission to foreign governments and as a result, alienates us from our own. You can't stand with one foot in two canoes."[22] Despite efforts by Elections Canada, a federal agency, to encourage voting, voter turnout from Kahnawake is almost nonexistent. Any Kahnawake resident who wants to vote has to go outside the nation's homelands to do so, as there are no polling stations in Kahnawake. Out of a population of ninety-three hundred, there are perhaps half a dozen who vote in each election according to band council spokesperson Joe Delaronde; all those who do vote are non-Natives married to Natives.[23]

Yet for other Native nations, such as the Hopi and Navajo nations in Arizona, involvement in the U.S. voting process is considered necessary to ensure that they have a voice in policies that potentially affect their communities. The Cherokee Nation in Oklahoma have also intensified their get-out-the-vote efforts by allocating $500,000 toward voter mobilization drives in 2006 and registering over twenty-five thousand new voters since the 2000 election. Several indigenous nations across the United States have taken the stance that voting and other forms of political participation, especially where there are a large number of Native voters who can be the swing vote in an election outcome, are the most pragmatic and effective ways to protect indigenous nationhood and promote issues of importance, such as religious freedom and hunting and fishing rights. According to the 2000 U.S. Census, there are seven states where the indigenous population represents 5 percent or more of the total population: Alaska, Arizona, Montana, New Mexico, North Dakota, Oklahoma, and South Dakota. Additionally, states such as California and Texas, have indigenous populations that exceed one hundred thousand people (see appendix D). Indigenous peoples in these states often seek to get out the vote in large numbers to influence a close election outcome as swing voters.

Do indigenous people have major concerns about compromising their self-determination by voting in U.S. elections? Results from a 2000 poll suggest not. According to an *Indian Country Today* poll of 450 indigenous community leaders, students, and scholars, 93 percent of those responding to the question "Should American Indians vote in U.S. elections?" believed that indigenous people should vote. Only 5 percent of those surveyed believed that indigenous people should not vote in U.S. elections, stressing that "political independence" is ideal in maintaining a government-to-government relationship.[24] Maqtew'kpaqtism (Mi'kmaq Nation), who opposes voting in U.S. elections, explains the reasoning behind his view: "If we vote in colonial elections, then why do we call ourselves a nation? Should we vote in Spain's elections? No! We are nations, not minority classes, and we have never surrendered our right to our Nation."[25]

For another question posed by the survey, "What kind of citizenship should natives have?" 88 percent of those responding favored dual citizenship, while 10 percent advocated tribal citizenship only. A small number of respondents (2 percent) favored complete assimilation into the U.S. system, indicating that indigenous people should possess U.S. citizenship only. Despite the apparent overwhelming support for voting in U.S. elections and holding dual citizenship in the survey results, this issue becomes much more complicated when Native scholars and researchers take a closer look at the implications of indigenous political mobilization in the U.S. electoral arena.

In 1997 political scientist Diane Duffy conducted extensive interviews to better understand indigenous perspectives on citizenship and found seven different categories of allegiance either to one's indigenous nation or to the U.S.:

1. *Indigenous nationalism:* The indigenous nation is the sole allegiance for Native people. This allegiance is expressive in positive indigenous (versus antiwhite) language.

2. *Measured separatism:* Primary allegiance is to the indigenous nation, but there is also some measured support for the United States and willingness to serve as allies with the United States in the armed services in battles with foreign countries.

3. *Anti-American:* Against the United States (versus solely for their indigenous nation). Adherents would under no circumstances serve in the U.S. military because they would consider it treasonous.

4. *Environmental allegiance:* Similar to indigenous nationalism, but allegiance is explicitly tied to all of creation and not simply humans.

5. *Assimilative:* The United States is perceived as the superior power, and the indigenous nation is subordinate.

6. *Co-opted or colonized:* Adherents refuse to conceive of a separate indigenous political consciousness that has merit and is deserving of allegiance.

7. *Apatriotic:* Adherents believe that patriotism is an irrelevant concept for Native peoples.[26]

Several of these categories are overlapping—for example, one can imagine an indigenous person who is assimilative (no. 5) in their value system as a result of being co-opted into a colonial institution (no. 6) such as the Bureau of Indian Affairs.[27] However, Duffy's typology provides a clearer picture regarding the legacies of colonialism and how indigenous identities have been altered. As Duffy's work suggests, strategies of "measured separatism" are often a precarious balance of loyalties. In terms of Wilkins's earlier question of whether indigenous nations can still legitimately assert their status as extraconstitutional sovereigns, a measured separatism strategy offers some direction for better understanding a balance of community loyalties and political aspirations.

Perhaps understanding the political aspirations of indigenous peoples is the best indicator of whether or not one should vote in U.S. elections. Legal scholar and member of the Small Robes Band of the Blood Indian Tribe of the Blackfoot Confederacy Leroy Little Bear describes an indigenous decision-making process for choosing whether or not to vote: "You should ask what your motive is for voting. If you're working for rights, go vote. If you're working towards sovereignty, don't vote. Rights are things that are granted to you. Sovereignty is something that you possess."[28]

As Little Bear points out, the decision of whether to vote or not depends on one's overall goal. If a person is seeking to engage in a legally constructed discourse for economic, social, cultural, civil, or political rights at the domestic level, then voting may be a viable option for achieving those aims. However, if a person is part of an indigenous nation that is seeking self-determination, other diplomatic strategies, such as treaty making, are more optimal ways to promote indigenous nationhood. Embedded in this discussion are fundamental tensions between the political roles of an individual who is a citizen of an indigenous nation and the responsibilities of an indigenous nation to their community members. There are trade-offs involved with each set of actions, but certainly one of the short-term dangers of voting in U.S. elections is the perception that indigenous peoples are regarded as interest groups within the U.S. political system rather than as nations, which has been a standard tactic for those policymakers invoking rich Indian racism.

Another possible, long-term danger in voting is co-optation, which is a process that can diminish the power of indigenous nations over time by challenging their distinctive nationhood status. Here we use the concept of co-optation in the way that sociologist Michael Lacy defines it: "Co-optation occurs if, in a system of power, the power holder intentionally extends some form of political participation to actors who pose a threat".[29] Taiaiake Alfred further describes how a process of co-optation takes place: "The complexity of indigenous-state relations gives agents of the state many opportunities and mechanisms to move indigenous leaders away from their communities, politically and ideologically, and towards the state."[30]

According to Lacy, powerful entities, such as state governors, historically promote their own legitimacy through twin processes of blunting and channeling.[31] Blunting simply means that an indigenous political agenda is shifted and altered to fit the dominant norms of institutional structures, such as a state or local agency. For example, translating indigenous powers of self-determination into an indigenous-state compact for casino operation on indigenous homelands would be one form of blunting. A channeling effect occurs when an indigenous nation stops acting outside the U.S. political system through extralegal activities, such as fish-ins or blockades, and confines their activities within official structures, such as voting in elections or working within state governmental procedures. For example, rather than organizing a grassroots effort to promote indigenous hunting and fishing based on prior treaty provisions, an indigenous community might channel most of their political efforts into putting a statewide referendum on the election ballot, where the general public can determine their hunting and fishing rights. The overall goal of co-optation is to stabilize government regimes, but these goals run counter to indigenous self-determination and decolonization strategies.

As Duffy's typology illustrates, there is a fine line between promoting indigenous nationalism and justifying measured separatism strategies. A key to overcoming the dangers of co-optation involves never sacrificing long-term opportunities to strengthen culture and community for short-term political gains at the voting booth. Overall, using a co-optation model of channeling and blunting techniques allows one to gauge the effects of indigenous political mobilization on indigenous nations themselves. Considering the dangers of co-optation, the pursuit of a measured separatism strategy becomes a precarious balancing act.

A brief look at an indigenous organization in Washington State illustrates some of the rationales for pursuing a measured separatism strategy. The First Americans Education Project (FAEP) was founded in 1999 by a group of indigenous leaders in the state of Washington who wanted to increase the involvement of Native peoples in the U.S. political process. With its twofold mission of increasing both education and direct political involvement, FAEP has had some notable success in the U.S. electoral process, such as mobilizing Native and non-Native voters to defeat anti-indigenous candidate Slade Gorton in the 2000 U.S. Senate election in Washington. In a 2001 interview with Russ Lehman, managing director of the First Americans Education Project in Washington, responded to a question about a possible compromise of indigenous nationhood with Native involvement in U.S. elections:

> Jeff Corntassel: Some indigenous scholars have questioned whether participation by Native people in external elections can compromise indigenous nationhood in the long run. Is this a concern?
>
> Russ Lehman: It's a terribly destructive attitude to have. To fail to participate in a system that impacts so much of their lives is wasteful and damages them in the long term. They should

be important participants in tribal governments. What happens in non-Indian governments affects their lives even more directly—air they breathe, schools they go to.[32]

Lehman's perspectives on this mirror those of the *Indian Country Today* survey results mentioned earlier, where 88 percent of those indigenous peoples surveyed regarded themselves as dual citizens. However, amid the current realities of the forced federalism era, indigenous peoples are increasingly treated by state policymakers as triple citizens: citizens of their indigenous nations, of the United States, and of the state in which they reside. This perception of triple citizenship contradicts historical evidence contained in several state disclaimer clauses specifying that states have no jurisdictional claims over indigenous nations (see chapter 1). Besides violating these Indian disclaimer clauses, states are asserting more and more jurisdictional oversight through compacting processes for gaming and taxation, which will be described in more detail in chapter 5. In short, devolution of power to states further confounds the abilities of indigenous nations to maintain measured separatism within the U.S. federal system.

Besides the long-term ramifications of *not* participating in external elections that Lehman points out, there are also potential long-term ramifications *for* lending legitimacy to the U.S. pluralist system, which may include compromising indigenous nationhood to the point where communities are legally and politically regarded as lobby groups rather than self-determining entities. Indigenous nations are exerting their influence and utilizing their resources in the U.S. electoral process through lobbying. Indigenous nation soft money donations to political parties have spiked up dramatically since 1988, from $113,671 in 1992 to $2.5 million in 2002.[33] The dangers of co-optation are real. Lawyer and researcher for the Samish Indian Nation Russel Barsh sees this trend in indigenous policy as problematic: "A case can be made that U.S. tribal governments have grown so integrated into the general institutional structure of the country that they are no longer able or willing to oppose it."[34] As the NGA and legislative evidence from chapter 2 demonstrates, since 1988 states generally have failed to view indigenous nations as part of a government-to-government relationship but instead see them as merely part of the service population or as a local interest group. One long-term risk that emerges for indigenous peoples is to become regarded

TABLE 3.1
Indigenous Nation Funds Paid to Lobbying Firms,
2000 and 2004 (in dollars)

Indigenous nation	2000	2004
Mashantucket Pequot Nation	120,000	180,000
Seminole Nation	160,000	480,000
Morongo Band of Mission Indians	120,000	180,000
Mississippi Band of Choctaw Indians	100,000	240,000
Eastern Band of Cherokees	n.d.	160,000
Pechanga Band of Luiseño Indians	30,000	160,000
Viejas Band of Kumeyaay Indians	160,000	120,000
Cabazon Band of Mission Indians	60,000	200,000
Salt River Pima-Maricopa Indian Community	40,000	600,000
Mohegan Nation	n.d.	140,000
Total	790,000	2,460,000

SOURCE: United States Senate Office of Public Records, http://sopr.senate.gov/

merely as wealthy constituents with special rights rather than as self-determining nations.[35]

Besides voting, lobbying has become a major activity for indigenous nations since 1988. However, rather than negotiating directly with federal policymakers, indigenous nations have begun contracting out their lobbying to firms in Washington, D.C. Table 3.1 tracks the steady increase in lobbying expenses for indigenous nations between 2000 and 2004 among the ten most politically active nations. The lobbying expenditures among those nations more than doubled over four years, going from $1 million to $2.5 million. All the listed nations operate casinos and have also been active in providing funds to political parties to influence policymaking decisions.

To put the figures in table 3.1 into proper perspective, lobbying has been a diplomatic strategy that indigenous nations have engaged in since first contact with colonial powers. In addition, other countries, such as the United Kingdom, spend millions each year to lobby the U.S. government regarding foreign policy decisions. In 2004 alone, the UK spent $27.5 million dollars lobbying U.S. policymakers.[36] That same year, Israel spent $1.1 million to lobby the U.S. government.[37] Even counties within the United States lobby decision makers in Washington, D.C.—Los Angeles County in California, for example, spent $1.1 million in lobbying costs in 2004.[38] Other countries around the world devote massive amounts of money to lobbying the U.S. government, but for some reason lobbying by indigenous nations is viewed with suspicion or worse, leading to the formulation of new state policies to limit or regulate indigenous lobbying behavior.

Overall, one can see how the actions of these politically and economically active indigenous nations can contribute to misleading impressions and social constructions of the rich Indian and emerging contenders—despite that their actions and resources represent a small percentage of all indigenous nations. Yet there are several downsides to the current lobbying practice of contracting out for non-Native lobbying firms. For one thing, indigenous nations historically have lobbied members of the executive branch and Congress themselves. Contracting out this duty to non-Native firms raises some serious questions about indigenous priorities and representation. And it creates potential for corruption and fraud, as with Jack Abramoff and Michael Scanlon's lobbying firm's disastrous involvement with the Tigua Nation in Texas to the tune of $4.2 million.

In addition, with this large amount of money leaving these nations, the question remains whether political solutions are being sought at the federal levels at the expense of local, community-based solutions. Part of the challenge put forward by Wilma Mankiller—"If we don't frame the issues, someone else will frame the issues for us"—should lead indigenous nations to reprioritize a principle of indigenous representation on their own terms to better manage the politics of perception.

Considering the risks in perception and policy, the question remains how indigenous peoples should participate in federal, state, and local elections. Part of this discussion is motivated by the legal imposition of U.S. citizenship on indigenous peoples in 1924 and the civil rights discourse during the 1950s and 1960s over extending the application of the right to vote to indigenous peoples, who were denied this right long after the 1924 Indian Citizenship Act went into effect. In Arizona and New Mexico, for example, Natives were denied the right to vote in state elections until 1948. This denial has led some indigenous peoples to demand a voice in the U.S. political system.

Returning to the motivations for voting that Little Bear described, are indigenous peoples seeking rights through voting or maintaining a measured separatism status as indigenous nations? Part of this discussion lies in how dual citizenship is perceived among indigenous peoples in the United States. Do indigenous peoples consider themselves first and foremost citizens of their nations with U.S. citizenship granted as an honorary or special diplomatic status allowing them to engage in external elections?

In a comprehensive study of state laws prohibiting the indigenous right to vote, political scientist Dan McCool finds three broad categories used by states to exclude the Native vote: constitutional ambiguity under provisions such as "Indians not taxed"; political and economic factors, such as not being regarded as official residents of a particular state; and cultural and racial discrimination, such as literacy tests.[39] Possibly responding to this longtime exclusion from the ballot box and the potential to be swing votes in close elections, Native nations increasingly tend to view voting as essential to their futures. In one of the earliest systematic looks at Native voting rights in the United States, political scientist Helen Peterson asserts that Native voters can be the deciding factor in close elections: "Organization is the Indians' best hope of having some part in determining their own future and in continuing to exist as Indian tribes in a nation committed to a philosophy of respect for cultural differences."[40] More recently, Bobby Barrett, vice chairman of the Viejas Nation in California, expressed the need for indigenous peoples to vote as part of their historical legacy: "Some people are having a hard time accepting that Indians are taking their rightful place in history. And part of that is participating in elections."[41]

Taking a stance similar to Barrett's, Chief Phillip G. Peters, Sr., of the Saginaw Chippewa Nation (Michigan) and supporter of the 1996 Native Vote campaign, which registered over fifteen thousand new indigenous voters, contends that voting is not an act of surrender to the U.S. government but gaining a voice in the U.S. government through dual citizenship: "Democracy has allowed many freedoms in this country, the right to vote is one of them. We, as dual citizens of this country, need to exercise the right to make our voices heard to maintain our inherent sovereignty."[42]

Seneca lawyer and professor Robert Porter presents a competing viewpoint regarding the motivations behind indigenous involvement in external elections: "Most of those Indian leaders supporting an increased role for Indians in the American political process appear themselves to already be a part of the American political establishment. This mentality suggests a predisposition in favor of federal, rather than tribal, solutions to the problems facing Indian people."[43] Porter's underlying thesis is that when indigenous people exercise their rights and obligations of U.S. citizenship, they jeopardize the ability of indigenous nations to continue an existence as separate, sovereign nations.[44] For Porter, the absence of a widespread consensus among Native peoples "as evidenced by the lack of Indian voters" makes the strategy of participating in external elections "inherently suspect."[45] He concludes that "voting in American elections, running for political office, and lobbying American officials totally concedes to the United States the controlling authority that it has long sought."[46]

Presenting a rebuttal to Porter, legal scholar John LaVelle (Santee Sioux Nation of Nebraska) concludes, "Like our ancestors, we must do battle for the rights of our tribes, for our survival as Indian nations and Indian people. Like they did, we must wage war on every front where our rights are threatened. American politics is one such battleground—a vast one, an important one, perhaps the most important one."[47] Continuing with his response to Porter, LaVelle interviews Frank LaMere, a citizen of the Winnebago Nation of Nebraska and member of the Democratic National Committee. In determining whether indigenous peoples should vote in U.S. elections, LaMere describes the calculated risks involved for indigenous nations getting out the vote: "Everything that can bring good to the nations must be acknowledged, political involvement included. Most nations agree with me on that point. It all has to do with education. Some nations seek to protect their sovereignty by expressing it to all who would listen. Other nations express their sovereignty in an arena where there are no guarantees, but where everyone must listen. That's the political arena. I will take chances in that arena. Many tribes take their chances in that arena."[48]

Whether agreeing with Porter or LaVelle, one must ultimately acknowledge the high risks of indigenous involvement in U.S. politics. The long-term dangers of voting are clear; forces of co-optation and assimilation undermine indigenous nationhood. As the past 230 years of federal indigenous policy suggests, the rights discourse is framed and controlled by state and federal policymakers and can turn against indigenous nations with or without their involvement in the electoral process. Little Bear exhorts indigenous people to deeply consider their motivations for voting: if you are pursuing self-determination and the promotion of nationhood, do not vote. In other words, act like a nation, not an interest group. Overall, a balance should be struck here by practicing diplomatic strategies that do not favor federal or state political solutions over indigenous nation solutions to the real challenges confronting indigenous communities.

The goal of this chapter is not to provide a definitive resolution to this ongoing debate but to outline some of the limitations and parameters of a measured separatism versus indigenous nationalism strategies. This discussion delves beneath the surface of poll results by providing a rudimentary guide for indigenous leaders and policy-making to assess the short- and long-term risks involved in that arena. The stakes for involvement in external elections are high and should be considered carefully.

RICH INDIAN RACISM AND THE 2004 U.S. SENATE ELECTION IN OKLAHOMA

During the 2004 U.S. elections, indigenous leaders mobilized for the largest ever get-out-the-vote effort in indigenous communities. As with previous elections, issue positions of candidates, whether treaty rights or natural resource protection, determined whether indigenous peoples would get out the vote, endorse certain candidates over others, or provide financial backing in swing states like South Dakota and Oklahoma.[49] Despite the strong indigenous turnout during the 2004 election, some indigenous candidates for federal offices, such as Kalyn Free (Choctaw Nation) and Brad Carson (Cherokee Nation) in Oklahoma, were not able to secure victories.[50]

One of the most hotly contested Senate campaigns of 2004 pitted Democratic candidate and former U.S. Representative Brad Carson, against Republican candidate Tom Coburn, who was an obstetrician from Muskogee and a former Oklahoma state representative. Given the retirement of Ben Nighthorse Campbell (Northern Cheyenne Nation) from the Senate after serving for twelve years, Brad Carson's election would have made him the only indigenous legislator in Congress.

Controversy arose during the campaign when Coburn, speaking to a small group in Altus, Oklahoma, on August 21, 2004, was recorded making the following statements:

Alright, listen, I know the tribal issues; I was a congressman where most of the Indians are in this state. The problem is, most of them aren't Indians. The average Cherokee quantum is $\frac{1}{512}$. Alright, most people in this room have more Cherokee in them than the Cherokee.

Alright, and they want to grow that, because as they grow their rolls, what happens? They get more money from the federal government. . . .

It is one thing for us to keep our obligations to recognize Native Americans, but it's a totally different thing for us to allow a primitive agreement with the Native Americans to undermine Oklahoma's future and that's what they're talking about doing and it's big money.[51]

Coburn's comments epitomize an attitude of rich Indian racism. The questioning of Tsalagi authenticity along with a portrayal of all Tsalagi actions to be motivated by greed reflects the racist imagery and stereotyping that has been frequently invoked in the forced federalism era. The response of the Cherokee Nation was swift and led Chief Chad "Corntassel" Smith and the tribal council to endorse U.S. Senate candidate Brad Carson, which was the first time that the Cherokee Nation had formally endorsed a candidate for U.S. office. According to Smith, the Cherokee Nation's unprecedented decision to endorse Carson was pretty straightforward:

Actually, until 2004 we had a policy that we would not contribute to a candidate or endorse a candidate, but the policy changed in 2004 because of a very clear distinction between two candidates running for the U.S. Senate. One was Brad Carson, who was a tribal member, and Tom Coburn, who had been a previous congressman from the second district, our district, and Carson, we thought, was . . . being a tribal member was one thing, but he was in support of the Cherokee Nation and was tremendous. Tom Coburn was very antagonistic to the Cherokee Nation Indians, and so in a rare situation—the only time we've ever done it—we endorsed and in acts of council supported Carson against Coburn.[52]

In contrast to the Cherokee Nation endorsement of Carson, some members of the United Keetoowah Band of Cherokee Indians in

Oklahoma staunchly supported Coburn, citing differences with candidate Brad Carson. Overall, while there was a lot of media attention resulting from Coburn's comments along with subsequent indigenous mobilization in Oklahoma ($126,300 in donations and massive get-out-the-vote campaigns), Coburn won with 53 percent of the vote in Oklahoma, compared to Carson's 41 percent.

Appendices E and F provide complete transcripts of interviews with Chief Smith and Brad Carson in which they each discuss their impressions of the 2004 race along with their reflections on future challenges that indigenous nations face. Both Smith and Carson identify several key themes of political mobilization, indigenous-state conflicts, and social constructions of rich Indians. Their valuable insights demonstrate the increasingly sophisticated and nuanced approaches indigenous leaders take when formulating diplomatic and political strategies. For Chief Smith successfully meeting the future challenges of forced federalism entails building indigenous leaders grounded in community values:

> The more you're in this office, it's not money, it's not resources; it comes down to a very simple thing of leadership and people who really believe in a long-term vision and are willing to work at it. Perhaps it's . . . there's so many competing interests, you know—consumerism, materialism, social pressures, and such—that many times people, our people, don't realize the great opportunities we have to rebuild the Cherokee Nation and how it really benefits them and their families. We get trapped in entitlement mentalities and social service mentalities and methamphetamine problems and alcohol problems, and I really do think the biggest challenge is challenging and developing leadership. Now, that leadership comes . . . folks that exercise and promote basic Cherokee attributes. And when you have those attributes, not only the individual but also the Cherokee community develops a positive quality of life.[53]

After losing the 2004 election for the U.S. House of Representatives, Choctaw Nation citizen Kalyn Free started a national organization called the Indigenous Democratic Network List (INDN's List) to recruit and train indigenous candidates for local and state offices.[54] Launched on February 28, 2005, this grassroots organization identifies

Democratic indigenous candidates running for state and local office across the United States and mobilizes the indigenous vote on their behalf. INDN's List had a strong record of success in the 2006 election, as sixteen of the twenty-two endorsed indigenous candidates won their elections.[55] After examining the extensive literature and first-hand accounts of indigenous strategies for managing the politics of perception, it is clear that theory has not kept pace with the contemporary realities of the forced federalism era. Other than the previously discussed social constructions frameworks and co-optation models, what are some other theories that might help explain the extensive involvement of indigenous peoples in the U.S. political system since 1988?

THEORIZING ABOUT INDIGENOUS POLITICAL MOBILIZATION

Consistent with indigenous scholarship on voting behavior, sociologist Stephen Cornell finds an underlying dilemma now confronting indigenous nations regarding their potential involvement in external political structures: "To the extent that Indians are trying to preserve modes of action and belief very different from those of the dominant society, the resources most Indians possess can be counterproductive. Their use is a form of incorporation: they facilitate action within the systems of the dominant society. To act is to enter those systems."[56] Cornell's research on indigenous politics emphasizes the importance of organizational networks, social cohesion, leadership, and money in facilitating the mobilization of indigenous nations during the 1960s and 1970s.[57] Yet the work of Cornell and others who emphasize resource mobilization theories fall short of explaining contemporary indigenous political mobilization outside of protest activities. Much of the research in this area deals with indigenous activism during the 1960s and 1970s and its subsequent effects on indigenous self-determination.[58] The confrontations between the U.S. government and indigenous peoples during this time, which ranged from the fish-ins beginning in 1964 to the eventual AIM occupation of Wounded Knee in 1973, forced issues of consequence, such as cultural integrity and autonomy, onto the federal as well as the global agendas.[59]

Stephen Cornell, Joseph Kalt, and other researchers with the Harvard Project on American Indian Economic Development, which was founded in 1987, have attempted to model conditions under which successful social and economic development can take place on indigenous homelands.[60] For the Harvard Project researchers, an indigenous nation must meet four key political conditions to engage in successful nation building:

1. *Self-rule:* Native nations must have genuine decision making power over their own affairs.

2. *Capable institutions of self-governance:* Native nations must have capable governing institutions that keep politics in its place, deliver on promises, administer programs and manage resources efficiently, and send a message to investors.

3. *Cultural match:* Native nations must create formal institutions that have the support of the people. The community has to have a sense of ownership about the institutions themselves.

4. *Strategic orientation:* Native nations must move away from a factional conflict approach to governance, focusing their energies less on crisis management and more on developing sustainable solutions to problems. For such nations, the key question becomes, what kind of society are we trying to build for the long term?[61]

According to the Harvard Project's data, the most successful indigenous nations in the area of economic development, such as Mississippi Band of Choctaw Indians and the White Mountain Apache Nation, use this model. However, this model is focused almost exclusively on a top-down structure of political authority and legitimacy. While the Harvard Project researchers contend that the model is flexible enough to accommodate the cultural diversity of indigenous nations, applications of their nation-building model ultimately privilege a centralized band council model of government to the exclusion of individual entrepreneurship and informal systems of governance (i.e., clans, societies, etc.). Furthermore, the idea that culture matters is paid little more than lip service in this economic development model— the priority is on generating a cash flow through political stability to secure economic and political power rather than revitalizing or regenerating cultural practices within community. Finally, the nation-building model proposed by the Harvard Project is virtually indistinguishable from other state-building models in western and eastern Europe that stress traditional capacity building and institutional legitimacy.[62]

The Harvard Project's institutional, top-down nation-building model stands in stark contrast to the notion of indigenous nationhood presented here. While indigenous nations do need to strive for economic self-sufficiency, the true sources of indigenous power lies within their informal governance relationships: the interrelationships between clan systems, confederations of families, homelands, language, ceremonial life, and sacred histories. Decision making and leadership arising from these community-based relationships will establish priorities that truly reflect nationhood and unity. The challenge is for indigenous nations to move beyond the rhetoric of nation-building models and find new solutions and tools to reshape their community relationships to confront encroachment from state and local governments. Aside from models of economic development on indigenous homelands, what are some other theories of indigenous political mobilization?

In her important work examining "the puzzle of Indian ethnic resurgence" between 1960 and 1990, sociologist Joane Nagel finds further support for the relationship between "movement resource acquisition" and the "extent of protest action" among indigenous peoples.[63] Her study suggests that federal government funding unwittingly promoted an indigenous ethnic renaissance by funding Native organizations and by providing increased incentives for indigenous ethnic identification and activism.[64] In sum, despite the promising application of resource mobilization theories to indigenous activism, this theoretical tool tends to exclude cultural and other informal leadership resources that may promote group mobilization. Also, this theory is predisposed toward explaining protest or violent political action and fails to account for other forms of political mobilization, such as party donations and candidate endorsement.

Applying models of pluralism to indigenous political behavior also has some serious shortcomings, as indigenous peoples are treaty-based nations, not interest groups trying to gain equality within the U.S. system. The pluralist model would view the co-optation of indigenous nations as a way to stabilize the regime. However, Emma Gross identifies the 1970s as a turning point where indigenous nations put their issues on the federal agenda.[65] Thus, according to Gross, indigenous peoples today are more likely to make their preferences known and policymakers are more likely to "respond by according them the right to participate in formulating the options and substance of formal policy."[66] In an important examination of the political and economic dimensions of indigenous gaming in New Mexico and Oklahoma, political scientist Dale Mason finds some basis for applying the tenets of the pluralist argument to indigenous nations. Mason concludes that the general trend of indigenous nations, states, and non-indigenous gaming interests moving from the courts to the legislature has greatly expanded the role of indigenous groups in shaping public policy.[67] Mason's findings also lend support to political scientist E. E. Schattschneider's "scope of conflict" model, where parties with an economic stake in a particular issue, such as indigenous nations operating casinos, will "seek the level or arena of government most likely to award them victory."[68] Ultimately, however, "tribal nations, generally—although this is changing for some tribes—do not consider themselves to be part of the pluralistic mosaic that is predominant in political science literature."[69]

The new social movements theory, which has its origins in earlier work by Karl Marx, Vladimir Lenin, and Antonio Gramsci, has been applied to several indigenous movements throughout the Americas when they have challenged state authority. Social movements can be broadly conceived as processes whereby social, cultural, and political actors produce meanings, negotiate and make decisions, communicate those meanings and decisions through contentious action against elites, and thereby challenge the rules and meanings constructed by state institutions. Sociologist Sidney Tarrow describes how social movements can be created: "Contentious politics is triggered when changing political opportunities and constraints create incentives for social actors who lack resources on their own."[70]

While indigenous nations in the United States have been experiencing changing political opportunities since 1988, a wider movement has not arisen that challenges the legitimacy of federal or state governments. Also, as Tarrow points out, social movements differ from other forms of collective action, such as voting or lobbying, in that they are "contentious challenges through disruptive direct action against elites."[71] Therefore, the new social movements theory does not apply to the political mobilization strategies that indigenous nations have used during the forced federalism era.

An internal colonial model potentially offers some insights into the mobilization strategies that indigenous peoples might employ to

promote decolonization and self-determination. Political scientist
James Tully defines internal colonialism as the situation where "the
colonizing society is built on the territories of the formerly free, and
now colonized, peoples. The colonizing or imperial society exercises
exclusive jurisdiction over them and their territories and the indigenous
peoples, although they comply and adapt, refuse to surrender their
freedom of self-determination over their territories and continue to
resist within the system as a whole as best they can."[72] Based on this
definition, a fundamental task of an internal colonial model would
be to explain how indigenous peoples "continue to resist within the
system." Sociologist Michael Hechter offers one explanation in his
well-known internal colonial model by outlining a cultural division
of labor among indigenous peoples, which in turn reinforces indigenous group solidarity. Based on Hechter's theory, the cultural
division of labor and increasing economic inequalities between the
core and periphery will mobilize the deprived cultural group toward
separatism.[73] Thus, when a person's life chances are affected by group
membership, she or he will make the critical choice to either leave
the community or adopt a strong nationalist identity. However, as
Wilkins points out in his comprehensive assessment of modernization, colonialism, and dependency models, internal colonialism
models "provide only a partial explanation and cannot cope with
tribal differentiation, especially as it pertains to socio-economic and
political disparities between various reservation communities."[74] An
additional problem with the application of an internal colonial model
to Native peoples is its reliance on a strict dichotomy, which tends
separates indigenous nations into simplistic categories of "traditional"
versus "progressive."[75]

In short, there are serious shortcomings and explanatory trade-
offs when attempting to apply theories of political mobilization to
indigenous peoples. Social constructions theory, discussed in chapter 2, still offers the most explanatory power when discussing how
indigenous political mobilization has been framed by state policymakers. Other theories of political mobilization offer only fragmented
perspectives on indigenous political mobilization since 1988. While
some combination of the theoretical tenets discussed earlier may
ultimately be the most useful strategy for comprehending contemporary indigenous political mobilization, it is important to note that

each indigenous nation has developed its own unique approaches to measured separatism and protection of indigenous nationhood. Given the current challenges to their nationhood, indigenous nations are making important decisions affecting the future of their communities.

CHAPTER FOUR

The Forced Federalism Survey

There is an awakening to political power that we can have. . . . We could have the "swing vote" if we vote together as Indians.

Vine Deloria, Jr., Standing Rock Sioux, 1968

Thus far, the picture of indigenous nations and their political mobilization has been provided largely through a social constructions model, which finds that states have been more prone to regulate indigenous economic activity given prevalent images of indigenous peoples as emerging contenders since 1988. To highlight the effects of social constructions on indigenous politics, the previous three chapters examined case studies of indigenous nations and their conflicts with state governors and policymakers in Arizona, Arkansas, California, Connecticut, Minnesota, Rhode Island, South Dakota, Texas, Virginia, and Washington, which are important to an understanding of indigenous political mobilization in the forced federalism era. Chapter 3 examined the reasons that indigenous peoples vote in U.S. elections and some of the potential effects of such a strategy.

However, a larger overview of indigenous political trends across the United States and how the politics of perception are being challenged in various political elections and state decision making contexts is in order. The forced federalism survey results, which have been used to examine the political activity of indigenous leaders between 1994 and 2000, offer a comprehensive view of how indigenous peoples are responding to increased state regulation and oversight of their nations.

When we first started the forced federalism surveys in 1994, our initial goal was to gauge indigenous political activity in states with large Native populations, such as Oklahoma and Arizona. We began by mailing a seven-question survey to the elected leaders of the 21 federally recognized nations in Arizona and the 39 federally recognized nations in Oklahoma after the 1994 U.S. elections. After receiving a high response rate to our initial surveys, we expanded the survey to a random sample of 108 indigenous nations in the continental United States. The initial survey was exploratory in that it was intended to gather basic information about the number of indigenous nations that participated in U.S. electoral processes. The survey also identified the reason(s) indigenous nations participated, how they participated, and the importance of federal, state, and local officials to the indigenous nations.[1] After an intensive period of follow-up, 42 of the 168 indigenous nations in the survey population responded to our inquiry (a 25 percent response rate).

Following the 1996 election, we added three questions to the initial survey instrument and expanded our survey population to include all indigenous nations in the continental United States. The three additional questions addressed the influence that indigenous nations perceived they had on the outcome of elections, the perceived attention that the federal, state, and local governments pay to Native concerns, and the specific issues that influenced participation in the election. After the follow-up process, we received 58 responses from 322 indigenous nations surveyed (an 18 percent response rate).

In 1998 the survey was distributed to an even larger pool by including 16 randomly selected indigenous nations from Alaska as well as all indigenous nations in the continental United States. After extensive follow-up, we received responses from 77 of 338 contacted nations (a 23 percent response rate). In 1998 the survey instrument was also expanded by two questions (see appendix G for sample survey). These two questions included whether the nation had negotiated a compact with the state and the content of the compact and the extent to which the nation perceived the compact had strengthened their sovereign rights.[2]

In 2000 the survey followed the same format as the 1998 survey instrument and was distributed to 322 nations. Out of 300 indigenous nations surveyed throughout the United States, 49 responded (a 16 percent response rate).

At first glance, the overall survey response rate may seem low, averaging 20.5 percent over the entire 1994–2000 period. However, three factors should be considered when surveying indigenous nations. First, a similar survey of 245 Native leaders in 1971 yielded a similar response rate of 23 percent.[3] Second, our results can be generalized, as we received responses from all regions of the country, including the ten states with the largest Native populations. Third, given cultural differences and distrust of government (state and federal) and research that asks specific questions about indigenous political support, we anticipated a response rate slightly lower than Theodore Taylor's 1971 survey given the higher risks to indigenous self-determination during the forced federalism era. The 168 total survey responses (see appendix A for a complete listing) present a valid picture of the nature and extent of indigenous political participation and the influences on these decisions for the years 1994, 1996, 1998, and 2000. To analyze the survey responses, we combined all four years into a workable data set. This allowed us to examine patterns of participation by year or combine the results to view the total participation of responding nations.

EXPECTATIONS

The era of forced federalism is marked by increased federal government pressure on indigenous nations to negotiate with state and local governments for jurisdiction on Native homelands. As a result, communication between indigenous nations and state and local policymakers has been steadily increasing since 1988. As indigenous nations have interacted more with state and local governments as perceived rich Indians on the political scene, one would expect that indigenous nations would also become more involved in the selection of federal, state, and local government officials. If indigenous nations can help elect officials friendly to their issues, or at least elicit promises of support for indigenous issues in return for financial or political assistance, contact with federal, state, and local governments is more likely to lead to an outcome deemed supportive of indigenous self-determination. States have engaged in more bureaucratic oversight and regulation of indigenous governance and economic development strategies since 1988 due to prevailing social constructions of indigenous peoples as rich, and indigenous peoples have been increasingly willing to challenge these state behaviors in the electoral arena. In the ongoing battle over the politics of perception, indigenous nations have turned to new political strategies in an attempt to (re)frame policy issues on their own terms.

We expect indigenous nations to support candidates for office who support Native issues, especially issues that address interaction with external governments, such as gaming and sovereignty. Further, participation in external U.S. elections is likely to take shape through efforts to mobilize members and get out the vote in support of favored candidates. Indigenous nations with increased financial resources are also more likely to make campaign contributions to office seekers in an effort to ensure the selection of favored candidates.

One final prediction was tested in all four surveys. Before 1988 indigenous nations were primarily concerned with maintaining good diplomatic relations with federal officials, including the president, U.S. senators, and members of the U.S. House of Representatives. Their importance in making federal law and policy and setting federal budgets made them important actors. Since the beginning of the forced federalism era, state and local elected officials are now claiming to have equal importance to federal officials in setting indigenous policy. Given the increased contact between indigenous nations and the governors of a state during the compacting process, our expectation was that state governors would be regarded as important to indigenous nations as federal elected officials are in policymaking. Unfortunately, the survey does not allow us to test this expectation before 1988. However, one can gauge from the surveys whether state governors have been elevated in their importance to indigenous nations since 1994.

We refined our survey instrument in 1996 and 1998 to further address the possible reasons for indigenous participation in the electoral process (see appendix G). While we expected a candidate's issue positions to drive the decision whether to support a candidate, issues may not be the sole reason that an indigenous nation becomes active in the electoral process. Instead, we expected Native participation to also be a reaction to changes brought about as a result of forced federalism and their own changing status as rich Indians. With that said, indigenous peoples have long shown a tendency to vote based on issues rather than let political party affiliation guide their decision to support candidates for office.[4] With this in mind, we identified three reasons for increased indigenous participation. First, if an indigenous nation has extensive contact with the state government, it is more likely to support a candidate or candidates for elective office. Second, if an indigenous nation feels it has a close relationship with the state, meaning the state pays attention to its concerns when making policy, it is likely to be more involved in the electoral process. Third, if an indigenous nation believes that it can make a difference in the outcome of an election, and possibly influence public policy, it is more likely to support a candidate.

Overall, our expectations about the political participation of indigenous nations reflect the exploratory nature of our study. We do not have the benefit of an ongoing survey that predates the beginning of the era of forced federalism. However, as evidenced by the increased NGA and legislative involvement detailed in chapter 2, we are guided by strong expectations about the changing relationship between indigenous nations and federal, state, and local governments.

SURVEY RESULTS

The first set of questions in the survey address whether indigenous nations are active in supporting candidates for external elections. The first two questions are about whether the indigenous nation had endorsed or supported a candidate in the recently held primary or general election. "Means of supporting a candidate" refers to any form of financial assistance, get-out-the-vote efforts, or volunteer activities, such as campaigning. Results are shown in table 4.1. Indigenous nations surveyed appear almost evenly split on their willingness to engage in the primary or general election, with a downward trend of participation after the 1996 election. Given that 1994 and 1998 are midterm elections, and thus elicit less interest and turnout, this finding suggests that indigenous nations may have responded to the more significant presidential election of 1996. However, this was not the case for the 2000 election.

Of greater interest is the level of overall participation when primary and general elections are combined. As expected, indigenous nations have remained active in the political process since 1994. In 1994 respondents were nearly evenly divided in their level of participation,

TABLE 4.1
Indigenous Nation Support of Electoral Candidates, 1994–2000

Percentage of respondents who supported a candidate	1994	1996	1998	2000
In a primary election	37	45	52	49
In a general election	37	53	46	43
In either a primary election or a general election	49	55	51	45

with 49 percent showing support for a candidate in either a primary or general election. By 1996, a presidential election year, the percentage of electoral participation increased, with 55 percent of indigenous nations surveyed supporting candidates for office. Contrary to expectations, however, political participation for indigenous leaders declined during the 2000 elections. Overall, these findings are important in conveying that in years 1994–98, over half of all indigenous nations surveyed were active in supporting a candidate or candidates for elective office (i.e., getting out the vote, campaigning, etc.).

Given that over half of all indigenous nations surveyed actively supported a candidate or candidates for office from 1994 to 1998, the question becomes, why were some candidates chosen over others? The survey provided as choices membership in the nation, political party of the candidate, issue positions of the candidate, and an "other" category, which was included to allow respondents to identify possible other reasons.[5] Respondents were asked to rank their reasons in order of importance: most important, somewhat important, or less important. If only one reason was marked, it was considered "most important."

As expected, indigenous nations based their political support predominantly on issue positions of the candidate. As shown in table 4.2, indigenous nations are much more likely to support a candidate who advocates for issue positions that favor Native people. A candidate's stance on key issues such as Native sovereignty and gaming were consistently mentioned by respondents over time as the main criteria for Native nations choosing to support one candidate over another. However, issues such as treaty rights, taxation, the environment, budget cuts, and education also figured prominently in survey

responses, demonstrating the interrelatedness of several issues associated with self-determination. In addition, depending on the political
context, certain issues were more prominent during each election
cycle.[6] The importance of the candidate's political party lags far
behind, suggesting that indigenous nations are sophisticated political
actors who do not rely solely on political party as the reason for
supporting a candidate. Membership in an indigenous nation does
not appear to be a major determinant of indigenous support, but
since so few indigenous people run for office, a candidate's membership in a particular nation is unlikely to be a factor for indigenous
voters who were surveyed. In fact, in during the 2006 election,
indigenous candidate Jack Jackson (Navajo Nation) had a difficult
time obtaining monetary support from other Arizona indigenous
nations during his campaign for the Arizona state legislature. In
total Jackson received a paltry $2,000 from one Arizona indigenous
nation, while his opponent, a non-indigenous candidate, Republican
Rick Renzi, received $80,000 from indigenous communities for his
campaign.[7] The critical issue leading to indigenous support in this
case was that Renzi was an incumbent who almost always took the
position favored by indigenous nations in the Arizona legislature.
This example supports our overall findings, which suggest that issue
positions and prior experience usually surpass indigenous identity in
terms of overall importance when determining the election support
of indigenous nations.

Since issue positions of a candidate for office were deemed the
most important factor influencing indigenous support for a candidate,
which issues are the most important ones for Native leaders? Two
issues immediately come to mind: economic development and indigenous self-determination. Due to increased indigenous-state compact
negotiations for casino gaming operations under IGRA, these issues
are the primary catalysts for increased indigenous-state contact in
the forced federalism era. State governors, and in some cases state
legislators, have become the key actors that indigenous nations have
to work with to secure compacts on anything from motor fuel taxation on indigenous homelands to casino operations. The first issue
is whether the economic benefits that are generated in a successful
gaming operation are likely to make gaming an important issue to
indigenous nations. A second related issue is the effect of indigenous-
state compacting on indigenous self-determination. By compelling

TABLE 4.2
Indigenous Nation Reasons for Supporting
a Political Candidate, 1994–2000

	1994	1996	1998	2000	Total
Total number of respondents	**42**	**58**	**77**	**49**	**226**
Issue positions	31	37	43	26	137
Most important	31	34	43	22	130
Somewhat important	1	2	3	6	12
Less important	1	1	1	0	3
Indigenous nation membership	9	8	8	11	36
Most important	2	3	1	1	7
Somewhat important	5	4	0	4	13
Less important	3	1	0	5	9
Political party	11	17	18	15	61
Most important	4	7	9	8	28
Somewhat important	5	5	6	2	18
Less important	5	4	4	5	18
Other	9	4	16	9	38

indigenous nations to operate on a government-to-government basis with states, the status of indigenous communities as treaty-based nations with exclusive diplomatic relations with the federal government has been undermined. As a result, we expected greater support for candidates who backed indigenous self-determination and treaty rights issues.

The results of the survey demonstrate that during the forced federalism era, gaming and self-determination issues clearly have the greatest influence on Native voters when backing a candidate for office (see table 4.3). Yet, it would be misleading to overstate these findings. These two issues are concerns that are likely to be addressed on a frequent basis by indigenous governments and federal, local, and especially state office holders. In other words, gaming and self-determination may not be the most important problems facing individual Native nations, but they are the most important issues facing indigenous governments when dealing with state and local officials. In part, this reflects a response to the increasingly regulatory

TABLE 4.3
Issues Important to Indigenous Nations, 1994–2000

	1994	1996	1998	2000	Total
Total number of respondents	**42**	**58**	**77**	**49**	**226**
Gaming	14	16	15	0	45
Sovereignty, treaty rights, self-determination	12	15	13	14	54
Other*	16	14	20	1	51

* Total of less frequent mentions, including education, taxes, English-only laws, wolf snare ban, equity, forestry, fishing, the environment, housing, health care, law enforcement, cultural integrity/preservation, agriculture, and others.

policies adopted by state policymakers in the areas of economic development designed to curtail or limit indigenous self-determination.

The "other" category is telling in that it exposes several key issues of concern to indigenous nations during the elections. These issues, such as fishing and cultural integrity/preservation, are also related to indigenous self-determination and were key factors in motivating political mobilization during the election cycles between 1994 and 1998.

The next survey question addressed the ways in which indigenous nations support candidates for office. It listed three possible means for indigenous nations to support candidates: providing financial resources, initiating get-out-the-vote efforts, and asking members to volunteer for a campaign.[8] The results reveal two main findings (see table 4.4). First, indigenous nations are more likely to engage in get-out-the-vote efforts and to contribute to candidates than they are to volunteer for a campaign. From a time management perspective, indigenous governmental leaders are in much stronger positions to advocate voting for a candidate or to provide financial support for a candidate, as these activities require less time and effort than working for a candidate. Second, the number of indigenous nations providing financial support to candidates from 1994 to 2000 is rather significant. In 1994 and 1998, more than 40 percent of all indigenous leaders surveyed provided financial resources to candidates, which demonstrates significant Native participation in U.S. electoral politics. One possible explanation for financial contributions to candidates is that those indigenous governments that have signed a compact with the state, and most likely those compacts for casino-style gaming, are likely to have had the financial resources necessary to support

TABLE 4.4
Types of Indigenous Support for Political Candidates, 1994–2000

	1994	1996	1998	2000	Total
Total number of respondents	**42**	**58**	**77**	**49**	**226**
Financial	18	18	32	20	88
Get-out-the-vote efforts	17	22	32	21	13
Volunteer	13	15	15	12	55
Other	11	19	15	6	51

candidates. These financial contributions, which have increased in scope and size since 1994, certainly form the crux of the emerging contender social constructions among state policymakers.

There appears to be a strong correlation between signing a gaming compact and providing financial support to a candidate. While only the 1998 and 2000 surveys asked whether an indigenous nation had signed a compact, they provide preliminary evidence for our contention that indigenous-state compacting led to increased political support for candidates for office during the 1998 and 2000 election campaigns. In other words, when an indigenous nation had negotiated a gaming compact with the state, they also tended to provide financial support for political candidates that same year (see table 4.5). Compacting is a rough measure of indigenous nations who have close contact with state governments. As a result of this increased indigenous-state contact, some nations have additional insight into the governmental and electoral processes. In addition, many of these compacts provide economic development and financial resources to indigenous nations. Motor fuel, tobacco, and taxation agreements are just a few examples of compacts negotiated between indigenous nations and state governments. In each case, the long-term rewards are financial and may be used to support a candidate for office.

In addition, indigenous nations may have a greater incentive to support candidates for office if their indigenous-state compact negotiations are being stalled, by a state governor, for example. This was certainly the case in Arizona in 1992, and it led to a showdown between indigenous nations and Governor Symington (see chapter 2).

TABLE 4.5
Correlation between Financial Support for Candidates and
Indigenous-State Compact, 1998 and 2000

	Pearson correlation
Signed an indigenous-state compact in 1998	.402
Signed an indigenous-state compact in 2000	.348

n = 73; significant at the .01 level

This indigenous-state conflict led indigenous nations to put gaming
on the ballot as a referendum issue in 1996 and also prompted greater
political activism that same year through the first ever American Indian
Voters Convention held in Phoenix, Arizona, which was attended by
more than five hundred people from all twenty-one federally recognized indigenous nations in Arizona. Being blocked from signing a
gaming compact may also be a motivation to financially support
candidates who are friendly to indigenous self-determination issues.
The motivations for financially supporting a candidate may be just
as strong when indigenous-state compacts are denied or challenged
by state officials as when they are negotiated successfully.

It follows from the preceding discussion that while candidates are
supported because of their issue positions, this does not explain why
an indigenous nation becomes involved in an election. The dynamics
of forced federalism have led to at least three possible reasons for
Native involvement in elections. First, contact with state policymakers,
in the form of government-to-government relations during the compacting process, provides an incentive for indigenous nations to
become politically active. Here, the goal is to positively affect the
outcome of an election in an effort to enhance Native political clout
in the indigenous-state relationship. In the future, involvement in
elections may advance an indigenous nation's efforts to secure an
agreement or compact. Despite expectations, the survey results
revealed no clear relationship between contact with the state system
as measured by compacting and indigenous political participation.

A second possible motivation for indigenous nations to participate
in the electoral process is the attention indigenous nations believe
the state pays to the concerns of indigenous nations when making
policy. If there is an apparent link between decision making at the
state level with the concerns of indigenous nations, indigenous

TABLE 4.6

Candidate Support and Governmental Attitudes
(Federal, State, and Local) toward Indigenous Nations, 1998 and 2000

	Level of Support			
Federal government	A good deal	Some	Not much	None
No electoral participation	8	20	28	5
Electoral participation	13	36	20	1
Total	21	56	48	6

$n = 131$ chi-square = 9.187; significant at the .05 level

	Level of Support			
State government	A good deal	Some	Not much	None
No electoral participation	3	16	25	16
Electoral participation	9	28	27	6
Total	12	44	52	22

$n = 130$ chi-square = 10.186; significant at the .05 level

	Level of Support			
Local government	A good deal	Some	Not much	None
No electoral participation	8	16	19	16
Electoral participation	15	28	19	8
Total	23	34	38	24

$n = 129$ chi-square = 7.184; not significant at the .05 level

governments may feel a sense of involvement in the system. Given the increased contact between governments, it is possible that a feeling of inclusion could foster additional involvement in the system. This sense of involvement may be perpetuated as electoral participation further influences candidates for office who are friendly to Native issues. In the 1998 and 2000 surveys, the question was asked "How much attention do you feel the federal, state, and local government pays to your government when making policy affecting American Indians?" Of key importance to the study of forced federalism is how indigenous nations perceive their relationship with the state government. Indigenous nations are more likely to support candidates for election if they feel the federal or state government pays attention to them when making policy (see table 4.6). Based on the survey results, even if state governments did not pay much attention ("not much" category) to indigenous nations, there was still a strong likelihood that they would mobilize to support candidates for office. The attitudes of local governments generally mirrored those of state governments in terms of influencing indigenous political behavior.

The third possible motivation for political participation by indigenous nations involves their sense of political efficacy, or their feeling that they could influence the outcome of an election. Indigenous nations may decide to back a candidate for office if they view their involvement as making a difference regarding which candidate will win the election. This can play out in a number of ways. Large nations, such as the Cherokees or Navajos, may feel that mobilizing their citizens in support of a U.S. candidate for office may also mean the difference in the election outcome. In local or close elections, smaller nations may also be able to mobilize their members to provide the winning margin of victory (i.e., swing votes). In other cases, many nations may pool their resources behind one candidate in an effort to further their common issues. In 2006, for example, the indigenous swing vote was instrumental in electing Democratic candidate Jon Tester to the U.S. Senate by the slimmest of margins (49 percent to opponent incumbent Republican Senator Conrad Burns's 48 percent). In Montana's reservation precincts, over 80 percent of all indigenous voters voted for Tester, which made difference in the election outcome.[9]

The survey asked respondents to identify how much influence they thought they had on election outcomes. The results revealed that an indigenous nation's perception of influence on political elections appears to play a significant role in determining if the nation will choose to support a candidate for election (see table 4.7). These findings are what one would expect: indigenous leaders only invest their time and effort into election campaigns where they think they can make a difference in the outcome.

This examination of the political motivations of indigenous leaders does not take into account their political legitimacy within their own nations and whether they are solely seeking political solutions at the federal and state levels at the expense of local, community-based solutions. However, the surveys have uncovered some of the reasons why indigenous voters might support candidates for office.

We took the investigation one step further by examining the motives for political participation using a more comprehensive statistical model, logistic regression, which is useful for calculating the likelihood

TABLE 4.7
Candidate Support by Indigenous Nations and Political Efficacy

Influence on electoral outcome	Level of Support			
	A good deal	Some	Not much	None
No electoral participation	4	13	17	24
Electoral participation	18	33	13	4
Total	22	46	30	28

$n = 126$ chi-square = 31.831; significant at the .001 level

of one event occurring over another. This model is also useful for modeling political behavior that is dichotomous (i.e., either yes or no). In this case, the dependent variable used in the analysis was whether or not indigenous political participation took place between 1998 and 2000 (see table 4.8). The connection between political participation and factors influencing indigenous mobilization was calculated by listing three logistic regression coefficients: perceived attention by state policy makers to indigenous issues, contact with the system (as measured by compacting), and indigenous feelings of political efficacy. This model allowed us to control for the effects of each of the three factors simultaneously. The result revealed that perceived indigenous influence in an election is the only statistically significant variable. This suggests compacting and perceived state concern for indigenous nations do not significantly influence indigenous rates of political participation. The only factor that appears to matter when deciding whether or not to support a candidate for office is whether an indigenous nation can influence the election outcome. This finding highlights the sophisticated political strategies that indigenous nations' leaders have taken regarding their decision to support candidates for office—they are pragmatic, and other factors, such as state attitudes and compact negotiations, do not appear to influence their final decisions.

A further examination of the relationship between perceived influence on election outcome and political support of office seekers allowed us to predict the probability of indigenous support. Indigenous nations that felt they had a great deal of influence on the election outcome were likely to endorse a candidate for election 87 percent of the time.[10] An indigenous nation that perceived they only had some influence on the election outcome endorsed a candidate 70

TABLE 4.8
Logistic Model of Indigenous Participation and
State Attitudes, 1998 and 2000

State attitude	.275 (.397)
Compact with state	.442 (.643)
Influence election	1.068* (.339)
Constant	3.968** (1.295)

n = 69; Log-likelihood–47.646; correctly classified = 72.46%. Standard deviations are given in parentheses.
**significant at the .01 level.   *significant at the .05 level.

percent of the time. Not surprisingly, indigenous nations that felt they had little influence on the outcome supported a candidate only 45 percent of the time, while indigenous nations who perceived they had no influence on the election outcome supported candidates for office only 22 percent of the time. These findings are consistent with expectations.

One final piece of evidence examining indigenous political mobilization between 1994 and 2000 relates to how indigenous nations rank the overall importance of state and federal elected leaders. We expected that as indigenous nations and states were compelled to work together in the compacting process, state leaders would become more important to indigenous nations when mobilizing politically. More specifically, we expected that the governor, as the person identified to work out compacting agreements with indigenous governments, would assume a role as important as federal officials. Federal officials, including members of the House of Representatives, senators, and the president have always been central players, given the important federal role in historic government-to-government relations. If, as expected, governors are perceived as important as federal officials, it would provide compelling evidence for the argument that indigenous-state intergovernmental relationships have changed dramatically.

The results show that four elected officials were important to indigenous nations, while five others were clearly less important (see table 4.9). Not surprisingly, the list of officials considered most important to indigenous nations included federal office holders such as the president, U.S. senators, and members of the House of Representatives. The fourth office of importance to indigenous nations

TABLE 4.9
Indigenous Nation Rankings of the Relative Importance of
Elected Officials, 1994, 1996, 1998, and 2000

Office	Average ranking		Most frequent placement	
	1994–98	2000	1994–98	2000
U.S. senator	2.72	2.83	2nd	1st
U.S. president	3.46	3.72	1st	3rd
U.S. representative	3.48	3.55	3rd	2nd
State governor	3.78	3.75	4th	4th
State senator	4.66	4.74	5th	6th
State representative	5.48	4.57	6th	5th
State attorney general	5.95	5.99	7th	7th
County official	6.55	6.44	8th	8th
Mayor/city official	7.54	7.54	9th	9th

was the state governor. In 2000, for example, the governor was in close competition with the U.S. president in terms of relative importance to indigenous nations responding to the survey. This result was also expected as the increased interaction in areas such as gaming and other forms of compacting have made governors important officials to indigenous nations.

REGISTRATION AND VOTER TURNOUT BY INDIGENOUS PEOPLE DURING ELECTIONS: TWO CASE STUDIES

Having examined the political behavior of indigenous nations using survey results from 1994 to 2000, we will now take an in-depth look at two state elections in South Dakota and Arizona to provide further insights into indigenous political mobilization during the forced federalism era. While there are many recent examples to draw on, these are two key examples of how indigenous peoples are mobilizing in ways predicted by the survey results. These two cases also demonstrate the multiple ways that indigenous nations are mobilizing to influence policy decisions at the state level. Finally, the indigenous populations in both states are significant (5 percent in Arizona and 8.2 percent in South Dakota), which makes the indigenous vote a possible swing vote in elections. The first example examines voter

registration and support in the 1996 race for U.S. Senator in South
Dakota. The second example considers indigenous vote choice on
Arizona Proposition 201, an initiative to allow nongaming indigenous
nations to negotiate compacts.

THE 1996 SOUTH DAKOTA SENATE RACE

The U.S. Senate race in South Dakota in 1996 was unique because it
was the only race that year in which a challenger, Tim Johnson (then
a Democratic member of the U.S. House of Representatives), was
able to defeat an incumbent Republican senator. The race was also
exceptional because it pitted a conservative Republican opposed by
most indigenous nations in South Dakota against a moderate Demo-
crat who received substantial backing from the nine reservations in
the state. Indigenous efforts to defeat incumbent Senator Larry Pressler
started two years before the election, when members of the Dakota
Territory Chairman's Council initiated efforts to register and educate
indigenous voters on the importance of participation in non-Native
elections.[11] Their plan was to work hard to elect a Senate candidate
friendly to Native issues. With relatively low voter registration in
predominantly Native counties, the first task was to register new voters.
Once these voters were registered, attention turned to educating voters
on their choices. Consistent with the survey findings, indigenous nations
showed strong support for the Democratic challenger based on his
issue positions relating to indigenous peoples. Finally, increased Native
voter turnout was expected to be crucial in what was shaping up to
be a very close race.

The success of efforts by indigenous leaders to register and mobilize
Native voters can be measured by examining county registration and
voter information for 1996. We did this by focusing on the six South
Dakota counties with a Native population of at least 50 percent,
which is a common cut-off point for gauging whether a county is
predominantly indigenous.[12] We also included information on registration and elections in years before 1996 to note the significant increase
in registration and turnout in indigenous communities.[13] The figures
in table 4.10 provide a good indication of the success of the registration efforts of Native leaders. Namely, in every county but Mellette,
voter registration increased—in most cases substantially—over the figures
from 1994. In Shannon County, which is contained in the Pine Ridge

TABLE 4.10
Voters Registered as Democrats in South Dakota's
Majority-Indigenous Counties, 1994 and 1996

County	Indigenous population (%)	Registered voters 1994	Registered voters 1996	Real change 1994–1996	Registration increase (%), 1994–1996
Bennett	50	881	992	111	13
Buffalo	79	665	697	32	5
Corson	50	998	1233	235	24
Dewey	70	1887	2104	217	12
Mellette	52	606	595	–11	–2
Todd	84	2044	2548	504	46
Shannon	95	2613	3817	1204	25
Ziebach	67	664	864	200	30

Reservation, voter registration increased by over 46 percent, and over one thousand more voters turned out in 1996 than in the 1994 election. Other predominantly Native counties experienced significant increases in registration and turnout, including Ziebach County, located on the Cheyenne Reservation, which saw an increase in voter registration of over 30 percent and a voter turnout increase of over 12 percent.

Based on these findings, increased voter registration and turnout is only important if it serves to increase support for the candidate friendly to Native issues. To measure how successful efforts by indigenous leaders to educate Native voters on the candidates were, we measured the change in support for incumbent Senator Pressler from his last election in 1990 to the year of his defeat in 1996. The results showed a change in voter choice that was driven by the candidate. In every county with a majority indigenous population in South Dakota, support for incumbent Senator Pressler dropped between the years 1990 and 1996. This decrease was significant, ranging from a 9 percent reduction to a 35 percent reduction in support. The efforts of indigenous leaders to register and turn out voters in support of a candidate favorable to Native issues produced impressive results. This evidence is indicative of the larger efforts of indigenous mobilization. With increased incentives to participate, indigenous people were becoming more active in the political process. As this example also illustrates, candidates were forced to consider the indigenous vote in South Dakota and elsewhere or face potential electoral defeat. Perhaps due to their success in 1996, the indigenous-state gaming compacts negotiated in 2000 contained provisions prohibiting indigenous nations in South Dakota from using funds generated by gaming in influencing the outcome of local, state, and federal elections within the state of South Dakota. (See appendix B for the full text of the compact.)

As the restrictive compacts of 2000 indicate, indigenous peoples may be victims of their own success in electoral politics. The widespread mobilization to support candidate Tim Johnson in 1996 led to greater oversight and regulation of indigenous nations gaming and political activities in subsequent years. While indigenous peoples got out the vote in massive numbers in 1996, they also got the attention of state policymakers as socially constructed emerging contenders on the political scene.

PROPOSITION 201 IN ARIZONA: THE FAIRNESS INITIATIVE

Efforts to influence the electoral process are not limited to candidate support. In a number of states, notably Arizona and California, indigenous nations have become active in the initiative process in an effort to shape their relationships with the governor and state government. In Arizona in 1996 and California in 1998 and 2000, citizen initiatives were placed on the ballot in an effort to secure the rights of indigenous governments to use gaming as a means for economic development on reservation land.

As discussed in chapter 2, the indigenous-state conflict leading up to Proposition 201 began in 1992, when former Arizona governor Fife Symington refused to negotiate five indigenous-state gaming compacts. After an FBI raid and tense standoff with the Fort McDowell Yavapai Nation, a federal mediator was called in to resolve the dispute. In February of 1993, a federal mediator, former Arizona Supreme Court justice Frank X. Gordon, sided with three of Arizona's indigenous nations by asserting that the governor could not unilaterally limit the number of slot machines operating in Native communities. In response to the mediator's decision, Symington called a special session of the state legislature to enact a bill that would criminally prohibit class III gaming in Arizona while leaving the state lottery and pari-mutuel betting at horse and dog tracks untouched. The conflict subsided when Secretary of the Interior Bruce Babbitt proposed a compromise position, linking the allocation of slot machines to the population size of particular indigenous communities; by April 1994 sixteen indigenous nations had entered into compacts with the state of Arizona.[14]

In May 1995 Governor Symington took a stand against indigenous gaming once again by refusing to negotiate any further indigenous-state compacts.[15] The Salt River Pima Nation took the issue to the voters in 1996 in the form of Proposition 201, which would aid the efforts of five indigenous governments who were being refused gaming compacts by Symington. While not all indigenous nations in Arizona were interested in operating a casino, for many Proposition 201 was about reaffirming the self-determining authority of indigenous nations, the ability to determine their own economic futures, with or without a casino. Asserting indigenous self-determination motivated a number of Native leaders, including Hopi chairman Ferrell Secakuku, Salt River Pima-Maricopa Indian Community president Ivan Makil, and Navajo president Albert Hale, to endorse the proposition before the election.[16]

Native support for Proposition 201 was also encouraged in 1996 at the first Arizona Indians Voters' Convention. At the convention, indigenous nations agreed to work together to pass Proposition 201 by registering voters and encouraging participation in the upcoming election. Participants at the convention also vowed to actively support candidates for office at all levels that were friendly to Native issues and encouraged others to participate in the upcoming election. In an era of forced federalism, the efforts of indigenous nations to mobilize in support of issues are especially important in framing the relationship between indigenous nations and state government.

To assess the effect of the Arizona indigenous vote in 1996, we gauged the effectiveness of efforts to turn out the vote in support of Proposition 201. To measure Native voting, we focused our analysis on two counties, Coconino and Apache. These two counties are ideally suited for analysis, as they have substantial indigenous populations and a large number of precincts located entirely on indigenous reservations.[17] In 1996 Coconino County had twenty-two precincts on reservation land, including seventeen on the Navajo (Diné) Reservation, three containing both Navajo and Southern San Juan Paiute land, and one each on the Hopi and Havasupai reservations.[18] Of the thirty-three reservation precincts in Apache County, thirty-two precincts are on the Navajo Reservation, with an additional precinct on the White Mountain Apache Reservation.

By focusing on reservation precincts, we were able to examine the vote choice of indigenous peoples with a high degree of accuracy despite the absence of polling or survey instruments. This approach follows previous work by political scientist Dan McCool, who analyzed indigenous voting in Arizona by measuring turnout and vote choice in reservation precincts.[19]

To measure the effectiveness of efforts to mobilize indigenous voters, we began with an analysis of vote choice in 1996. We expected, given the high stakes for Native people in 1996 and the efforts of indigenous leaders to mobilize Native voters, that there would be a significant difference between levels of indigenous and non-indigenous support for Proposition 201. Indigenous voters supported Proposition 201 at a much higher rate than non-indigenous people (see table 4.11). For even though there was a high level of support, with nearly 64 percent of the state's population supporting the proposition, an even greater level of indigenous voters supported the proposition. In both Apache and Coconino counties, the proposition was supported in reservation precincts by nearly seven out of ten voters. In Apache County reservation support was nearly 6 percent greater than off the reservation. Similarly, large discrepancies were apparent in Coconino County, where levels of support on the reservation exceeded non-reservation precincts by nearly 8 percent. Finally, our findings suggest that when we control for a number of possible influences by looking at precincts within the same county, we see strong evidence that reservation voters favored Proposition 201 more than voters off the reservation.

Even after Symington's resignation in 1997, conflicts persisted over the renegotiation of indigenous-state gaming compacts, with Arizona state legislature refusing to approve seventeen indigenous gaming compacts in 2002. For indigenous nations engaging in gaming, the Fort McDowell community's 1992 blockade represents a pivotal point in gaming rights in Arizona and around the country, as well as exhibiting the perils of forced federalism.

This example of indigenous political mobilization in Arizona has several implications. Proposition 201 passed by a wide margin in 1996, with approval from nearly two-thirds of Arizona voters. However, this case also illustrates the potential dangers of voter backlash and being forced to put one's self-determination powers up for a popular vote, which could backfire if a gaming proposition is defeated. In 2003

TABLE 4.11
Voter Support for Proposition 201
in Cococino and Apache Counties, Arizona, 1996

Support	Apache County	Cococino County
Reservation precinct support (%)	69.2	69.0
Non-reservation precinct support (%)	63.4	61.2
Difference	+5.8	+7.8
Reservation precinct support (%)	69.2	69.0
Statewide support* (%)	63.9	63.9
Difference	+5.3	+5.1

*Statewide support for Proposition 201 was 858,903 votes.

the Passamaquoddy and Penobscot nations lost a similar referendum to run casinos by nearly a two-to-one margin in Maine, and in 2006 the Narragansett Nation lost a ballot initiative in Rhode Island to operate a Harrah's Narragansett casino by a wide margin (63 percent against and 37 percent for). Putting gaming and other indigenous self-determination issues up for a popular vote will increasingly become a risky strategy given the realities of rich Indian racism.

Furthermore, issues that affect indigenous people are likely to work their way onto the political agenda of Native leaders. Indigenous leaders in turn are likely to advocate support for issues that have direct and indirect effects on indigenous nations. Native support for Proposition 201 also reaffirms the findings in our surveys of indigenous nations. Clearly a salient issue motivates political participation of indigenous leaders and Native voters. The support of issues can be clearly stated at events like the Arizona Indian Voters Convention and shared with others in an effort to mobilize the electorate. Interestingly, Navajo and Hopi support for Proposition 201 did not translate into support for gaming on either reservation, as neither nation entered into a gaming compact after the passage of Proposition 201.

In an era of forced federalism we expected indigenous governments to participate in the political process to increase their influence through government-to-government relations at the state and federal levels. Our expectations were borne out when we examined the political participation of indigenous people from three perspectives. First, by surveying indigenous leaders, we were able to discover why candidates for non-reservation elections were supported—their position on issues important to indigenous people—and to identify the efforts undertaken to support favored candidates. We also identified the factors that influenced Native involvement in the electoral process by suggesting that the stronger the feeling that an indigenous nation can influence the outcome of the election, the more likely they are to support candidates for office. Importantly, this feeling of political efficacy emerged in our examination of the vote choice of Native voters. As our overview of the 1996 U.S. Senate election in South Dakota indicates, efforts of the Dakota Territory Chairman's Council to promote the candidacy of challenger Tim Johnson were successful, as predominantly Native counties provided strong support for the challenger in 1996. This support was much higher than in the prior U.S. Senate race of incumbent Larry Pressler in 1990.

A new expectation for the forced federalism era is the introduction of ballot propositions aimed at clarifying the relationship between indigenous nations and state governments. In both California and Arizona, ballot propositions have been successful in securing the rights of Native governments to engage in casino-style gaming. However, in Maine a Native gaming ballot initiative failed in 2003 by a wide margin. What led to its demise? As expected, Maine's governor, John Baldacci, openly campaigned against the referendum. Those campaigning against the referendum portrayed indigenous peoples as rich Indians and emerging contenders—they played on fears of traffic and crime drawn from experiences with gaming operations by Pequots and Mohegans in nearby Connecticut. In addition, groups such as the Audubon Society, child welfare advocates, and Maine's well-known corporate entity L.L. Bean all teamed up to denounce the referendum, citing fears of overcrowding, corruption, and crime.[20] While a referendum strategy offers an alternative to dealing with uncooperative state governors, the changing social constructions of indigenous peoples as emerging contenders may eventually lead to more incidents of backlash at the voting booth.

We tested the expectation that indigenous voters would support issues of importance to indigenous nations by examining precinct level voting patterns in Arizona. Despite relatively high levels of support from non-indigenous voters, a clear difference emerged as reservation voters outpaced non-reservation voters in their support of Native issues. This strong showing in reservation precincts also supports the role of indigenous leaders who worked to mobilize voters in the electoral process.

Finally, can indigenous participation in the political process backfire? The answer is somewhat mixed. On one hand, it appears unlikely if indigenous peoples form a significant segment of the voting population in their state. In fact, a close showing in a race with heavy indigenous participation may encourage an office holder to work harder to secure the Native vote. However, as the backlash toward indigenous peoples in South Dakota and Maine illustrate, managing the politics of perception is just as important as supporting the winning candidate in an election. In the future, the outcome of close elections may be decided by the indigenous swing vote. This was definitely the case in South Dakota in 1996, and in Washington in 2000, when the indigenous vote was mobilized in part by the First Americans Education Project to defeat anti-indigenous candidate Slade Gorton in the U.S. Senate election. Thus far, the backlash over socially constructed images of indigenous peoples as emerging contenders has yet to manifest itself widely in electoral politics. During the 2004 elections, for example, indigenous gaming referenda were passed in Wisconsin for the development of a Menominee casino and in Oklahoma for the approval of indigenous-state compacts expanding the range of slot machines in Native-run casinos. Even amid two major referendum victories during the 2004 election cycle, the state of Nebraska voted down a series of initiatives that would have allowed casinos, directly affecting the Winnebago Nation's plans to bid to run an urban casino.[21]

Thus, while it makes sense for elected officials to pay attention to Native issues, the general public is also weighing in on indigenous-run casinos. Until indigenous peoples reframe political issues on their own terms and manage the politics of perception effectively, the potential for backlash is always near the surface.

With an increased involvement in state and local elections, at what point do indigenous peoples get co-opted into a pluralist, interest group mentality? Is this a new form of diplomatic engagement with state governments through lobbying and endorsement of political candidates for office? Going back to the quote from Leroy Little Bear, it really gets down to the motivations of those participating in U.S. elections: "You should ask what your motive is for voting. If

you're working for rights, go vote. If you're working towards sovereignty, don't vote."[22] If indigenous peoples have increasingly become
more politically active in state and federal elections since 1988, what
is it that they are working toward? One has to consider the long-term
costs to indigenous nationhood as well as the immediate gratification
of an electoral triumph. The following chapter takes a closer look at
the indigenous-state compacting process and how it poses something
of a dilemma for indigenous nationhood: at one level, state compacts
confer a recognition on indigenous nations as governments and
major political actors, but these compacting agreements also impose
limits on the forms of self-determination that they can exercise.

CHAPTER FIVE

Negotiating Compacts between Indigenous Nations and States

We've evaluated all the risks. It's time for us to put our treaties in the courts. It's for the economic future of our nation.

Arthur Montour, Seneca Tribal Council leader, 2003

The previous chapter discussed the increased rates of participation of indigenous nations in the U.S. election processes in response to changing indigenous-state relationships. Since 1988 most indigenous-state intergovernmental relations have been through the negotiation of compacts covering issues such as gaming, motor fuels taxation, tobacco taxation, cross-deputization agreements, Temporary Assistance to Needy Families (TANF), motor vehicle licenses, and so on. This chapter will develop our understanding of the reasons behind indigenous nation involvement in state governmental politics through compacting. Indigenous nations are responding to strong incentives at the state and federal levels of government that are prompting their increased activity in the U.S. political process. Efforts by indigenous nations to expand their influence in the compacting process are key to understanding political participation in the forced federalism era. By expanding their influence in the compacting process, indigenous nations claim to be securing economic and political benefits that uphold indigenous self-determination. However, signing compacts with states has important long-term political implications for indigenous jurisdictional claims, as Oren Lyons, faithkeeper of the Onondaga Nation, points out: "Yes, in the 'compacts,' as they

107

are called. You see, Indians have a funny way of thinking. They think any kind of agreement they sign is a treaty. Really, it is a business agreement, and you give up what they say they want in the process. You give up jurisdiction. . . . And their rationale is, 'Well, we will make enough money to secure our future . . .' But money is not your future. Look what is happening now: land and jurisdiction on the land, that's your future."[1]

As we see from the discussion of voting in chapter 3, there are several political strategies relating to nationhood and measured separatism that caution against extensive indigenous involvement in the U.S. political system. Whether one votes in U.S. elections and engages in state compact negotiations depends on the motivations: securing state-granted rights that are renegotiable every election cycle or seeking out other diplomatic strategies that will enhance indigenous self-determination. Do indigenous-state compacts secure a self-determining future for indigenous nations, or do they create additional bureaucratic oversights that hinder relationships to community and homelands? A dilemma arises over the negotiation of indigenous-state compacts: state compacts confer a recognition on indigenous nations as governmental entities and major political and economic actors, but these compacting agreements also impose limits on the forms of self-determination that indigenous peoples can exercise on their homelands. The negotiation of indigenous-state compacts ultimately cedes regulatory oversights to state governors and legislatures to further challenge the governing authorities of extra-constitutional indigenous nations. State policymakers are increasingly invoking rich Indian images to erode indigenous self-determining authority even further.

This chapter begins with a comparison of treaties and gaming compacts to accentuate and differentiate the powers of treaty rights versus those of compacts. The next section examines the incentives for indigenous nations and states to participate (or not participate) in the compacting process. The third section suggests that subsequent compacts and intergovernmental agreements may consequently be influenced by indigenous political participation. Finally, the chapter concludes with additional evidence to further illustrate the ways in which indigenous nations are active in the political process through mobilizing voters and supporting candidates for office.

TREATIES VERSUS INDIGENOUS-STATE COMPACTS

Treaties are international, legally binding agreements between two or more sovereign entities.[2] There are over 379 ratified treaties between indigenous nations and the U.S. government still in force. Appendix C lists one example of a treaty negotiated between the Cherokee Nation and the U.S. government in the 1785 Treaty of Hopewell. As one can see from the treaty provisions, this is an agreement between sovereign powers. Article 5, for example, states that any person who encroaches on Tsalagi hunting grounds will "forfeit the protection of the United States, and the Indians may punish him or not as they please." Article 12 is interesting in that it allows Tsalagis to "send a deputy of their choice, whenever they think fit, to Congress." By codifying the ability to send Tsalagi delegations to Congress the treaty acknowledges the diplomatically recognized government-to-government relations between the Cherokee Nation and the United States.[3]

While the 1785 treaty and 378 other ratified treaties between the United States and indigenous nations are still in force, they are often denied their true international standing as agreements between sovereigns. For example, the United Nations' *Study on Treaties, Agreements, and Other Constructive Arrangements between States and Indigenous Populations* found that "the dominant viewpoint . . . asserts that treaties involving indigenous peoples are basically a domestic issue, to be construed, eventually implemented and adjudicated via existing internal mechanisms, such as the courts and federal (and even local) authorities."[4]

This process of "domesticating" indigenous treaties started early in the United States, with Chief Justice John Marshall's creative legal fiction in *Cherokee Nation v. Georgia*—"domestic dependent nations." Despite its legal veneer, the domestication of indigenous treaties is fundamentally challenged by Native peoples around the world as they promote the political and cultural standing of existing treaties and agreements in venues such as the United Nations Intercessional Working Group on the Draft Declaration on the Rights of Indigenous Peoples, the Inter-American Court of Human Rights, and the International Labor Organization. Nor is this a problem unique to indigenous peoples in the United States. In Canada, the ongoing British Columbia Treaty Process has been structured to promote federal and provincial supremacy regarding indigenous issues and requires that indigenous peoples "surrender their Aboriginal title to the Crown, whereupon it becomes vested in the province."[5]

The Nisga'a final agreement, which was voted on by only 61 percent of Nisga'a's eligible voters, went into effect on May 11, 2000, effectively extinguished the Nisga'a original title to their homelands. Additionally, the final agreement made no mention of the word "treaty" anywhere in the text of the document.[6] The government of Canada and negotiators in British Columbia have hailed the Nisga'a final agreement as a model for other indigenous nations to emulate because it subordinates Nisga'a political status to that of Canada, which is a clear example of domestication. As James Tully points out, "As far as I am aware, this is the first time in the history of Great Turtle Island that an indigenous people, or at least 61 percent of its eligible voters, has voluntarily surrendered their rights as indigenous peoples, not to mention surrendering over 90 percent of their territory, and accepted their status as a distinctive minority with group rights within Canada. This appears to be the first success of strategies of extinguishment (release) and incorporation by agreement."[7]

A similar process of domestication of indigenous issues is taking place in the United States with the institutionalization of the indigenous-state compacting process. The indigenous-state compacting process technically began in 1978 with passage of the Indian Child Welfare Act, but the passage of the Indian Gaming Regulatory Act (IGRA) in 1988 has become the driving force behind most indigenous-state compacts today. IGRA is also the impetus for most of the ongoing indigenous-state jurisdictional conflicts, as evidenced by ongoing indigenous-state conflicts in California, Arizona, and New York. By 2004, 255 gaming compacts had been negotiated between indigenous nations and states. Yet 26 of these compacts have been superseded or declared void, a clear indicator of jurisdictional conflict. Ironically, the indigenous-state compact procedure under IGRA, which was originally developed to avoid litigation, has resulted in more litigation than any other provision of IGRA.[8]

As a binding agreement between two parties, the indigenous-state compact was originally designed to enable states and indigenous governments to draw up and ratify agreements that "provide for the application of civil, criminal, and regulatory laws of either entity over Indians and non-Indians as the parties may see fit to agree."[9] For the purpose of this research, a compact is a "negotiated agreement between two political entities that resolves questions of overlapping jurisdictional responsibility."[10] Compacts may include agreements over policy relating to gaming, taxation, environmental, social service, and other matters.

Occasionally referred to as the "new treaties," indigenous-state compacts do not hold the same legal status as treaties, as they can be superseded by federal law and do not involve transfers of federal trust land.[11] As Oren Lyons points out, compacts are business agreements, first and foremost. In addition, unlike treaties, compacts are regarded as domestic agreements that yield forms of indigenous jurisdiction to states and have no standing under international law. This reflects the ongoing U.S. domestication of indigenous issues. While indigenous treaties have been repeatedly broken by the U.S. government, indigenous nations continue to abide by the terms of some 379 ratified treaties as valid claims to self-determination and, more recently, to circumvent state jurisdictional claims. Special rapporteur Alfonso Martinez draws a similar conclusion in his United Nations treaty study: "In the case of Indigenous peoples who concluded treaties or other legal instruments with the European settlers and/or their continuators in the colonization process, the Special Rapporteur has not found any sound legal argument to sustain the argument that they have lost their international juridical status as nations/peoples."[12]

One final factor that differentiates treaties from compacts is their relative durability. While treaty-based law is held in perpetuity according to the principle of *pacta sunt servanda* ("the treaty must be upheld"), indigenous-state compacts are often short-term resolutions that must be renegotiated every ten to fifteen years.[13] The indigenous-state compacting process generally adheres to a philosophy of *rebus sic stantibus* ("by way of changing conditions"), exhibited by the unilateral invalidation of over twenty-six compacts by governors in Arizona, California, and New Mexico since 1993. For all these reasons, indigenous-state compacts are not "new treaties" but tenuous business agreements that undermine the once exclusive federal-indigenous trust relationship.

THE COMPACTING PROCESS

Indigenous-state compacts address disputes in two main areas: environmental and property concerns and indigenous government and finance.[14] This two-fold categorization allows for a convenient placement of fish and game management, zoning agreements, water rights, and protection of oil, gas, and timber into an environmental and property category. Indigenous government and finance focuses on intergovernmental relations, which includes taxation; law enforcement; social services, including health, education, and welfare programs; and gaming agreements. The identification of gaming as a separate category signals the central role that it plays in the indigenous-state compacting process and thus the genesis of the forced federalism era.

In the years since its passage, IGRA has taken on considerable importance in regulating the role of federal and state government relationships with indigenous nations. Much like the language from the 1787 Northwest Ordinance, the federal government mandates that states negotiate "in good faith" with indigenous nations. There is little recourse for indigenous nations, however, should states fail to meet this directive. The secretary of the interior approves all negotiated compacts between indigenous nations and states before they go into effect.[15] In the 2000 gaming compact between the Sisseton-Wahpeton Sioux Tribe and the state of South Dakota, for example (see appendix B), indigenous nations are forced to negotiate provisions that entitle state officials to inspect casinos, that require background investigations of indigenous casino developers and the licensing of casino employees, and that stipulate that indigenous nations pay a portion of the state's expenses for establishing and maintaining regulatory agencies.[16]

For both indigenous nations and states, compacting represents one alternative to litigation, which is a costly option.[17] However, the indigenous-state compact procedure under IGRA has resulted in more litigation than any other provision of IGRA.[18] Given the state assertions of jurisdiction over indigenous issues, under the regulatory policies of IGRA, both parties enter into the compacting process with vastly different incentives guiding their negotiation strategies. Taking the example of gaming, indigenous nations cede some of their jurisdictional powers in exchange for the promise of economic benefits that might allow indigenous peoples to reduce the level of poverty and unemployment in their communities. For states, gaming raises moral, regulatory, infrastructure, and law enforcement concerns that are offset by potential and economic benefits for surrounding communities and a negotiated percentage of gaming revenues (as with the NGA regulatory oversight of gaming). According to some policymakers, compacting represents an opportunity for indigenous nations and states to work in a government-to-government relationship to solve a pressing policy issue. However, states have historically been the deadliest enemies to indigenous nations. Indigenous peoples have long memories of historic state encroachment onto their homelands and jurisdictions and should only cautiously enter into indigenous-state agreements during an era of forced federalism.

For indigenous nations, the intent of IGRA is clear: it offers states jurisdictional oversight of indigenous economic self-determination. However, the economic development achieved through gaming is premised on enhancing an indigenous nation's self-sufficiency and reducing unemployment. Funds from gaming may also be used to expand health care facilities, build houses, develop infrastructure, increase educational funding for Native schools, provide education funding, and so on. However, are these economic opportunities worth the jurisdictional compromises that go along with problems of sudden wealth? Some 224 indigenous nations have negotiated gaming compacts with their respective state governments, but questions of long-term ramifications linger.

Often viewing indigenous nations as competitors when it comes to economic development, state governments have been reluctant to negotiate gaming compacts in light of the economic potential for indigenous gaming and its potential competition with state-run gaming establishments. Gaming establishments on indigenous lands are perceived by policymakers as diverting income away from state budgets. With seven states receiving over $100 million each in tax revenue from state-run casinos in 1995, a loss of these tax dollars would be problematic for their budgets. As a result, indigenous casinos have been viewed as a threat to state budgets if they are not taxed and regulated in the same way as non-indigenous casinos.

Since IGRA, states can negotiate agreements with indigenous nations for the amount of remuneration for the services provided by a state. Funding for services is not equal to the revenues generated by non-indigenous casinos. Thus, states have limited economic incentives to negotiate gaming compacts. However, governors and other state officials can gain tremendous political capital by appearing to confront or stand up to perceived emerging contenders who benefit from state services, for example, California governor Arnold Schwarzenegger, who focused much of his 2004 campaign asserting that "Indians must give their fair share."

For indigenous nations, gaming can be a threat to cultural values—the type of economic development pursued must be appropriate to the cultural and economic needs of the community and its citizens. Indigenous values and cultural integrity are potentially undermined by casino gaming.[19] According to IGRA policy, gaming proceeds are to be diverted to one of five areas: to fund tribal government operations or programs, to provide for the general welfare of the Indian tribe and its members, to promote tribal economic development, to donate to charitable organizations, or to help fund operations of local government agencies. Given these IGRA specifications, a number of indigenous nations contend that gaming is a way to preserve culture through increased language programs and cultural centers and to reacquire indigenous homelands.

However, the revitalization of culture and community through gaming is not so clear cut. The experiences of the Oneida Nation in Wisconsin illustrate how the trade-offs of engaging in the indigenous-state compact system can affect indigenous communities. The Oneida story is similar to the experiences of the other 223 indigenous nations signing gaming compacts with state governments. Since the Oneida Nation entered into their first gaming compact with the state of Wisconsin in 1991, there have been strong state regulatory effects on their nationhood and jurisdiction. Oneida historian Loretta Metoxen discusses some positive and negative sides to gaming since that time: "We have done great things with our gaming profits. We've purchased a lot of land, and land is the basis of an Indian nation. We've provided great scholarship resources for post-secondary students, which is a great opportunity for those students." According to Metoxen, Oneidas have also used gaming revenues to purchase property and homes for Oneida citizens. Social services are also provided through gaming revenues.[20]

"On the other side, most of the gaming dollars are spent in Green Bay and Appleton," Metoxen said. "Most all of the 3,000 people who work here spend all their money in the local towns, including buying houses, paying rent, buying food, cars and other consumer products. They don't buy on the reservation, so that multiplier affect is not on the reservation."[21] Metoxen also acknowledges another downside to gaming: gambling addiction. Most important, as Ron Hill, Oneida cultural wellness facilitator, states: "It [gaming] has led to a loss of our sovereignty."[22]

By running a successful casino, the Oneida Nation often receives comments about how they are "wealthy." Yet there are no millionaires—the Oneida wealth is tied to jobs and further economic development.[23] However, the lingering image of the Oneidas and other indigenous nations operating casinos as rich Indians remains embedded in the minds of the general public and policymakers. It is also clear that the future of the Oneida casino is now inextricably linked to the future of the Oneida Nation. When asked what an end to gaming would entail for the Oneida Nation, Metoxen replied, "[It] would cause great chaos in our community. If people were cut off from their bread and butter we would have no way of taking care of all our folks. That is a threat and we have to remain ever vigilant."[24] Metoxen illustrates the strong gravitational pull that gaming and other forms of economic development have in slowly redirecting indigenous priorities away from community, homelands, and culture and toward protection and maintenance of the economic engine and the political clout that goes with it.

Similarly, states are faced with competing ideological and political views on negotiating gaming compacts. State citizens often claim that gaming violates their moral views and also tend to voice concerns over organized and other gambling related crimes within state boundaries. These public views become especially pronounced when indigenous nations put a casino ballot initiative up for a popular vote. IGRA attempts to address these issues by suggesting that a state cannot refuse to negotiate with indigenous nations if it does not prohibit similar types of gaming. Yet states have often acted to limit the amount and types of games that indigenous nations can offer.

A final disincentive for indigenous nations is that compacting with state governments means they are forced to cede some of their jurisdictional powers. This has put pressure on indigenous leaders to consider how the loss of jurisdictional powers will affect the community when considering whether to enter into compact negotiations. Based on current trends, economic opportunity appears to trump concerns over loss of jurisdiction for some impoverished Native communities. Several indigenous nations have decided that the sacrifice of jurisdictional powers is not an acceptable trade-off; 60 percent of all federally recognized indigenous nations do not operate casinos.

Clearly IGRA and compacting is a compromise solution to a complex problem facing indigenous nations, states, and the federal government. As a result, both indigenous nations and states pressure each other to negotiate optimal compacts. This includes a significant effort on the part of indigenous nations to become politically active by supporting candidates for office and mobilizing indigenous voters.

INDIGENOUS-STATE GAMING COMPACTS

Since 1988 and the passage of IGRA, indigenous nations have negotiated over 255 compacts with states over the establishment of class III gaming. In addition, a number of states have become active in seeking cooperative agreements with indigenous nations in areas beyond gaming. This section examines two aspects of the forced federalism era. First, it provides an overview of the states that have negotiated gaming compacts, the ratification date of these compacts, and the limitations that are contained within them. Second, it examines other types of compacting that are taking place in the forced federalism era.

Table 5.1 provides an overview of the indigenous nations and states that have entered into gaming compacts. After the passage of IGRA in 1988, 224 indigenous nations in twenty-eight states entered into gaming compacts. The first indigenous nation to sign a gaming compact, the Cabazon Band of Cahuilla Mission Indians, negotiated it with the state of California in March 1990. That the Cabazon Nation was the first to sign a compact is not surprising, as IGRA was a direct response to the Supreme Court's ruling that the state of California had no authority to regulate indigenous gaming within the Cabazon Nation.[25] Despite the large number of compacts negotiated in California, Arizona, New Mexico, Minnesota, and Washington, the institutionalization of an indigenous-state compacting system has not prevented a number of high profile indigenous-state conflicts from occurring over the scope and scale of gaming in each state.

More important for our research is the overwhelming evidence that a large percentage of indigenous nations have entered the forced federalism era by negotiating a compact that covers some form of issue impacting indigenous homelands, whether over hunting and fishing, cross-deputization, gaming, or other policy areas. In fact, of

TABLE 5.1

Indigenous-State Gaming Compacts by State, 1988–2000

State	Number of compacting nations	Date of approval of initial compact
Arizona	17	July 15, 1992
California	60	March 27, 1990
Colorado	2	July 6, 1992
Connecticut	2	April 10, 1991
Idaho	3	February 5, 1993
Iowa	3	February 24, 1992
Kansas	4	June 23, 1993
Louisiana	3	October 29, 1992
Michigan	11	November 19, 1993
Minnesota	11	March 27, 1990
Mississippi	1	January 15, 1993
Montana	6	June 24, 1992
Nebraska	1	December 31, 1990
Nevada	6	March 27, 1990
New Mexico	16	March 15, 1995
New York	2	June 4, 1993
North Carolina	1	September 22, 1994
North Dakota	5	December 3, 1992
Oklahoma	8	April 7, 1995
Oregon	9	November 20, 1992
Rhode Island	1	December 5, 1994
South Dakota	9	July 30, 1990
Washington	20	September 25, 1991
Wisconsin	11	January 24, 1992

SOURCE: Bureau of Indian Affairs Tribal-State Compact List (as of July 6, 2000), http://www.doi.gov/bia/gaming/gamcmpt.pdf (accessed January 12, 2001).

the 336 federally recognized indigenous nations in the continental United States, 212, or 63 percent, have entered into some form of a compact, whether gaming or otherwise, with a state. That nearly two-thirds of all indigenous nations have negotiated compacts with state governors serves to recognize their decision making authority while also limiting indigenous self-determination powers.

OTHER INDIGENOUS-STATE COMPACTS

Forced federalism is not restricted to gaming compacts. Compacts are likely to appear in other areas where indigenous nations and states have mutual interests, such as natural resource protection. This section takes a look at Arizona and Oklahoma to provide additional details of state challenges to indigenous self-determination. Given the large indigenous population in Oklahoma (273,230) and Arizona (255,879), these are especially appropriate states to examine, as a sizeable Native population provides many opportunities for indigenous governments to influence state policymaking.

There are twenty-one federally recognized indigenous nations within the state of Arizona. These twenty-one indigenous governments, as self-determining nations, are charged with providing a wide range of social services to citizens residing on the reservation. These services include family support, childcare, job training, food and nutrition programs, transportation, assistance for needy families, and game and wildlife protection. Indigenous nations are increasingly required to enter into agreements with the state of Arizona in an effort to facilitate the provision of these services.

According to the data in table 5.2, during the year 2000, indigenous nations in Arizona were involved with ninety agreements with the Arizona Department of Economic Security, Department of Fish and Game and Department of Transportation to facilitate service provision on the reservation. Among the agreements reached between the indigenous nations and state are nine registration agreements that facilitate more effective childcare on five reservations. Also, thirteen indigenous nations signed agreements that facilitated job training and placement under the job training and partnership act. Similarly, fifteen indigenous governments had agreements with the state for services to the elderly, including meal provision, transportation, counseling, and housekeeping. Indigenous-state agreements have also been signed in the area of food distribution or food stamp programs and TANF. Clearly, the indigenous nations and the state of Arizona have actively pursued mutual agreements in social services. But are these nation-building activities? Such a bureaucratized relationship tends to treat indigenous nations as an interest group or domestic dependent nation.

TABLE 5.2
Indigenous-State Agreements in Arizona, 2000

Indigenous nation	Number of agreements	Department making agreement
Ak-Chin	2	Economic Security
Cocopah	4	Economic Security
Colorado River	4	Economic Security
Fort McDowell Yavapai	2	Economic Security, Game and Fish
Fort Mojave	4	Economic Security, Game and Fish
Fort Yuma	3	Economic Security
Gila River	4	Economic Security
Havasupai	2	Economic Security
Hopi	4	Economic Security
Hualapai	5[a]	Economic Security, Game and Fish
Kaibab-Paiute	2	Economic Security, Game and Fish
Navajo	14	Economic Security, Game and Fish, Transportation
Pascua Yaqui	6	Economic Security
Salt-River Pima-Maricopa	7	Economic Security
San Carlos Apache	7[b]	Economic Security, Game and Fish
San Juan Paiute	2	Economic Security
Tohono O'Odham	6	Economic Security
Tonto Apache	1	Economic Security
White Mountain Apache	9	Economic Security, Game and Fish, Transportation
Yavapi-Apache	1	Economic Security
Yavapai-Prescott	1	Economic Security
Total	90	

NOTE: Agreements include intergovernmental agreements, memorandum of understanding, and registration agreements for child care centers. Departments examined include Economic Security, Game and Fish, and Transportation (motor fuels).
[a]An earlier fish and game agreement expired in 1975.
[b]Two earlier fish and game agreements expired, one in 1975 and another in 1998.

TABLE 5.3

Indigenous-State Tobacco Agreements in Oklahoma, 1992–2004

	Number of agreements signed
1992	5
1993	7
1994	2
1995	1
1996	3
1997	2
1998	8
1999	3
2000	0
2001	1
2002	0
2003	39
2004	7
Total	78

SOURCE: Oklahoma Indian Affairs Commission, http://www.state.ok.us/~oiac/tobacco.htm.
NOTE: Tobacco agreements were necessitated by the Supreme Court ruling in *Oklahoma Tax Commission v. Citizen Band of Potawatomi,* 489 U.S. 505 (1991).

Beyond social services, indigenous nations and the state of Arizona have forged agreements in the area of wildlife and environmental protection and fuel taxes. Consistent with forced federalism, twelve of sixteen wildlife agreements between nine indigenous governments and the state have been implemented after 1988. This is consistent with earlier findings (see table 2.1). Of the twelve cooperative agreements with the Department of Fish and Game, the subject of these agreements cover a host of projects including wildlife law enforcement, habitat management, and species-specific tracking programs.

The thirty-seven federally recognized indigenous nations in Oklahoma have also been active in forging agreements with the state. Given the large population of Native peoples in Oklahoma, nearly 8 percent of the population, numerous cooperative agreements have been worked out. Besides IGRA, two important Supreme Court rulings set the stage for cooperative agreements in Oklahoma. The first, in 1991, affirmed Native sovereign immunity and allowed indigenous nations to sell goods to members free from state taxation.[26] However, the ruling did allow for the collection of taxes on goods sold to

TABLE 5.4
Indigenous-State Motor Fuel Agreements in Oklahoma, 1996–2004

	Number of agreements signed
1996	3
1997	6
1998	8
1999	3
2000	7
2001	4
2002	1
2003	1
2004	1
Total	34

SOURCE: Oklahoma Indian Affairs Commission, http://www.state.ok.us/~oiac/motorfuels.htm.
NOTE: Motor fuel agreements were necessitated by the Supreme Court ruling in *Oklahoma Tax Commission v. Chickasaw Nation*, 115 S.Ct. 2214 (1995).

nonmembers. In response, indigenous nations and the state have entered into cooperative agreements to collect revenue on highly lucrative tobacco sales on reservation land. These agreements provide much needed revenue for indigenous nations through a negotiation process with Oklahoma. The figures in table 5.3 provide an overview of tobacco agreements in Oklahoma through 2004.

A second Supreme Court ruling favoring Oklahoma indigenous nations in 1995 set the stage for additional negotiations with the state of Oklahoma. In the 1995 ruling, Oklahoma's motor fuel laws were found to be invalid on Native lands and could not be applied to sales of motor fuel by indigenous nations.[27] Following the ruling, indigenous nations and the state worked together to forge a compromise that would allow motor fuel tax revenue to be collected by the state and returned to indigenous nations for use by their governments (see table 5.4). That thirty-three indigenous nations have signed cooperative agreements since 1995 is additional evidence of a shift to indigenous government–to–state government relations.

While the evidence presented regarding indigenous-state compacts has been drawn from the states of Arizona and Oklahoma, it nonetheless reflects intergovernmental cooperation in areas such as policing and resource management and conflictual relations in areas relating to economic development, such as gaming and motor fuels compacts. Namely, since the passage of IGRA, indigenous governments and state governments have entered a new, turbulent phase of government-to-government relations. Depending on the issue being negotiated, there may be a greater state tendency toward conflict (usually economic development issues) or cooperation (natural resources, law enforcement, etc). The example of indigenous-state compact negotiations in California illustrates the contentious and politicized relations that may develop between state governors and indigenous nations, especially when the governor draws on images of rich Indians in setting policy.

PLAYING THE POLICY LOTTO IN CALIFORNIA

Indigenous efforts to influence the compacting process are not limited to supporting candidates or providing campaign funds for friendly office seekers. In a number of states, notably Arizona and California, indigenous nations have become active in the initiative process in an effort to shape the policy environment and terms of gaming compacts. In Arizona in 1996 and California in 1998 and 2000, indigenous groups placed citizen initiatives on the ballot in an effort to secure the rights of indigenous governments to use gaming for economic development on reservation land.[28] In each case indigenous nations accused the current governor of refusing to negotiate gaming compacts in "good faith." In each state the governor had previously agreed to and signed gaming compacts, but was reluctant to enter in to further negotiations. We now look to indigenous mobilization in California to see how indigenous peoples have played the policy lotto by subjecting their jurisdictional powers to a popular vote.

The history of efforts of indigenous nations in California to engage in gaming as a means of economic development predates IGRA. In fact, IGRA is a direct result of the *California v. Cabazon* (1987) decision that placed regulation of indigenous gaming solely in the hands of the federal government. In response to the Cabazon decision, Congress passed IGRA and compelled the state of California and the Cabazon Nation to agree on a compact for class III gaming on reservation land. Initially, the compacts agreed to by indigenous nations and the state limited class III gaming to pari-mutuel wagering on horse races.[29] Additional efforts by indigenous nations to negotiate for gaming on Native reservations was met with stiff resistance by Governor Pete Wilson and Attorney General Dan Lungren. In response, a number of indigenous nations in California expanded their casinos to include games that the governor was unwilling to approve. At the same time, indigenous nations sought negotiations and undertook legal challenges to secure the right to expanded gaming.

By 1998, with their legal avenues exhausted and threats of closure of their casinos, indigenous nations began searching for a resolution to the impasse over indigenous gaming. One answer came in the form of a negotiated compact between the Pala Band of Mission Indians, a nongaming nation, and Governor Wilson. The Pala Compact, as it became known, was opposed by most of California's indigenous nations because it provided many restrictions on the type of games allowed and relied on video lottery terminals instead of the more lucrative video slot and poker machines. For nations that had the banned machines in their casinos, the solution would seem to lie elsewhere.

A second response to the impasse was an initiative for a statute change placed on the general election ballot in November of 1998, which would permit casino-style gaming on indigenous territories. This would allow indigenous nations that currently operated casinos to continue their operation in terms decided by California voters. The initiative strategy was risky in that it put the gaming issue and aspects of Native self-determination before voters who would be subject to a political campaign. Yet the initiative strategy was deemed a necessary reaction to elected officials who had opposed indigenous gaming and only reluctantly agreed to a more restrictive form.

The campaign for Proposition 5, the Tribal Government Gaming and Economic Self-Sufficiency Act of 1998, pitted all but 5 of California's 107 indigenous nations against Nevada casinos, California card rooms, and other anti-indigenous gaming interests.[30] The efforts of indigenous nations paid off on November 3, as Proposition 5 passed with 63 percent of the vote. California voters overwhelmingly agreed with the indigenous supporters of the gaming initiative, and it appeared that the indigenous gaming issue had been definitively resolved.

Within days, lawsuits challenging the constitutionality of the proposition were filed in the state capital in hope of blocking the implementation of Proposition 5. In August 1999 the California Supreme Court threw out Proposition 5 on the grounds that indigenous casinos, with slot machines and house-banked card games, were regarded as

similar to those in Nevada and New Jersey, and the California constitution specifically prohibited similar casinos.

Indigenous nations were again left with the option of negotiating
compacts with the governor or placing Proposition 5 on the ballot as
a constitutional initiative. By this time the political landscape had
changed—Grey Davis replaced Pete Wilson as governor in 1998, and
the passage of Proposition 5 provided strong evidence that voters
would support indigenous gaming. In addition, indigenous nations
that had previously opposed Proposition 5 were now supporting it.
In this environment, negotiators from the indigenous nations and
Governor Davis's office hammered out an agreement that would allow
slot machines and house banked card games. The compacts would
also limit the number of indigenous casinos and types of games permitted but would create a revenue sharing plan where gaming revenue
would be distributed to the nongaming nations in California.

The electoral process was to remain the final hurdle in securing
indigenous gaming in California, since the agreement was to be placed
on the ballot as Proposition 1A, a change to the state constitution to
allow gambling on Native lands. In April 2000, facing little of the
organized opposition that its predecessor had, Proposition 1A was
passed with nearly 65 percent of the vote.[31] By 2000 sixty indigenous
nations had signed compacts with the state of California for gaming
on reservation land.[32]

The story of indigenous nations in California finally securing the
right to engage in gaming on indigenous reservations is important
for showing how indigenous political mobilization has largely been a
reaction to imposed regulations by state governors. The 1987 Cabazon
decision forced Congress to come up with a means for indigenous
nations and states to reach agreements on gaming issues. Initially,
indigenous nations and California's governor signed compacts allowing
a pari-mutuel wagering but nothing else. As indigenous governments
sought the right to expand their gaming operations, the governor's
reluctance to negotiate was met with the legal challenges allowed by
IGRA. Having little success in the courts, indigenous nations pursued
a political solution. By using the initiative process to change the laws
of the state to include provisions for indigenous gaming, indigenous
nations won a major political and economic victory with the passage
of Proposition 5 in 1998. While subsequent legal challenges to Proposition 5 overturned its passage, the support it had garnered with

the general public was evident when the next round of negotiations began. How could the governor oppose negotiations or oppose terms of a compact that were similar to one supported by over 60 percent of the population? This made Native efforts to secure gaming compacts that were favorable to them much easier. By 2000 the efforts of groups allied against indigenous gaming also disappeared in light of strong public support. Indigenous nations had become players in the electoral process and were willing to use elections to secure their interests despite the risks of putting their self-determining authority up for a popular vote.

However, the story of indigenous gaming in California took an even more unexpected turn. In 2001 Governor Grey Davis froze all ongoing negotiations with indigenous nations over gaming compacts, claiming that a pending lawsuit against the state's previous gaming compacts warranted stopping any future negotiations. When Governor Davis was recalled by California voters in 2003, the newly elected governor, Arnold Schwarzenegger, who had focused much of his campaign asserting that "Indians must give their fair share," renegotiated five indigenous nation–state compacts. These five indigenous nations now collectively contribute to an unprecedented $1 billion bond fund for the state and pay approximately $150 million a year in taxes to the state until the compacts expire in 2030. In addition, the state of California is allowed greater regulatory power in tort law, mitigation, the environment, and state inspection of machines.[33] While few examples are as extreme as the players in the policy lotto in California, this example emphasizes the risks involved when indigenous nations put their jurisdictional powers up for a popular vote.

FOLLOWING THE MONEY IN STATE POLITICS

Given the increasing interaction between indigenous nations and states, issues of concern to Native people reach the state policy agenda with much frequency. In this context, indigenous nations have accelerated efforts to seek influence in the U.S. political process through campaign contributions.

A 1999 report by the National Institute on Money in State Politics outlined the contributions of indigenous and non-indigenous gaming interests in state politics.[34] The findings of the report suggest that

TABLE 5.5

Indigenous Campaign Contributions in Six States, 1990–2000

	Number of gaming nations	Year of first compact	Dollars contributed					
			1990	1992	1994	1996	1998	2000
California	60	1990	0	0	1,137,968	893,364	5,712,822	2,035,104
Idaho	3	1993	1,600	0	72160	2,000	29,077	31,750
Nevada	6	1990	1,000	0	0	1,500	0	203,711
New Mexico	16	1995	0	79,500	23,300	122,163	136,000	121,025
Oregon	9	1992	500	0	5,000	2,450	68,995	84,690
Washington	20	1991	1,745	23,505	3,860	2,9547	81,040	45,891

SOURCE: Heather Cafferty, "Gambling across State Lines" report issued by the National Institute on Money in State Politics, http://www.followthemoney.org/issues/gamble.html for years 1990–98. Figures for 2000 from http://www.followthemoney.org state campaign finance database.

the 1990s saw considerable growth in the amount of money coming from indigenous and non-indigenous gaming organizations. While non-indigenous gaming dominated the contribution list, in a number of states with indigenous gaming indigenous nations became much more active in providing money in state elections as the decade progressed. While state-level campaign finance data is scarce for a number of states in the report, we see indigenous nations contributing to state campaigns where the information is available. In addition, the findings are more telling when the date of the initial compacts signed by indigenous nations and states are included (see table 5.5).[35]

The clear trend indicates that indigenous nations were providing money for campaigns by the year 2000. Moreover indigenous nations were unlikely to make major contributions to state elections before signing gaming compacts. Following the signing of a gaming compact, indigenous nations within these states significantly increased the amount of money they contributed to state candidates. These findings are not surprising given the financial limitations of indigenous nations before compacting and the contact with state officials required by the compacting process. From a financial perspective, the purpose of gaming compacts is to provide financial resources to indigenous nations that have few resources.

Thus, using scarce resources in a political campaign prior to compacting was unlikely since the money was just not available. Gaming

TABLE 5.6

Money Donated to U.S. Political Parties by Indigenous Nations
with Casinos versus Non-Indigenous Casinos, 1990–2006

	Compacts signed	Native gaming dollars	Non-Native gaming dollars	Native dollars as percentage of non-Native dollars
1990	15	1,750	462,549	.004
1992	49	144,721	1,409,998	11
1994	52	662,250	2,325,499	28
1996	39	2,003,049	5,068,408	40
1998	38	1,564,644	4,982,544	31
2000	71	4,378,217	8,081,850	54
2002	n/a	6,812,446	8,189,302	83
2004	n/a	7,470,889	3,764,947	198
2006	n/a	5,772,906	8,619,827	67

SOURCES: Indigenous-state compact information is published in the *Federal Register* by the Office of Indian Gaming Management, Bureau of Indian Affairs, Office of the Commissioner. Information about monetary contributions by indigenous nations was obtained from the Center for Responsive Politics, http://www.opensecrets.org (accessed February 1, 2006).

effectively changed political priorities of indigenous nations by channeling most of their energies into U.S. elections. In addition, as a reflection of this newfound political clout, indigenous interactions with members of the state executive and legislative branches have been fundamentally different during the forced federalism era than they had been previously.

Table 5.6 provides yet another perspective on how indigenous nations are using campaign donations to influence the compacting process. Based on the tremendous increases in party donations, indigenous nations are mobilizing with newfound monetary resources to meet the threats of forced federalism. To provide some perspective on relative contributions from various sectors of the gaming industry, indigenous gaming moneys are compared with total contributions from non-indigenous casinos and gaming facilities for each election cycle. Indigenous gaming contributions to U.S. political parties start at a miniscule amount (.004 percent) compared to other non-indigenous casino donations in 1990. However, by 2000 indigenous gaming contributions are 54 percent of the overall contributions to political parties by gaming interests. In 2004 indigenous gaming monetary donations to political parties actually far exceeded those given by non-indigenous casinos. While indigenous monetary influence is exaggerated by perceptions of rich, emerging contenders throughout the 1990s, the 2002 and 2004 election cycles demonstrate that indigenous gaming monetary donations rival those donations from other non-indigenous casinos.

This is the picture of indigenous nations running casinos that policymakers focus on the most: the rich Indian social construction. The expanding resource base of the top twenty gaming indigenous nations is really the force behind the largest donations (see table 5.6). The Mashantucket Pequots (Connecticut) donated the most in 2000, with $533,748.[36] While most of the Pequot donations went to the Democratic Party in 2000 (67 percent of all donations), this changed markedly in 2006, with 50 percent of the Pequot campaign contributions targeting the Republican Party. Other top contributors in 2000 came primarily from California, Minnesota, and Arizona. The donations to party candidates from the top twenty indigenous contributors almost doubled in 2004, going from $4.4 to $7.5 million. However, this figure went back down to $5,772,906 in 2006 , further illustrating that indigenous campaign contributions vary according to the issues at stake as well as whether the election cycle takes place during a presidential race.

In 2006 the Morongo Band of Mission Indians (California) was the top donating indigenous nation and provided $353,409 to both Democratic and Republican candidates. The level of indigenous involvement in 2006 continued to reflect the occurrence of conflicts with state governments—indigenous nations from California, Arizona, and Minnesota continue to be the highest monetary contributors. Given the indigenous-state conflicts that have been recurring for these nations, the campaign funding becomes an additional strategy to fund candidates and parties who are friendly to indigenous issues.

It is important to consider that each of these top twenty donating nations already have a high stake in the U.S. and state policy process and that they have continued to contribute to political parties as a form of insurance for their investments. Most indigenous nations who operate casinos are unable to make such large contributions

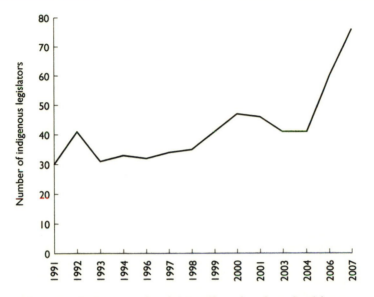

Figure 5.1. Indigenous Candidates Elected to State Legislatures,
1991–2001

and have sought other forms of political influence to achieve their
needs. In addition, with the exception of 2004, indigenous nation
campaign contributions from nations with casinos are usually far less
than the monetary donations from non-indigenous casino operators.

As a result of the compacting process, indigenous nations have
been seeking more direct ways to influence state governors and legislatures. Since 1988 Native interests have been more likely to be debated
in state legislatures and between governors and legislators.[37] With
financial resources available, indigenous nations have also looked
to state legislators for influence as other compacts and intergovernmental agreements were being negotiated.

Moreover, an increasing number of indigenous peoples have been
running for state legislative posts to directly influence policymaking.
As seen in figure 5.1, there has been a steady increase in the overall
number of indigenous peoples serving as state legislators across the
United States, going from thirty in 1991 to forty-six by 2001. This
figure went down slightly in 2004 to forty-one Native legislators but
increased dramatically to seventy-six Native legislators in 2007. Overall,
the marked increase in Native peoples elected to state legislatures
demonstrates a sustained trend over time of direct involvement in

the legislative process.[38] This trend will only continue to grow as indigenous organizations emerge to identify and support indigenous candidates for office. As mentioned in chapter 3, a national organization called the Indigenous Democratic Network List (INDN's List), has now been created to recruit and train indigenous candidates for local and state offices. Besides mobilizing on behalf of Democratic indigenous candidates running for state and local office across the United States, the organization also trains potential candidates to be stronger candidates and keep INDN's List members informed of political events and news headlines through newsletters, e-mail alerts, direct mail, and a website.[39] With a growing number of indigenous peoples elected to state legislatures, one might expect legislative policymaking outcomes to reflect these changing demographics. However, if indigenous peoples become so embedded in U.S. politics, might it compromise their claims at extraconstitutional and distinct self-determining nations?

As the above examples suggest, indigenous efforts to influence state elections have an effect beyond the initial gaming compact. In a number of states, compacts need to be updated regularly. This means that indigenous nations involved in the process are constantly gearing up for the next gubernatorial election or future state assembly elections. Once again we return to a dilemma in indigenous-state compacting: state compacts confer a recognition on indigenous nations as governmental entities and influence as major political and economic actors, but these compacting agreements impose limits on the forms of self-determination that indigenous peoples can exercise on their homelands. Having a voice in the policymaking process in the future comes at a great cost of ceding jurisdiction on indigenous homelands. In addition, the proliferation of nongaming compacts means that indigenous nations and states are interacting even more frequently regarding policy and how it relates to Native and non-Native interests. In this new political landscape, efforts to curry favor with elected officials friendly to indigenous issues should be balanced with efforts to seek out local, community-based solutions to the issues confronting indigenous nations.

The evolving government-to-government relationships between indigenous nations and states since 1988 have resulted in one key change in political behavior. Namely, indigenous nations have become more active in the political process in an effort to influence the outcome of state and federal elections. If states and indigenous nations are negotiating compacts on such a wide range of issues, having helped elect a governor, state senator or representative is a pragmatic decision for affecting future policymaking decisions. The importance of state governors in the compacting process makes them especially prominent figures in future compact negotiations and election campaigns. Over the past two decades, no single piece of legislation has been more important than IGRA, as it has become a source of significant economic growth for a large number of indigenous nations. At the same time, this economic growth and involvement in the U.S. electoral process comes at a great cost—in the words of Ron Hill, Oneida cultural wellness facilitator: "It [gaming] has led to a loss of our sovereignty."

A key factor in the overall increase of negotiated indigenous-state compacts is the availability and potential availability of monetary resources to use in the electoral process. In several cases, compacting has been overutilized, as indigenous nations have agreed to engage in state compacting procedures when treaty rights would suffice. However, before signing gaming compacts, few indigenous nations had the financial resources available to contribute to candidates for office (as exhibited by the relatively small $1,750 donation by indigenous nations in 1990). This meant that previous strategies for compact negotiation did not include significant contributions to candidates for office. Thus, after negotiating compacts, the financial resources became available and have been used to support Native-friendly candidates. However, as the donations to political parties have risen, to over $7 million in 2004, indigenous nations are increasingly subject to regulatory policies by state and local government and backlash from the general public when it comes to putting one's jurisdiction up for a popular vote. Managing the politics of perception has turned out to be much more costly than a $7 million donation—emulating the electoral politics of the U.S. system has not insulated indigenous nations from public backlash and regulatory policies that are fueled by rich Indian images. Rich Indian imagery, along with involvement in the compact system, has effectively limited the self-determining authority of indigenous nations while adding regulatory oversight from state actors, such as governors and state legislators. For these reasons, engaging in indigenous-state compacting in the areas of economic development (i.e., gaming, taxation, etc.) has not allowed indigenous nations to represent themselves on their own terms. When gaming and taxation are negotiated through compacts, state policymakers have been given the upper hand in managing the politics of perception.

Finally, while contact with state officials was not uncommon prior to IGRA, indigenous nations were not previously compelled to negotiate for jurisdictional powers with state officials. Once compacting became more frequent, indigenous nations had developed contacts with leading state officials and have identified candidates friendly to indigenous issues in the state house and governor's mansion. As a result, establishing and continuing relationships with members sympathetic to Native issues and helping get them elected has become part of a new indigenous political strategy in the forced federalism era. In addition, there has been a steady increase in the overall number of indigenous peoples serving as state legislators across the United States, going from thirty in 1991 to forty-six by 2001. With the creation of groups like INDN's List supporting the election of indigenous candidates for office, this trend will only continue in states with long histories of conflict over indigenous compacting, such as South Dakota, which had four indigenous state legislators in 2004, and New Mexico, which had five.

These ideas build on the survey findings reported in chapter 4, where gaming and self-determination issues were a primary concern to more indigenous nations than any other issue. Indigenous nation–state compacts have become the primary means to resolve intergovernmental jurisdictional questions but only in certain bureaucratic policy areas, such as cross-deputization agreements and wildlife management. As stated earlier, the indigenous-state compact procedure under IGRA has resulted in more litigation than any other provision of IGRA.[40] Conflicts over taxation run a close second to gaming, whether through direct intervention by the state, as in the previously discussed Narragansett example in Rhode Island (chapter 2), or through litigation, as evidenced by the court cases filed in Oklahoma over motor fuels tax compacts. Evidence of the rapid growth in indigenous-state agreements suggests that in some areas, including social services, game and wildlife management, and cross-deputization agreements, the compacting process has been less contentious. However, new compacts agreements come at a high price—they cede some indigenous jurisdiction and increase the involvement of state officials in decision making on Native homelands.

Indigenous-state negotiations are highly contested in areas of tobacco taxation, motor fuels taxation, and gaming. The question that remains is whether indigenous nations have become so entrenched in U.S. politics that they have jeopardized their status as distinct indigenous nations. Rich Indian racism continues to be propagated by state policymakers as they have benefited politically and economically from challenging the identities and self-determining authorities of indigenous nations.

CHAPTER SIX

Conclusions

Again, were we to inquire by what law or authority you set up a claim, I answer, none! Your laws extend not into our country, nor ever did. You talk of the law of nature and the law of nations, and they are both against you. . . . You say: Why do not the Indians till the ground and live as we do? May we not, with equal propriety, ask, why the white people do not hunt and live as we do?

Cherokee peace chief Kai-yah-teh-hee, or First-to-kill (aka Old Tassel), 1785 speech to the U.S. Congress

This book began by identifying a new era in indigenous policy: forced federalism (1988–present). The forced federalism era differs markedly from the previous self-determination era, which entailed providing indigenous nations with greater administrative control over the contracting of education, health care, and other services on their homelands. Since IGRA and the devolution of federal powers to state governments, indigenous nations have been forced into dangerous political and legal relationships through compacts with state governments that challenge their nationhood. This off-loading of federal powers to state governments undermines the once exclusive federal government–to–indigenous government relationship based on 379 prior treaties, direct consultation with Congress on indigenous affairs, federal statutory obligations, and court decisions.

Therefore, given the widespread devolution of federal powers to states, indigenous nations have become more vulnerable to the jurisdictional claims of local governing bodies, such as state and municipal policymakers. Invoking rich Indian images, these local governing agencies are more likely to exercise their newly created jurisdictional claims to implement regulatory policies targeting indigenous nations (i.e., taxation, gaming, etc.) in ways that benefit state policymakers economically and politically.

The forced federalism project is the only one of its kind to systematically examine the political, economic, and cultural implications of the contemporary era using case studies, interviews, survey results, opinion polls, and data from various organizations. The findings of this comprehensive study provide a clearer picture of indigenous lobbying, political mobilization strategies, and the increasing regulatory oversight of state actors (governors, legislatures) in indigenous policy during the 1990s and into the twenty-first century.

During the forced federalism era, state governors and policymakers have increasingly treated indigenous nations as wealthy interest groups. Consequently, new challenges to indigenous nations have arisen from prevalent and damaging stereotypes of Native peoples as rich Indians. As Wilma Mankiller argues, "Perception is as much of a threat as anti-sovereignty legislation. We have to regain control of our image."[1] This book has documented several of the strategies that indigenous nations have employed to regain control of their image.

The newly invented rich Indian image is grounded in prevalent public perceptions that indigenous peoples are all wealthy as a result of operating casinos, and this image has supplanted other historical stereotypes of indigenous peoples, such as the noble savage and childlike Indian. According to Katherine Spilde, contemporary rich Indian racism motivates policymakers to deny indigenous nationhood and self-determination in two ways: "by insisting tribes prove that they still need sovereign rights to be self-sufficient" and "by invoking the notion that gaming tribes are less 'authentically' Indian, diminishing their claims to political independence."[2]

As state governors and other policymakers tend to portray indigenous nations as moneyed casino cultures, their dominant strategy has been one of extensive regulation in an attempt to curtail perceived indigenous gaming wealth and political clout through the negotiation of indigenous-state compacts. For indigenous nations, managing the politics of perception entails finding new political mobilization strategies that will enhance indigenous self-determination and nationhood.

It is apparent from the findings in chapter 2 that the most effective approach to predicting state policymaking decisions in the forced
federalism era has been Anne Schneider and Helen Ingram's social
constructions model, which exposes existing power relations between
policymaking elites and indigenous communities. The prevalent social
constructions of indigenous peoples today are those of the rich Indian
and emerging contender in state and federal politics. Consequently,
the policy benefits offered to indigenous peoples as emerging contenders perceived as having "special rights" are predictably symbolic,
hollow, and deceptive, while governors and other state officials
emphasize the importance of regulating or restricting indigenous
political and economic behavior through indigenous-state gaming
compacts. Evidence from seven case studies in chapter 2 lends further
support for this finding. The analysis also demonstrates that the
emerging contender stereotype overlaps with other social constructions of indigenous peoples as dependents or militants, especially
when economic self-determination strategies by indigenous nations
are considered. However, the predominant image guiding policy
decisions since 1988 is that of the rich Indian.

Findings from chapter 2 also demonstrate that state policymakers
tend to deal with emerging contenders as economic competitors to
be extensively regulated and monitored, as exhibited by the several
National Governors' Association's policies enacted between 1993 and
2003. Finally, according to state legislative data examined between
1994 and 2003, prospects for indigenous-state cooperation are greater
in areas of environmental policy (i.e., wolf recovery, forest land
management, hunting and fishing rights, etc.) than with economic
development policies (i.e., gaming, motor fuel taxation, etc.). Overall,
gaming and related economic activities were often targeted with
regulatory state policies, while environmental issues were more
likely to result in the enactment of nation-building policies by the
state legislatures. It follows that rather than being viewed as a zero-
sum issue, environmental resources are more likely to be perceived
as shared and, therefore, are less contentious than Native economic
development initiatives. However, this may change in the future, as
water and other natural resources become scarcer.

After examining the ways in which indigenous-state intergovernmental relations have shifted with an emphasis on regulatory policies
and invocations of rich Indian images since 1988, we turned to the

question of how indigenous peoples have responded to this jurisdictional encroachment to frame the politics of perception on their own terms. In examining the existing gaps between theory and practice when it comes to understanding indigenous political behavior, chapter 3 took a historical survey of diplomatic strategies, such as treaty making and lobbying, that have been practiced by indigenous peoples long before first contact with colonial powers. It also examined the political and cultural implications for indigenous peoples voting in U.S. elections. While indigenous peoples often justify voting in U.S. elections given their potential as a swing vote in close elections and long-term influence on policymakers, the findings suggest that there is a fine line between such a measured separatism strategy and cooptation into the U.S. system. A critical distinction in this discussion is to understand the political aspirations of indigenous peoples as the best indicator of whether or not one should vote in U.S. elections.

In addition, when examining contemporary indigenous lobbying behavior, it was noted that although other countries and governmental entities throughout the world devote massive amounts of money to lobbying the U.S. government, comparable lobbying activity by indigenous nations is often met with suspicion and state regulatory oversight. If lobbying continues to be a cornerstone of indigenous diplomacy, it should not be contracted out to non-indigenous firms, as the Abramoff and Scanlon scandal has indicated (see chapter 1). Rather, it should be undertaken by indigenous peoples to frame policy issues on their own terms. Moreover, the vast amounts of money spent on lobbying should be balanced by other priorities of indigenous governance, such as language revitalization programs and other educational programs.

Finally, chapter 3 reviewed some promising theoretical models for examining indigenous political and economic mobilization, ranging from the Harvard Project on American Indian Economic Development's nation-building model to Sidney Tarrow's new social movements theory. All of them had significant shortcomings, and the social constructions model offered the most explanatory power for understanding how indigenous political mobilization have been framed in political and social contexts, such as U.S. elections and indigenous-state compact negotiations.

Chapter 4 presented findings from the forced federalism surveys of 168 indigenous nations during the 1994, 1996, 1998, and 2000 elections. It is clear from these results that indigenous people are mobilizing politically (i.e., getting out the vote, endorsing candidates for office, lobbying, etc.) with unprecedented numbers and resources to support elected officials and candidates that claim to be friendly to indigenous self-determination and gaming and economic development issues. Indigenous nations today act in a number of different ways to influence policy, going well beyond oversimplified notions that the only two available choices are litigation or cooperation.

Several key findings emerge from the survey results presented in chapter 4:

1. Candidates for U.S. elections were supported by indigenous nations based on their positions on issues (versus political party affiliation) important to indigenous people.

2. The most important issues for indigenous governments when dealing with state and local officials were gaming and self-determination.

3. The stronger the feeling that an indigenous nation could influence the outcome of the election, the more likely they were to support candidates for office, whether at the state or federal level.

4. The importance of state governor as a key political actor to indigenous nations has risen in prominence since 1994; governors were consistently ranked as the fourth most important elected official for indigenous peoples to work with— behind U.S. senators, presidents, and U.S. representatives.

5. There is a strong correlation between indigenous nations signing a gaming compact and then providing financial support to a U.S. candidate for political office; in the era of forced federalism, compacting is an accurate measure of whether indigenous nations have close contact with state governments.

6. Indigenous nations, such as those in California and Arizona, are increasingly bypassing state policymakers and putting their gaming rights up for a popular vote. So far this strategy has been successful; however, in Maine, a Native gaming ballot initiative failed in 2003 by a wide margin because of rich Indian racism. This strategy will become ever more risky, given increasing tendency for policymakers and the general public to

frame indigenous issues to fit their demands for the regulation of rich Indians.

7. In the future the outcome of close elections, as in the 1996 elections in Arizona and South Dakota, may continue to be decided by the indigenous swing vote in states where a high concentration of Native voters is present. For example, there are six states in which the indigenous population represents 5 percent or more of the total population (see appendix D).

After documenting the extensive indigenous involvement in the U.S. system, it appears that the extraconstitutional and self-determining status of indigenous nations is being challenged by state governments. While the donation of money to political party candidates and mobilization to get out the vote may lead elected officials to pay attention to Native issues in states with large numbers of Native peoples, the question of long-term effects arises: are political solutions being sought at the state and federal levels at the expense of local, community-based solutions?

Chapter 5 examines the implications the indigenous-state compact system for indigenous self-determination that lead to four possible conclusions. First, indigenous treaties and compacts are different in terms of their recognition of indigenous nationhood. Compacts are essentially business agreements that limit indigenous jurisdictions, while treaties are international, legally binding agreements between two or more sovereign entities.

Second, an examination of indigenous-state negotiated agreements and compacts in Arizona and Oklahoma found that there is some cooperation in largely bureaucratic domains, such as health contracting, cross-deputization, game and fish, and transportation. However, when negotiating more substantial economic issues, such as indigenous tobacco sales and motor fuel taxation in Oklahoma, it appears that litigation usually preceded an indigenous-state agreement. The negotiation of indigenous-state gaming compacts continues to be the most contentious—especially when framed by the rich Indian imagery promoted by policymakers to set further limits on indigenous jurisdiction. As stated earlier, the indigenous-state compact procedure under IGRA has resulted in more litigation than any other provision of IGRA.[3] Conflicts over taxation run a close second to gaming, whether through direct intervention by the state as in the controversy over the opening of the Narragansett tax-free smoke shop in Rhode Island (see chapter 2) or through litigation, as evidenced by the court cases filed in Oklahoma over motor fuels tax compacts.

The case study of California was most telling about the nature of these new conflicts. After several lawsuits and voter referendums taking place between 1998 and 2003, five indigenous nations renegotiated compacts with the governor to collectively contribute to an unprecedented $1 billion bond fund for the state and pay approximately $150 million a year in taxes to the state until the compacts expire in 2030. In addition, the state of California is allowed a greater control over the tribes in regulating tort law, the environment, inspection of machinery, and mitigation.

Third, before signing gaming compacts, few indigenous nations had the financial resources available to contribute to candidates for office. This meant that previous strategies for compact negotiation did not include significant contributions to candidates for office. Thus, after negotiating compacts, the financial resources became available and have been used to support Native-friendly candidates for state and federal office-holders. However, as the donations to political parties have increased indigenous nations are progressively more subject to regulatory policies by state and local government and backlash from the general public when it comes to putting one's jurisdiction up for a popular vote. For these reasons, a social constructions model continues to be the best way to predict future state and local regulatory policies targeting indigenous nations because of widespread perceptions of rich Indians.

Finally, while contact with state officials was not uncommon before the IGRA, indigenous nations were not previously compelled to negotiate for jurisdictional powers with state officials. However, establishing and continuing relationships with members sympathetic to Native issues and helping get them elected has become part of a new indigenous political strategy. There has also been a steady increase in the overall number of indigenous peoples serving as state legislators across the United States. With the creation of groups like INDN's List supporting the election of indigenous candidates for office, this trend will only continue in states with long histories of conflict over indigenous compacting.

Since the passage of IGRA, indigenous-state compacts have been touted as the primary means to resolve intergovernmental jurisdictional questions during the forced federalism era, but they are found to be highly problematic in terms of the limits placed on indigenous jurisdictions. Moreover, compacts negotiated over gaming or taxation have been notoriously contentious and costly.

During the forced federalism era, indigenous nations have been compelled to deal with states as equals, which undermines the exclusive and historic relationship with the federal government. While not all the changes resulting from the transfer of federal powers to states have resulted in conflict, the adjustment has been turbulent and has led to the invocation of rich Indian images by state policymakers that challenge the self-determining authority of indigenous nations. Ultimately, the long-term solutions to confronting rich Indian racism do not arise from emulating the lobbying and political behavior of other U.S. citizens; rather, the strength of indigenous nations comes from protecting indigenous homelands and regenerating cultural and political forms of governance. With these findings in mind, what are some plausible recommendations for indigenous nations regarding their interactions with state governments today?

SUGGESTED FUTURE STRATEGIES

Given the rich Indian messages being conveyed by contemporary state and federal policymakers, the need to reframe policy issues on our own terms while avoiding the pitfalls of ceding jurisdiction and control to state governments is critical to the future of indigenous nations. What is the future of indigenous-state relations and what are some of the issues that will come to the forefront for the next generation of indigenous leaders to confront? In my interviews with Chief Chad Smith and Brad Carson (see appendices E and F), Jeff Corntassel asked them both about the future of indigenous self-determination, and they each identified several areas that are likely to provoke indigenous-state conflicts over the next twenty years. For example, Chief Smith mentioned water rights as one of the biggest challenges of the future. He also mentioned the importance of revitalizing indigenous languages, education, leadership, and "overcoming entitlement mentalities."

Similarly, Brad Carson raised several questions that indigenous leaders will have to address soon:

Well, I think the conflicts are all going to spring from the very notion of sovereignty itself. For example, if the Cherokee Nation, or the Choctaws, or the Chickasaws, the Seminoles, any of the thirty-nine federally recognized tribes that make their home in Oklahoma, are they states within states, or are they have a slightly different status? And that plays out in everything from water rights to environmental rules; that is a growing dispute all across the country. Do tribes have the right to set their own water and air standards? Do tribes have the right to issue their own hunting licenses? Their own fishing licenses? Do they have the right to regulate oil and gas drilling, which is something that is an important part of the Oklahoma economy? In Oklahoma, because of the many tribal actors, it is in some ways a state that has within it thirty-nine kind of "duty free" zones, where generally applicable sales taxes are either less or not present at all. How does this affect the ability of the government to raise revenues to fund programs like public education or transportation?

Smith's and Carson's responses point to the need for new strategies to confront future challenges to indigenous nationhood, ranging from protecting water rights to the revitalization of indigenous languages. While each community will set their own strategies to enhance their self-determining authority, the following seven strategies are possible paths to overcoming some of the threats to indigenous nationhood that have arisen in the forced federalism era.

Implement self-determination accords: Frank Pommersheim points out the need for sovereignty accords, which are indigenous-state agreements or guides to serve as starting points toward resolving historical animosities often existing between indigenous nations and states. Similar accords have been successfully negotiated in Washington and South Dakota and apply a philosophy of "the utmost good faith" to future indigenous-state interactions.[4]

By taking an important, symbolic step of asserting indigenous self-determination, even if only possible through a declaration by an indigenous nation, the parameters for an indigenous-state relationship are framed on indigenous terms. Moreover, indigenous-state self-determination accords emphasize their nationhood status while tending to avoid costlier avenues of litigation as a primary means of resolving indigenous-state conflicts.[5] This option is one diplomatic strategy that serves as an alternative to party donations and getting out the vote as viable strategies for influencing policy.

Emulate leaders: Most indigenous nations regard "leadership by example" as a necessary quality for generating respect and for identifying leaders that others will want to follow. A Tsalagi notion of leadership is no different: a person starts with a vision for the people, then supports that vision by taking action to inspire others, makes the vision a valued relation (relational) to others, and finally offers some direction for others to take action. How have other Native communities and leaders dealt with indigenous-state disputes around the country either historically or in the contemporary era? Are treaty rights invoked, as with the Yakama Nation (Washington), who used their 1855 treaty to combat the problems of alcohol in their community? Are other, more forceful strategies warranted? For example, when New York governor George Pataki proposed collecting a state-based cigarette tax on indigenous reservations, two hundred Native leaders from the state held a summit in 1996 to refute Pataki's claims and reaffirm their self-determination. After two direct confrontations with the Senecas and community members from other indigenous nations, Pataki decided by 1997 that he would not enforce the state taxation scheme.

Another example of leadership is that of the Nez Perce Nation in Idaho. In 1995 the U.S. Fish and Wildlife Service entered into an unprecedented agreement with the Nez Perces to restore the gray wolf to the region based on prior treaties between the federal government and the Nez Perces. Given the centrality of the wolf to Nez Perce culture and this exercise of their self-determination powers, the Nez Perces' "Gray Wolf Recovery and Management Plan" was a good fit for community members to safeguard an endangered species. In the agreement, the Nez Perces assumed full jurisdiction of the reintroduction and recovery of gray wolves in Idaho, and so far, this initiative has been successful, with twelve wolf packs now active in Idaho.

The strategy of emulating other nations also holds benefits for pursuing economic self-sufficiency. Outside the sphere of gaming, indigenous nations are finding effective ways to promote their nationhood and engage in innovative economic initiatives. For example, the Cabazon Band of Cahuilla Mission Indians in California owns First Nation Recovery, Inc., which is a tire recycling plant that grinds rubber to produce asphalt for state roads—four million tires are recycled every year. Another innovative community strategy includes creating an online news service: Indianz.com on the Winnebago Reservation.[6] Historic acts of resistance and leadership undertaken by indigenous peoples, whether by Tsalagis, such as Dragging Canoe, Redbird Smith, and Kai-yah-teh-hee (aka Old Tassel), or others, also inspire indigenous nations to action by invoking their sacred histories.

Act like a nation: Oren Lyons, faithkeeper of the Onondaga Nation, once said, "If a nation feels like a nation, acts like a nation, then you will be a nation."[7] Lyons put this statement to the test by traveling to Geneva with a Six Nations passport in 1977 (rather than a U.S. or Canadian passport), and, consequently, Swiss authorities now recognize Six Nations passports. "Acting like a nation" was certainly the mantra of indigenous communities of the Northwest as they asserted treaty-based fishing rights beginning with fish-ins during the 1970s. They have now achieved greater cooperation with the state of Washington. Indigenous nations have maintained their communities and peoplehood since time immemorial and have done so by asserting rather than negotiating their powers. As findings from the American Indian Policy Center state, "Many tribes are now recognizing that far too much of their effort and time is spent examining issues from a non-native perspective."[8]

As treaty-based nations, indigenous communities have several diplomatic strategies to draw on, such as requiring passports for those U.S. citizens who travel onto indigenous homelands, demanding U.S. accountability within global forums, and reinstituting inter-indigenous treaty making.

Act globally: Long before the establishment of the UN Working Group on Indigenous Populations in 1982, Deskaheh, chief of Six Nations of Grand River, petitioned the League of Nations through the government of the Netherlands in April 1923. As his petition stated, "We have exhausted every other recourse for gaining protection of our sovereignty by peaceful means before making this appeal to secure protection through the League of Nations. If this effort on our part shall fail we shall be compelled to resist by defensive action upon our part this British invasion of our Home-land, for we are determined to live the free people that we were born."[9]

Despite being unsuccessful in his effort to secure support from all the countries in the League of Nations, Deskaheh's words are just as prescient today as indigenous peoples struggle to "live the free people that we were born."

Given the shortcomings of the "International Decade of the World's Indigenous Peoples" (1995–2004), indigenous delegates should be selective regarding their participation in global forums.[10] However, acting globally is one way to demonstrate the truly international personality of indigenous nations and avoid the trap of domestication.

Interestingly, only one indigenous nation responding to the forced federalism surveys was both a top monetary contributor to political candidates and participant at the UN Working Group on Indigenous Populations in Geneva (for both 1998 and 2000 election years). This was out of a total pool of fifty-nine top indigenous contributors, demonstrating that the newfound indigenous monetary resources are not being used globally to promote indigenous diplomatic strategies.

Indigenous nations can seek remedial action and demand U.S. accountability within organizations such as the Unrepresented Nations and Peoples Organization in Geneva or the Inter-American Commission on Human Rights in Washington, D.C. Also, indigenous nations can make global declarations stronger political instruments by "having them reflect consensus and unity within indigenous communities, better communicating the meaning of indigenous self-determination, and by articulating strategies to build a new relationship with states."[11]

In 1979 the Commission on Security and Cooperation in Europe (CSCE) issued a report examining the U.S. compliance with the Helsinki Final Act (1975). In the report issued by the CSCE, a global, independent agency, they found the U.S. commitment to indigenous nations and peoples to be lacking and called for an "intensified cooperation between concerned government agencies and the Native peoples themselves."[12] It is time to hold the U.S. government more accountable to international indigenous rights instruments, such as the Helsinki Final Act, by calling for an update to the 1979 report. The CSCE recommendation for "intensified cooperation" has not yet occurred during the forced federalism era. As transnational action networks, strategic alliances among indigenous nations, global agencies, and grassroots groups can help publicize and rectify human rights abuses outside U.S. borders. These are just some of the potential strategies for bypassing state government jurisdictional claims and strategizing as nations.

Strengthen indigenous governance: Because of the Indian Reorganization Act (1934) and Public Law 280 (1953), some community forms of conflict resolution, such as peacemaking, have been replaced with litigation and other non-indigenous techniques for dispute resolution.[13] Ongoing intracommunity conflicts occurring in communities such as the Mescalero Apache Nation (New Mexico), Confederated Salish and Kootenai Nations (Montana), Saginaw Chippewa Nation (Michigan), Catawba Nation (South Carolina), and elsewhere attest to the shortcomings of modeling indigenous governments after Western political systems. Intracommunity disputes have intensified in frequency and scope during the 1990s as indigenous governments seek legitimacy through formal institutions that mirror state and federal systems. At the same time, they must fend off attacks on their autonomy from external state and federal government actors. Given these struggles, the American Indian Policy Center recommends that "instead of deferring resolution of problems to outside communities or courts, American Indians can build their own nation for internal problem-solving, calling on traditional Indian values and beliefs."[14]

This strategy emphasizes the links between spirituality and politics and calls for a regeneration of indigenous principles, such as *Gadugi,* or community camaraderie, on indigenous homelands. Peoplehood models, which stress the interrelationships between language, homelands, sacred histories, and ceremonial cycles, also offer strategies for indigenous community regeneration. Many answers lie in our indigenous languages and cultures, as each indigenous nation has their own traditional principles for community building and self-determination. For example, Kanien'kehakas (Mohawks) use the word *Onkwehonweneha,* which roughly translates as the "way of the original people" or "Native way." Tsalagis (Cherokees) have the tradition of *Wi-Gaduwaga,* which translates into "I will always be up above in all things that influence me in life; in the uppermost; for us to follow or emulate."[15] Given that Western words and models for these phenomena undermine indigenous nationhood, it is time to express indigenous self-determination on our own terms.

Practice insurgent education: Most of the challenges to indigenous nationhood today stem from ignorance and ethnocentrism. Taking advantage of any and all opportunities to educate policymakers and the general public on the history of indigenous self-determination is critical. For example, the indigenous nations of Virginia continue to honor the terms of the 1646 and 1677 treaties with Virginia by offering an annual tribute to the governor. This is not merely a symbolic act but fulfills the terms of an international agreement as well educating citizens of Virginia about the sacred, binding nature of treaties. Similarly, the Cherokee Nation has recently sought to reinstate the practice of sending Cherokee delegates to the U.S. Congress as outlined by Article 12 of the 1785 Treaty of Hopewell.

A more aggressive example of educating by reminding occurred in 2000, when indigenous voters reminded Washington residents that they have extensive influence in state policymaking and even election results. The First Americans Education Project (FAEP), founded in 1999, was designed to educate legislators about indigenous self-determination while encouraging Native people in the state of Washington to mobilize politically on issues relevant to indigenous nations. As FAEP director Russ Lehman points out, this is "issue advocacy for Indians and only Indians—on our own terms."[16]

Indigenous people at any place and at any time can undertake insurgent education. For example, after the police raid of the Narragansett Smoke Shop in 2003, the nation transformed the shop into the Narragansett Sovereignty Protection Headquarters. People in the shop educated the public about Narragansett history and nationhood while selling T-shirts proclaiming "Sovereignty" and "Homeland Security: Fighting terrorism since 1492. In support of the Narragansett Tribe, July 14, 2003."[17]

Insurgent education about indigenous histories and culture has to be provided to indigenous citizens as well so that people can be in a position to educate others. For example, the Cherokee Nation has required that all of its employees take a Cherokee Nation history course, which has provided a stronger sense of pride and a better understanding of the struggles for self-determination. In addition, these educational opportunities offer indigenous peoples tools to counter the influences of colonialism in their communities and put forward strategies for community regeneration. One example is provided by Tsalagi scholar and activist Andrea Smith, who contends, "Because sexual violence has served as a tool of colonialism and white supremacy, the struggle for sovereignty and the struggle against sexual violence cannot be separated."[18]

Renew inter-indigenous treaty making: Vine Deloria, Jr., and Raymond DeMallie have urged indigenous leaders to "seriously consider the feasibility of conducting their own form of diplomacy with other Indian nations."[19] This is part of a larger strategy of reframing the politics of perception on indigenous terms. Increasingly, regional coalitions are forming, such as the coalition of large, land-based indigenous nations, led by the Navajo (Diné) Nation and the Montana-Wyoming Tribal Leaders Council. These coalitions have met with some success in mobilizing large numbers of indigenous and non-indigenous people to affect the state and federal policymaking processes. Despite their success so far, inter-indigenous treaties would make these alliances even stronger through the renewal of sacred compacts with other indigenous nations.

New indigenous alliances of peace and friendship hold even greater urgency for those communities bisected by colonial borders, such as the Akwesasne Mohawks (United States and Canada), Tohono O'odhams (United States and Mexico), and Kickapoos (United States and Mexico). Renewed treaty making between indigenous nations would promote strength and unity. Since the United States has not honored indigenous treaties for the most part, it is time for indigenous peoples to lead by example and demonstrate once again their communities' approaches to principles of respect and diplomacy.[20] New inter-indigenous treaties might include those that affirm alliances, protect indigenous peoples when they cross borders, and establish new trade arrangements, further illustrating the wide spectrum of indigenous powers of self-determination. Of course, these are only a few examples of the multiple possibilities for promoting new treaty diplomacies and unity among indigenous peoples.[21]

A moneyed casino culture is not a sustainable indigenous future. As Oren Lyons states, "Land and jurisdiction on the land, that's your future."[22] Whether in ten or twenty years, casinos will run their course as economic and political powerhouses for indigenous nations, and what will remain? The power of indigenous nations ultimately lies in our relationships to the land, language and communities, and so on. There is great potential for applying a peoplehood model when seeking to regenerate indigenous relationships through reconnections to language, homelands, sacred histories, and ceremonial life.[23] These are the true powers of indigenous self-determination.

As this book has demonstrated, the long-term solutions to confronting rich Indian racism do not arise from emulating the lobbying and political behavior of other U.S. citizens; instead, the strength of indigenous nations comes from protecting indigenous homelands and regenerating our cultural and political forms of governance. Casinos and other forms of economic development being promoted on indigenous homelands have a strong pull that, despite the best of intentions, can distract leaders and community members from our real priorities as indigenous nations: regenerating cultural practices and self-determination. Lobbying and other diplomatic strategies have reflected the pull of casino cultures during the forced federalism era, but these priorities should be shifted back toward a focus on nationhood. We are not just confronting hostile legislation and policy-makers but also the politics of perception. It is time to take back our futures as indigenous peoples and represent ourselves on our own terms.

Indigenous Nations Participating in the Forced Federalism Survey, 1994–2000

Indigenous nation	Location by state
Absentee-Shawnee Tribe	Oklahoma
Agua Caliente Band of Cahuilla	California
Alabama-Coushatta Tribe of Texas	Texas
Alabama Quassarte Nation	Oklahoma
Aroostook Band of Micmac Indians	Maine
Assiniboine and Sioux Tribe	Montana
Barona General Business	California
Bear River Band of Rohnerville Rancheria	California
Benton Paiute Reservation	California
Big Sandy Rancheria	California
Bishop Reservation	California
Blue Lake Rancheria	California
Bridgeport Indian Colony	California
Cabazon Band of Mission Indians	California
California Valley Miwok Tribe	California
Catawba Nation	South Carolina
Cahto Indian Tribe of the Laytonville Rancheria	California
Cayuga Nation	New York
Cedarville Rancheria Community Council	California
Chemehuevi Tribal Council	California
Cherokee Nation	Oklahoma
Cheyenne-Arapaho Tribe of Oklahoma	Oklahoma

Indigenous nation	Location by state
Cheyenne River Sioux Tribe	South Dakota
Chickasaw Nation	Oklahoma
Chico Rancheria	California
Chippewa Cree Business Community	Montana
Citizen Potawatomi Nation	Oklahoma
Choctaw Nation	Oklahoma
Coast Indian Community of Yurok Indians of the Resighini Rancheria	California
Coeur d'Alene	Idaho
Colorado River Tribal Council	Arizona
Colville Business Council	Washington
Confederated Tribes of Coos Lower Umpqua and Suislaw Indians	Oregon
Confederated Tribes of the Grand Ronde Community	Oregon
The Confederated Tribes of Siletz Indians	Oregon
Cortina Rancheria	California
Delaware Tribe	Oklahoma
Dry Creek Rancheria Band of Pomo Indians	California
Eastern Band of Cherokee Indians	North Carolina
Eastern Shawnee Tribe	Missouri
Elem Indian Colony	California
Elko Band Council	Nevada
Fallon Paiute-Shoshone Tribe	Nevada
Fond du Lac Reservation	Minnesota
Forest County Potawatomi Indian Community	Wisconsin
Fort Independence Indian Community	California
Fort McDermitt Paiute and Shoshone Tribe	Nevada
Fort Mojave Tribal Council	California
Fort Peck	Montana
Fort Sill Apache Tribe	Oklahoma
Gila River Indian Community	Arizona
Grand Traverse Band of Ottawa and Chippewa	Michigan
Ho-Chunk (Winnebago) Nation	Wisconsin
Hoh Tribal Business Community	Washington
Hoopa Valley Tribe	California
Hopland Band of Pomo Indians of the Hopland Reservation	California

Indigenous nation	Location by state
Houlton Band of Maliseet Indians	Maine
Hualapai Tribe	Arizona
Huron Potawatomi	Michigan
Ione Band of Miwok Indians	California
Iowa Tribe of Oklahoma	Oklahoma
Jamestown S'Klallam Tribal Council	Washington
Jena Band of Choctaws	Louisiana
Jicarilla Apache	New Mexico
Kaibab Paiute Tribe	Arizona
Karuk Tribe of California	California
Kaw Nation	Oklahoma
Kickapoo Tribe	Oklahoma
La Jolla Band of Luiseno Indians	California
Lac Vieux Desert Band of Lake Superior Chippewa Indians	Michigan
Larsen Bay Village	Alaska
Leech Lake Reservation Business Committee	Michigan
Little Traverse Bay Bands of Odawa Indians	Michigan
Lovelock Paiute Tribe	Nevada
Lower Elwha Klallam Tribe	Washington
Loyal Shawnee Tribe	Oklahoma
Lummi Nation	Washington
Mandan, Hidatsa, and Arikara Nation	North Dakota
Match-E-Be-Nash-She-Wish Band of Pottawatomi Indians	Michigan
Menominee Indian Tribe of Wisconsin	Wisconsin
Mesa Grande Band of Diegueno Mission Indians of the Mesa Grande Reservation	California
Metlakatla Indian Community	Alaska
Mill Lacs Band of Chippewa Indians	Minnesota
Minnesota Chippewa Tribe	Minnesota
Modoc Tribe	Oklahoma
Mohegan Tribe	Connecticut
Muckleshoot Indian Tribe	Washington
Muscogee (Creek) Nation	Oklahoma
Native Village of Chuathbaluk	Alaska
Native Village of Port Heiden	Alaska
Native Village of South Naknek	Alaska

Indigenous nation	Location by state
Navajo Nation	Arizona
Nez Perce Tribe	Idaho
Ninilchik Village Tribe	Alaska
Nooksack Indian Tribe	Washington
North Fork Rancheria	California
Northwestern Band of Shoshoni Nation	Idaho
Ogala Sioux Nation	South Dakota
Oneida Indian Nation	New York
Osage Nation	Oklahoma
Otoe-Missouria Tribe	Oklahoma
Ottawa Tribe	Oklahoma
Pala Band of Mission Indians	California
Passamaquoddy Tribe	Maine
Pawnee Tribe	Oklahoma
Penobscot Nation	Maine
Picayune Rancheria of the Chukchansi Indians	California
Pleasant Point Reservation	Maine
Poarch Band of Creek Indians	Alabama
Ponca Tribe	Oklahoma
Prairie Island Indian Community	Minnesota
Pueblo of Isleta	New Mexico
Pueblo of Pojoaque	New Mexico
Pueblo Of Santa Ana	New Mexico
Pueblo of Santa Clara	New Mexico
Pueblo of Zia	New Mexico
Pyramid Lake Paiute Tribe	Nevada
Quapaw	Oklahoma
Quartz Valley Reservation	California
Ramah Navajo Chapter	New Mexico
Red Lake Band of Chippewa Indians	Minnesota
Redding Rancheria	California
Reno-Sparks Indian Colony	Nevada
Round Valley Indian Tribes	California
San Juan Southern Paiute Tribe	Arizona
Sauk Suiattle Indian Tribe	Washington
Sault Ste. Marie Tribe of Chippewa Indians	Michigan
Scotts Valley Band of Pomo Indians	California
Seminole Nation of Oklahoma	Oklahoma

Indigenous nation	Location by state
Seneca-Cayuga Tribe	Oklahoma
Sherwood Valley Rancheria	California
Shingle Springs Rancheria	California
Shoshone-Paiute Tribes of Duck Valley	Nevada
Skokomish Tribal Nation	Washington
Smith River Rancheria	California
South Fork Band Council	Nevada
Spokane Tribe of Indians	Washington
St. Regis Mohawk Indian Nation	New York
Summit Lake Paiute Tribe	Nevada
Suquamish Tribe	Washington
Swinomish Indian Tribal Community	Washington
Sycuan Business Committee	California
Te-Moak Tribes	Nevada
Timbisha Shoshone Tribe	California
Tonkawa Tribe	Oklahoma
Tonto Apache Tribe	Arizona
Torres Martinez Desert Cahuilla Indians	California
Trenton Indian Service Area	North Dakota
Tulalip Tribes	Washington
Twin Hills Village Council	Alaska
United Keetoowah Band of Cherokee Indians	Oklahoma
Upper Lake Band of Pomo Indians	California
Wampanoag Tribe of Gay Head (Aquinnah)	Massachusetts
Washoe Tribe (Woodfords Community Council)	Nevada
Wells Indian Colony Band Council	Nevada
Wiyot Tribe (Table Bluff Reservation)	California
Yavapai-Apache Indian Community	Arizona

Gaming Compact between the Sisseton-Wahpeton Sioux Tribe and the State of South Dakota, 2000

67016   **Federal Register**/Vol. 65, No. 217/Wednesday, November 8, 2000/Notices

DEPARTMENT OF THE INTERIOR
Bureau of Indian Affairs
Indian Gaming
AGENCY: Bureau of Indian Affairs, Interior.
ACTION: Notice of Approved Tribal-State Compact.

SUMMARY: Pursuant to Section 11 of the Indian Gaming Regulatory Act of 1988 (IGRA), Pub. L. 100-497, 25 U.S.C. § 2710, the Secretary of the Interior shall publish, in the **Federal Register**, notice of approved Tribal-State Compacts for the purpose of engaging in Class III gaming activities on Indian lands. The Assistant Secretary—Indian Affairs, Department of the Interior, through his delegated authority, has approved the Amended Gaming Compact between the Sisseton-Wahpeton Sioux Tribe and the State of South Dakota, which was executed on August 24, 2000.
DATES: This action is effective November 8, 2000.
FOR FURTHER INFORMATION CONTACT:
George T. Skibine, Director, Office of Indian Gaming Management, Bureau of Indian Affairs, Washington, DC 20240, (202) 219-4066.
Dated: October 25, 2000.
Kevin Gover, Assistant Secretary—Indian Affairs.
[FR Doc. 00-28587 Filed 11-7-00; 8:45 am]
BILLING CODE 4310-02-P

AMENDED GAMING COMPACT
BETWEEN THE SISSETON-WAHPETON SIOUX TRIBE
AND THE STATE OF SOUTH DAKOTA

This Amended Compact is made and entered into as of the _____ day of August, 2000, by and between the Sisseton-Wahpeton Sioux Tribe (Tribe), and the State of South Dakota (State).

WHEREAS, the Tribe is a federally recognized Indian Tribe in northeastern South Dakota; and

WHEREAS, the Constitution of the Tribe provides for adequate authority for negotiations and agreements with state government; and

WHEREAS, the State has, through constitutional provisions, legislative acts, and regulations, authorized limited gaming activities to be conducted in Deadwood, South Dakota; and

WHEREAS, the Congress of the United States has enacted the Indian Gaming Regulatory Act, Public Law 100-497,102 Stat. 2426,25 U.S.C. § 2701, *et seq.* (1988), which requires Indian tribes to operate Class III gaming activities in "Indian country" pursuant to a Tribal-State Compact entered into for that purpose; and

WHEREAS, the Tribe operates gaming activities in accordance with a Tribal/State Gaming Compact entered into on April 1, 1991; and

WHEREAS, the Tribe intends to operate slot machines and other gaming at locations specifically identified within this Compact; and

WHEREAS, the Tribe and the State desire to negotiate a Tribal-State Compact to permit the operation of such slot machines and other gaming; and

NOW, THEREFORE, in consideration of the foregoing, the Tribe and the State hereby do promise, covenant, and agree as follows:

1. *Declaration of Policy*

In the spirit of cooperation, the Tribe and the State hereby set forth in joint effort to implement the terms of the Indian Gaming Regulatory Act. The State recognizes the positive economic benefits that gaming may provide to the Tribe. The Tribe and the State recognize the need to ensure that the health, safety and welfare of the public and the integrity of the gaming industry in Indian Country and in South Dakota is protected.

2. *Purpose and Scope of Compact*

This Compact and the Tribe's gaming regulations and ordinances shall govern the regulation and operation of Class III blackjack, slot machines, be placed at and pari-mutuel wagering on horses and dogs conducted at the gaming establishments identified in paragraph 8.5. The purpose of this Compact is to provide the Tribe with the opportunity to operate slot machine and other gaming activities in a manner that will benefit the Tribe economically, that will insure fair operation of the games, and that will minimize the possibility of corruption.

3. *Type of Gaming Permitted*

3.1 The Tribe shall operate slot machines pursuant to the terms of this Compact and the Tribe's gaming regulations and ordinances For the purposes of this Compact, the term "slot machines" is defined in South Dakota Codified Laws 42-7B-4 (21), except that the term "slot machines" does not include "video lottery machines" as defined by SDCL 42-7A-1 (13).

Slot machines operated by the Tribe pursuant to this Compact may be linked or connected by means of telecommunications, satellite or technologic or computer enhancement to slot machines or video lottery machines operated by another tribe or tribes on "Indian lands" (as that term is currently defined in the IGRA, 25 U.S.C. § 2703(4)) pursuant to the terms of a tribal/state compact, approved by the Secretary of the Interior pursuant to 25 U.S.C. § 2710, authorizing such other tribe or tribes to similarly operate slot machines or video lottery machines through linkages or connections with the slot machines or video lottery machines operated by other tribes.

3.2 The Tribe shall operate pari-mutuel wagering on horses and dogs pursuant to the terms of this Compact and the Tribe's gaming regulations and ordinances. The Tribe may operate pari-mutuel wagering on horse and dog races occurring within or without the United States.

3.3 The Tribe shall be allowed to operate an unlimited number of tables of Class III blackjack at Dakota Connection as may be authorized by state law.

3.4 The Tribe shall be permitted to operate such other gaming as may be authorized by state law, upon written amendment of this agreement.

4. *Operation of Slot Machines and Pari-Mutuel Wagering on Horses and Dogs*

4.1 The Tribe shall operate its slot machine gaming activities pursuant to this Compact and the ordinances and regulations enacted by the Tribe which ordinances and regulations shall be at least as stringent as those adopted by the State of South Dakota in SDCL 42-7B-4 and ARSD 20:18, *et seq.* All such ordinances and regulations shall be made available to the State.

4.2 The Tribe shall operate its pari-mutuel wagering on horses and dogs gaming activities pursuant to this Compact and the ordinances and regulations enacted by the Tribe, which ordinances and regulations shall be at least as stringent as those adopted by the State of South Dakota in SDCL 42-7-56 and ARSD 20:04:15, *et seq.*, and 20:04:15.01, *et seq.*, for greyhound racing and in SDCL 42-7-56 and ARSD 20:04:30, *et seq.*, for horse racing.

In consideration for the limited right of conducting pari-mutuel wagering with the use of private-side runners, the Tribe will voluntarily donate an equal share of twenty-five percent (25%) of its net revenue from the described wagering to all K-12 public schools located within the original boundaries of the Lake Traverse Reservation as described in Article III of the Treaty of February 19, 1867. The initial donation to each of the schools will occur one (1) year from the publication date in the Federal Register and annually thereafter. In the event the Tribe ceases pari-mutuel wagering with the use of private-side runners, the Tribe shall notify the State in writing and payment to the described educational facilities will no longer occur.

4.3 The Tribe shall appoint a Tribal Gaming Commission which shall supervise the gaming activities, issue licenses as provided herein, inspect all premises where gaming is conducted and otherwise be responsible for enforcing the Tribe's Gaming Ordinances and regulations.

The Sisseton-Wahpeton Sioux Tribal Gaming Commission shall have primary responsibility for the supervision and regulation of gaming conducted under the authority of this Compact. This shall include, but not be limited to, the licensing of gaming employees and the inspection and regulation of all slot machines and pari-mutuel operations. Any discrepancies in the gaming operation and any violation of Tribal Gaming Commission regulations and rules or this Compact shall be immediately reported to the Tribal Gaming Commission and the South Dakota Commission on Gaming for appropriate action by the Tribal Gaming Commission pursuant to the terms of this Compact.

4.4 *Disciplinary Action For Misconduct By Licensees*

Any suspected violation of any law or rule, adopted in this Compact, shall be reported to the Tribal Gaming Commission and the South Dakota Gaming Commission. If either the State or the Tribe concludes that a violation has occurred, the violation will be addressed by the Tribe within five (5) days. If, after consultation with the Tribal Gaming Commission and after efforts to resolve any difference of opinion reflecting an appropriate penalty for such violation have been made, the executive director of the South Dakota Gaming Commission concludes that the disciplinary action undertaken by the Tribal Gaming Commission is inadequate, a more severe penalty shall be imposed by the Tribal Gaming Commission as requested by the executive director of the South Dakota Gaming Commission.

5. *Criminal Jurisdiction*

5.1 All criminal matters arising from or related to Class III gaming shall be dealt with according to applicable Tribal, State, or Federal law. Nothing in this compact shall deprive the Courts of the Tribe, the United States, or the State of South Dakota of such criminal jurisdiction as each may enjoy under applicable law.

5.2 The Tribe has adopted and agrees to adopt gaming ordinances and regulations to regulate gaming in the gaming establishments identified in paragraph 8.5, which ordinances and regulations are at least as stringent as those statutes and administrative rules adopted by the State of South Dakota to regulate gambling in Deadwood,

South Dakota, and to regulate pari-mutuel wagering on horses and dogs. The Tribe shall furnish the State with copies of such ordinances and regulations and shall advise the State of any amendment, revision or rescission of the gaming regulations. The Tribe agrees that in no event shall it amend, revise or rescind any gaming regulations which would result in the tribal regulations being less stringent than the statutes and rules adopted by the State of South Dakota.

6. *Civil Jurisdiction*

6.1 All civil matters arising from or related to Class III gaming shall be dealt with according to applicable Tribal, State, or Federal law. Nothing in this compact shall deprive the Courts of the Tribe, the United States, or the State of South Dakota of such civil jurisdiction as each may enjoy under applicable law. Nothing in this provision shall be construed to be a waiver of the sovereign immunity of the Sisseton-Wahpeton Sioux Tribe.

7. *Licensing of Gaming Operators and Employees*

All individuals who operate or manage a gaming operation under the authority of this Compact shall be licensed by the Tribal Gaming Commission. All individuals employed to work directly with the gaming operation shall be licensed by the Commission.

The Sisseton-Wahpeton Sioux Tribal Gaming Commission shall have primary responsibility for the licensing of individuals who operate or manage a gaming operation or who are employed in the tribal gaming operation. Any person seeking to be licensed hereunder shall first submit an application to the Tribal Commission which application shall include a written release by the applicant authorizing the State to conduct a background investigation of the Applicant on behalf of the Tribal Gaming Commission. The State shall agree to conduct an investigation of the applicant on behalf of the Commission, upon receipt of the executed release and payment of the fee as provided in the South Dakota Commission on Gaming rules and regulations for such investigations. The State shall provide the Commission with a written report regarding each applicant within 30 days of the receipt of the request and fee or as soon thereafter as practical.

The Commission shall not issue a license to any unsuitable applicant. A suitable applicant is one who is determined suitable by the Tribal Gaming Commission according to tribal ordinance and by the South Dakota Gaming Commission pursuant to SDCL ch. 42-7B and SDCL 42-7-56 and the South Dakota Gaming Commission rules and regulations.

Because each licensee must, in any case, be relicensed annually, the State agrees not to require additional relicensing of any person to operate, manage or be employed in any gaming operation conducted under the authority of this Compact, provided that the person has obtained the applicable license to operate, manage or be employed in any gaming operation in Deadwood, South Dakota, or has obtained applicable license to operate, manage or be employed in any gaming operation in Deadwood, South Dakota, or has obtained the applicable license to operate, manage or be employed in any pari-mutuel gaming operation conducted pursuant to the laws and regulations of the State of South Dakota or any such gaming operations conducted under the authority of a compact between the State of South Dakota and any Indian tribe.

Should the Tribal Gaming Commission disagree with the State's determination on suitability, the Tribal Gaming Commission may invoke the following arbitration procedure:

The dispute shall be determined by a three-person binding Arbitration Board. One member of the Board shall be selected by the Tribal Gaming Commission, one member shall be selected by the State Gaming Commission, and one member shall be jointly selected by the State Gaming Commission and the Tribal Gaming Commission. Within thirty (30) days of the signing of this Agreement, the parties hereto shall appoint the members to the Arbitration Board for a three-year term. In the event of death, resignation, or expiration of a term, new members shall be appointed on the same basis as the original members. The Arbitration Board shall determine whether the applicant is deemed suitable, taking into consideration the ordinance and regulations adopted by the Tribal Gaming Commission and the statutes and rules adopted by the State of South Dakota. The Arbitration Board shall further decide the suitability issue in the best interest of the public. If permitted by law, either the State or the Tribe may appeal the arbitration decision to federal district court.

8. *Regulatory standards for Gaming*

In recognition of the valid public policy interests of the State, which are similarly appreciated as desirable by the Tribe, the following regulatory standards are established for gaming operated and played within the gaming establishments identified in paragraph 8.5.

8.1 *No Credit Extended*

All gaming shall be conducted on a cash basis. Except as herein provided, no person shall be extended credit for gaming by the gaming facilities operated under this compact, and no operation shall permit any person or organization to offer such credit for a fee. This restriction shall not apply to credits won by players who activate play on gaming machines after inserting coins or currency into the game, and shall not restrict the right of the Tribe or any other person to offer check cashing or to install or accept bank card or credit card transactions in the same manner.

8.2 *Minimum Age for Players*

Any participant in a game authorized by this Compact shall be twenty-one (21) years of age or older at the time of participation. No licensee may permit any person who is less than twenty-one (21) years of age to participate in a game authorized by this Compact. A violation of this provision shall subject the participant or licensee to punishment under applicable Tribal or State law.

8.3 *Technical Standards for Slot Machines*

All slot machines operated and played within the establishments identified in paragraph 8.5 pursuant to this Compact shall meet or exceed the hardware and software specifications set forth by the South Dakota Gaming Commission and SDCL 42-7B-43 prior to play. Slot machines prototypes will be tested and approved prior to play by the State according to State procedures.

8.4 *Approval of Slot Machines*

No slot machine shall be operated in the gaming operations identified in paragraph 8.5 unless:

1) The slot machine is purchased, leased or acquired from a manufacturer or distributor licensed to sell, lease or distribute slot machines by the State, pursuant to SDCL ch. 42-7B and ARSD 20:18, and

2) The slot machine or a prototype thereof, has been tested, approved and certified by a gaming test laboratory as meeting the requirements and standards of this Compact. For purposes of this Compact, a gaming test laboratory shall be a laboratory agreed to and designated in writing by the South Dakota Gaming Commission and the Tribal Gaming Commission.

8.5 *Number of Slot Machines*

The number of slot machines permitted to be operated under this Compact shall be limited to a cumulative total of two-hundred fifty (250) slot machines in the tribal gaming establishments located at Dakota Sioux Casino, a facility five miles north of Watertown on Sioux Valley Road or at Dakota Connection Casino, a facility two miles east of Sisseton on Highway 10. There shall be no limits placed on the number of blackjack tables that may be operated at Dakota Connection Casino.

The Tribe shall be entitled to have up to ten (10) slot machines to be used to replace slot machines which are out of service as a result of mechanical problems. These additional slot machines are only to be used in such an event and shall not be operated in addition to the maximum number of slot machines authorized by this provision. Further, these additional slot machines shall meet the requirements of paragraph 8.3 of this Compact.

8.6 *Slot Machines Inspection Procedure*

The South Dakota Gaming Commission agents shall be authorized to inspect (not to include audits) the slot machines operated in the tribal gaming establishments in accordance with the laws and rules adopted in this Compact.

Any periodic inspection of slot machines shall only occur if the state inspector is accompanied by a member of the Tribal Gaming Commission, or a designee. Any such testing shall be carried out in a manner and at a time which will cause minimal disruption of the gaming operation. The Tribal Gaming Commission and the South Dakota Gaming Commission shall be notified of all such testing and the results of such testing.

8.7 *Remedies for Non-Complying Slot Machines*

Upon inspection pursuant to paragraph 8.6, the State may designate slot machines which it believes do not comply with tribal gaming laws. The machines shall immediately be removed temporarily from play or sealed. Within five days of receipt of such written designation, the Tribe shall either:

1) accept the finding of noncompliance, remove such slot machines from play, and take appropriate action to ensure that the Tribe, manufacturer, distributor or other responsible party cures the problem; or

2) contest the finding of noncompliance before the Arbitration Board as provided in paragraph 7 above. In the event the Arbitration Board finds that the slot machine is noncomplying, such slot machine shall be removed from play. Slot machines removed from play pursuant to this section may be returned to play only after such slot machine comes into compliance with the provisions of 8.4 herein. Nothing in this section shall limit the rights or remedies available to the parties under any other provision of this Compact or under the IGRA.

8.8 *Approval and Inspection of Pari-Mutuel Wagering Equipment*

All equipment used by the Tribe, including electrical or mechanical tote board devices, in conducting pari-mutuel wagering shall be of a type and meet the standards for size and information display set forth by the South Dakota Gaming Commission.

The South Dakota Gaming Commission agents shall be authorized to inspect (not to include audits) the equipment used by the Tribe in conducting pari-mutuel wagering to determine that it is in accordance with the laws and rules adopted in this Compact.

Any periodic inspection of pari-mutuel wagering equipment shall only occur if the state inspector is accompanied by a member of the Tribal Gaming Commission, or a designee. Any such inspection shall be carried out in a manner and at a time which will cause minimal disruption of the gaming operation. The Tribal Gaming Commission and the South Dakota Gaming Commission shall be notified of all such inspections and the results of such inspections. If the results of any such inspection reveal that the equipment fails to meet applicable standards, the Tribe will not use such equipment until the equipment meets the applicable standards.

8.9 *Limit on Wagers*

The amount of a bet in any slot machine or any Class III blackjack game may not be more than five dollars on the initial bet or subsequent bet subject to rules promulgated by the Tribal Gaming Commission. Slot machines operated in the establishments identified in 8.5 and Class III blackjack games at Dakota Connection Casino may in the future offer such higher bet limits which are consistent with South Dakota statute and regulation and which are authorized by the Tribal Gaming Commission.

There shall be no wager limitation on pari-mutuel wagers placed on horse and dog races authorized under this Compact.

9. *Accounting and Audit Procedures*

The Tribe shall adopt accounting standards which meet or exceed those standards established in Chapter 20:18:22 of the South Dakota Rules and Regulations for Limited Gaming.

The Tribe shall conduct independent audits of the gaming operation and provide copies to the State. At the request of the Tribe and at the Tribe's expense, the State may in its discretion audit the tribal operation. The Tribe shall engage an independent certified public accountant to audit the books and records of all gaming operations conducted pursuant to this Compact and shall make copies of the audit and all current internal accounting and audit procedures available to the State upon written request. The Tribe shall permit the State to consult with the auditors before or after any audits or periodic checks on procedures which may be conducted by the auditors, and shall allow the State to submit written or oral comments or suggestions for improvements regarding the accounting and audit procedures. Within 30 days of receipt of any written or oral comments, the Tribe shall:

(a) accept the comments and modify the procedures accordingly; or

(b) respond to the comments with counterproposals or amendments.

10. *Duration*

This Amended Compact shall become effective upon execution by the Governor of the State and the Chairman of the Tribe, approval by the Secretary of the Interior and publication of that approval in the Federal Register pursuant to the IGRA.

The terms of this Compact shall be subject to review at four (4) year intervals dating from the date of execution of this Compact. Prior to the expiration of the four (4) year period, each party to the Compact may give notice to the other party of provisions it believes requires review or amendment. Such notice shall be in writing and shall be sent by certified mail to the Governor of the State or Chairman of the Tribe at the appropriate governmental office. If no notice is given by either party prior to the expiration of the four (4) year period or any subsequent four (4) year period, the Compact shall automatically be extended for an additional four (4) years. If, in the notice, a party states that termination of this Compact should not result from any failure of the parties to reach agreement with respect to changes in the provisions noticed for review or amendment, the Compact shall also automatically be extended for an additional four (4) years.

Upon receipt of such notice, the parties shall engage in good faith efforts to resolve the issues identified in the notice.

Except as otherwise provided in the second paragraph of this section, in the event the parties are unable to resolve the issues identified in the notice upon expiration of the four (4) year period or any subsequent four (4) year period, this Compact, unless earlier terminated by agreement of the parties, shall remain in effect for 180 days thereafter. The parties shall have until the expiration of the 180 days to continue to negotiate and remedies available under the Indian Gaming Regulatory Act shall apply. The State and the Tribe may agree in writing to extend the negotiating period without prejudice to the rights of either party.

Upon the expiration of the negotiating period, or any extension thereof, the Compact shall terminate unless the parties, in writing, agree otherwise.

Either party may terminate this Compact upon a substantial breach by the other party regardless of any other provision of this Compact. Upon identification of what either party believes to be a substantial breach of the terms of this Compact, such party shall notify the other party in writing, via certified mail, return receipt requested, as to the nature of the substantial breach. The complaining party may terminate this Compact in writing after at least 30 days have elapsed from receipt of the notice of noncompliance by the other party, unless the breach has been remedied and the cause of the breach has been dealt with in a manner acceptable to the complaining party or unless the responding party has presented a plan to deal with the breach which is acceptable to the complaining party.

Notwithstanding any other provision of this Compact including the paragraph immediately above, it is agreed between the parties that on the day that it becomes illegal as a matter of South Dakota law to operate slot machines or Class III blackjack or to conduct pari-mutuel wagering on horses and dogs, as the case may be, within the State of South Dakota, this Compact shall expire and be of no further force with respect to the illegal gaming activity.

11. *General Provisions*

The following conditions shall be applicable throughout the term of this Agreement:

11.1 The parties hereto agree that in the event that a dispute arises as to an interpretation of the provisions of this Compact, in any of the rights, responsibilities or obligations attaching to the parties hereto, either party may commence an action in federal district court for the purpose of resolving such dispute.

11.2 The parties hereto agree that the Tribe will be responsible for the costs incurred by the State and associated with the State's performance of its responsibilities as provided for herein. The intent of this Compact is to provide for the reimbursement for the costs and expenses of the State in performing its responsibilities as provided herein. The parties agree that this provision does not require payment by the Tribe of court costs or attorney's fees in litigation. The parties also agree that this provision does not require payment by the Tribe of costs incurred by the State of South Dakota for law enforcement officers of the State except that such payment is required with regard to costs incurred for law enforcement officers of the State who are agents and employees of the South Dakota Commission on Gaming.

The hourly rate to be paid to the State for its services pursuant to paragraph 11.2 of the attached Compact is fifty dollars ($50.00). Travel, per diem, and other expenses shall be paid to the State at the rates set out in South Dakota Administrative Rules, ARSD 05:01:02. Should the rates set out in the Administrative Rules be changed during the time of this Compact, the rates to be paid to the State shall likewise be altered.

11.3 Unless otherwise indicated differently, all notices, payments, requests, reports, information or demand which any party hereto may desire or may be required to give to the other party hereto, shall be in writing and shall be personally delivered or sent by telegram or first class certified or registered United States mail, postage prepaid, return receipt requested, and sent to the other party at its address appearing below or such other address as any party shall hereinafter inform the other party hereto by written notice given as aforesaid:

Notice to the Tribe shall be sent to:
Chairman's Office
Sisseton-Wahpeton Sioux Tribe
Box 509
Agency Village, SD 57262

Notice to the State shall be sent to:
Governor's Office
500 East Capitol
Pierre, SD 57501

All notices, payments, requests, reports, information or demand so given shall be deemed effective upon receipt or if mailed, upon receipt or the expiration of the third day following the day of mailing, whichever occurs first, except that any notice of change of address shall be effective only upon receipt by the party to whom said notice is addressed.

11.4 This Agreement is the entire Agreement between the parties and supersedes all prior agreements whether written or oral, with respect to the subject matter hereof. Neither this Agreement not any provision herein may be changed, waived, discharges, or terminated orally, but only by an instrument in writing.

11.5 This Agreement may be executed by the parties hereto in any number of separate counterparts with the same effect as if the signatures hereto and hereby were upon the same instrument. All such counterparts shall together constitute but one and the same documents.

11.6 The State and/or the Tribe may not assign any of its respective right, title, or interest in this agreement, nor may the State and/or the Tribe delegate any of its respective obligations and duties under this Agreement, except as expressly provided herein. Any attempted assignment or delegation in contravention of the foregoing shall be null and void.

11.7 Nothing in this Compact shall be construed to limit the rights or remedies available to the parties hereto under the Indian Gaming Regulatory Act.

11.8 This Compact shall not be construed to waive or diminish the sovereignty of the Sisseton-Wahpeton Sioux Tribe or the State of South Dakota, except as specifically provided by the terms of the Compact set forth above.

11.9 This Agreement may be amended or modified in writing at any time subject to any federal approval of such amendment or modification required by the Federal Indian Gaming Act.

11.10 The Tribe hereto agrees that none of the funds generated by gaming conducted under this Compact shall be used by the Tribe or its agents to influence the outcome of any local, state, or federal election conducted within the State of South Dakota.

IN WITNESS WHEREOF, the parties hereto have caused this Agreement to be executed as of the date and year first above written.

SISSETON-WAHPETON SIOUX TRIBE

_____   By:_____
(Date)   Andrew J. Grey, Sr.,
                                                             Tribal Chairman

STATE OF SOUTH DAKOTA

_____   By:_____
(Date)   William J. Janklow, Governor
                                                             State of South Dakota

BUREAU OF INDIAN AFFAIRS

_____   By:_____
(Date)   Assistant Secretary

Treaty with the Cherokees, 1785

Nov. 28, 1785. 7 Stat., 18.

Articles concluded at Hopewell, on the Keowee, between Benjamin Hawkins, Andrew Pickens, Joseph Martin, and Lachlan M'Intosh, Commissioners Plenipotentiary of the United States of America, of the one Part, and the Head-Men and Warriors of all the Cherokees of the other.

The Commissioners Plenipotentiary of the United States, in Congress assembled, give peace to all the Cherokees, and receive them into the favor and protection of the United States of America, on the following conditions:

ARTICLE 1.
The Head-Men and Warriors of all the Cherokees shall restore all the prisoners, citizens of the United States, or subjects of their allies, to their entire liberty: They shall also restore all the Negroes, and all other property taken during the late war from the citizens, to such person, and at such time and place, as the Commissioners shall appoint.

ARTICLE 2.
The Commissioners of the United States in Congress assembled, shall restore all the prisoners taken from the Indians, during the late war, to the Head-Men and Warriors of the Cherokees, as early as is practicable.

ARTICLE 3.

The said Indians for themselves and their respective tribes and towns do acknowledge all the Cherokees to be under the protection of the United States of America, and of no other sovereign whosoever.

ARTICLE 4.

The boundary allotted to the Cherokees for their hunting grounds, between the said Indians and the citizens of the United States, within the limits of the United States of America, is, and shall be the following, viz. Beginning at the mouth of Duck river, on the Tennessee; thence running north-east to the ridge dividing the waters running into Cumberland from those running into the Tennessee; thence eastwardly along the said ridge to a north-east line to be run, which shall strike the river Cumberland forty miles above Nashville; thence along the said line to the river; thence up the said river to the ford where the Kentucky road crosses the river; thence to Campbell's line, near Cumberland gap; thence to the mouth of Claud's creek on Holstein; thence to the Chimney-top mountain; thence to Camp-creek, near the mouth of Big Limestone, on Nolichuckey; thence a southerly course six miles to a mountain; thence south to the North-Carolina line; thence to the South-Carolina Indian boundary, and along the same south-west over the top of the Oconee mountain till it shall strike Tugaloo river; thence a direct line to the top of the Currohee mountain; thence to the head of the south fork of Oconee river.

ARTICLE 5.

If any citizen of the United States, or other person not being an Indian, shall attempt to settle on any of the lands westward or southward of the said boundary which are hereby allotted to the Indians for their hunting grounds, or having already settled and will not remove from the same within six months after the ratification of this treaty, such person shall forfeit the protection of the United States, and the Indians may punish him or not as they please: Provided nevertheless, That this article shall not extend to the people settled between the fork of French Broad and Holstein rivers, whose particular situation shall be transmitted to the United States in Congress assembled for their decision thereon, which the Indians agree to abide by.

ARTICLE 6.
If any Indian or Indians, or person residing among them, or who shall take refuge in their nation, shall commit a robbery, or murder, or other capital crime, on any citizen of the United States, or person under their protection, the nation, or the tribe to which such offender or offenders may belong, shall be bound to deliver him or them up to be punished according to the ordinances of the United States; Provided, that the punishment shall not be greater than if the robbery or murder, or other capital crime had been committed by a citizen on a citizen.

ARTICLE 7.
If any citizen of the United States, or person under their protection, shall commit a robbery or murder, or other capital crime, on any Indian, such offender or offenders shall be punished in the same manner as if the murder or robbery, or other capital crime, had been committed on a citizen of the United States; and the punishment shall be in presence of some of the Cherokees, if any shall attend at the time and place, and that they may have an opportunity so to do, due notice of the time of such intended punishment shall be sent to some one of the tribes.

ARTICLE 8.
It is understood that the punishment of the innocent under the idea of retaliation, is unjust, and shall not be practiced on either side, except where there is a manifest violation of this treaty; and then it shall be preceded first by a demand of justice, and if refused, then by a declaration of hostilities.

ARTICLE 9.
For the benefit and comfort of the Indians, and for the prevention of injuries or oppressions on the part of the citizens or Indians, the United States in Congress assembled shall have the sole and exclusive right of regulating the trade with the Indians, and managing all their affairs in such manner as they think proper.

ARTICLE 10.
Until the pleasure of Congress be known, respecting the ninth article, all traders, citizens of the United States, shall have liberty to

go to any of the tribes or towns of the Cherokees to trade with them, and they shall be protected in their persons and property, and kindly treated.

ARTICLE 11.
The said Indians shall give notice to the citizens of the United States, of any designs which they may know or suspect to be formed in any neighboring tribe, or by any person whosoever, against the peace, trade or interest of the United States.

ARTICLE 12.
That the Indians may have full confidence in the justice of the United States, respecting their interests, they shall have the right to send a deputy of their choice, whenever they think fit, to Congress.

ARTICLE 13.
The hatchet shall be forever buried, and the peace given by the United States, and friendship re-established between the said states on the one part, and all the Cherokees on the other, shall be universal; and the contracting parties shall use their utmost endeavors to maintain the peace given as aforesaid, and friendship re-established.

In witness of all and every thing herein determined, between the United States of America and all the Cherokees, we, their underwritten Commissioners, by virtue of our full powers, have signed this definitive treaty, and have caused our seals to be hereunto affixed. Done at Hopewell, on the Keowee, this twenty-eighth of November, in the year of our Lord one thousand seven hundred and eighty-five.

Benjamin Hawkins, [L. S.]
And'w Pickens, [L. S.]
Jos. Martin, [L. S.]
Lach'n McIntosh Koatohee, or Corn Tassel of Toquo,
   his x mark, [L. S.]
Scholauetta, or Hanging Man of Chota, his x mark, [L. S.]
Tuskegatahu, or Long Fellow of Chistohoe, his x mark, [L. S.]
Ooskwha, or Abraham of Chilkowa, his x mark, [L. S.]
Kolakusta, or Prince of Noth, his x mark, [L. S.]
Newota, or the Gritzs of Chicamaga, his x mark, [L. S.]

Konatota, or the Rising Fawn of Highwassay, his x mark, [L. S.]
Tuckasee, or Young Terrapin of Allajoy, his x mark, [L. S.]
Toostaka, or the Waker of Oostanawa, his x mark, [L. S.]
Untoola, or Gun Rod of Seteco, his x mark, [L. S.]
Unsuokanail, Buffalo White Calf New Cussee, his x mark, [L. S.]
Kostayeak, or Sharp Fellow Wataga, his x mark, [L. S.]
Chonosta, of Cowe, his x mark, [L. S.]
Chescoonwho, Bird in Close of Tomotlug, his x mark, [L. S.]
Tuckasee, or Terrapin of Hightowa, his x mark, [L. S.]
Chesetoa, or the Rabbit of Tlacoa, his x mark, [L. S.]
Chesecotetona, or Yellow Bird of the Pine Log, his x mark, [L. S.]
Sketaloska, Second Man of Tillico, his x mark, [L. S.]
Chokasatahe, Chickasaw Killer Tasonta, his x mark, [L. S.]
Onanoota, of Koosoate, his x mark, [L. S.]
Ookoseta, or Sower Mush of Kooloque, his x mark, [L. S.]
Umatooetha, the Water Hunter Choikamawga, his x mark, [L. S.]
Wyuka, of Lookout Mountain, his x mark, [L. S.]
Tulco, or Tom of Chatuga, his x mark, [L. S.]

Top Twenty Indigenous Populations by State, 2000

	Indigenous population	Percentage of indigenous peoples in relation to the total state population
California	333,346	1.0
Oklahoma	273,230	7.9
Arizona	255,879	5.0
New Mexico	173,483	9.5
Texas	118,362	6.0
North Carolina	99,551	1.2
Alaska	98,043	15.6
Washington	93,301	1.6
New York	82,461	0.4
South Dakota	62,283	8.2
Michigan	58,479	0.6
Montana	56,068	6.2
Minnesota	54,967	1.1
Florida	53,541	0.3
Wisconsin	47,228	1.0
Oregon	45,211	1.3
Colorado	44,241	1.0
North Dakota	31,329	5.0
Illinois	31,006	0.2
Utah	29,684	1.3

SOURCE: U.S. Bureau of the Census, Census 2000, http://www.census.gov (accessed September 1, 2004).

Interview with
Chad "Corntassel" Smith

The following is a full transcription of an interview with Chad "Corntassel" Smith, principal chief of the Cherokee Nation, July 1, 2005.

Jeff Corntassel: Okay, so I'll start off. This is relating to my book project *Forced Federalism,* and so getting to the 2004 general election, did the Cherokee Nation endorse one or more candidates during that election?

Chad "Corntassel" Smith: Actually, until 2004 we had a policy that we would not contribute to a candidate or endorse a candidate, but the policy changed in 2004 because of a very clear distinction between two candidates running for the U.S. Senate. One was Brad Carson, who was a tribal member, and Tom Coburn, who had been a previous congressman from the second district, our district, and Carson, we thought, was . . . being a tribal member was one thing, but he was in support of the Cherokee Nation and was tremendous. Tom Coburn was very antagonistic to the Cherokee Nation Indians, and so in a rare situation— the only time we've ever done it—we endorsed and in acts of council supported Carson against Coburn.

JC: Okay, and in what ways did you all support Carson?

CS: I publicly came out in favor of him and expressed towards our government by announcing that we were financially supporting him, so we did it on an official level and publicly supporting him at press conferences and such. We, the council procured tribal funds to support him by contributing to his campaign. And we did grass roots work, organized people, got people out to vote—the classic things that are involved in the campaign.

JC: Sure, to mobilize folks. And I remember just reading about this election from afar, and it was a pretty ugly campaign, especially given some of the things Coburn said about the Cherokee Nation, about Cherokee treaties being "primitive agreements" . . .

CS: Yes.

JC: And was that one of the issues that prompted Cherokee involvement? Or were there some other issues that also were at play?

CS: Early on there was the situation [that] we knew Coburn's history and we knew Carson's history. It made it easier to support Carson when Coburn had made some very derogatory comments towards the Cherokee Nation. I can send you the CD that we developed. . . . One of the things that we did to support him, we sent it out to 22,000 households that lived in Oklahoma, Cherokee households, a CD. We mailed it to them, and in that CD there was an introduction by myself and quotes and parts of a speech from Carson when he accepted an honor from us on a Cherokee holiday, dealing with Coburn's very hostile comments made in western Oklahoma in which he said treaties are a form of primitive agreements, certain parts of the relationship with Cherokees are a joke. The only part that we did not publish was he went on to say that we were corrupt and we had Swiss bank accounts. We didn't want to republish that slander, but it was very hostile sentiment by Coburn.

JC: Definitely. Obviously Coburn was the one who ultimately got elected, but how do you think Cherokee involvement impacted the overall outcome? It wasn't the favorable outcome you were hoping for, but did it have an impact slightly or did it pave the way for strategizing future elections?

CS: Well, politics is a strange animal. With American politics, sometimes you're condemned if you don't and sometimes you're condemned if you do. And even if you lose, if you put up a strong fight the next time around, people pay attention to you. And even when people get into office, even if they're the worst sort, who you have to tend to when you get into political office is the people who fought against you because you don't want to have to fight against them the next try. So it worked for us because even though we backed Carson against Coburn and he lost, it was well worth the effort of standing up and saying, you know, we're just not going to take this. And if you're going to slap us around, we're going to stand up, and then you're going to have to slap us around in public. We don't like it, and we're not going to take it. Actually, I think it worked out. Coburn has not been openly hostile to us since that time. He's been decidedly moderate. Many of his peers and other Republicans have made excuses for him. You know, if you get in the fight, you've got to fight. You can't be bashful about it.

JC: Well, does the fact that Coburn won with such hostile statements about Tsalagis as well as other Native folks, does that say something about the political climate in Oklahoma today? Is that something that is fairly recent, or is that something that you see as an ongoing thing?

CS: I think there are certain tiers; I think there's always an apathy about tribes and the underlying antagonism by the general public. There's always sometimes a petty jealousy that the Indians are getting away with something in Oklahoma, and that's widespread. But it doesn't rise to the level of blatant racism. So when Coburn says that stuff, it may stick with a few folks, especially on the west side, but the rest of the state, even though it might have some appeal to it, I think the rest of the state says, "You know, this guy's sort of out there". But I think Coburn's win had very little to do with Indians. Oklahoma voted two to one for Bush, even though it's highly Democratic, it had what's called "Bush Democrats" who believed in defending the country and believed in the western man kind of swagger to Bush, and they supported him, and Coburn rode his coattails. But it is interesting that Coburn got a lower percentage riding Bush's coattails than any other federal Republican in the race.

JC: It is pretty telling.

CS: He won by 53 percent, and there's an independent that got six points, and I think Carson got forty-one. I think that Coburn had the same charisma that resonated in Oklahoma City but worked as well in the public debates. But the primary reason Carson lost is the Bush factor; second one is that he didn't do well in televised debates; third one is that it got so hostile and vicious at the end that the independent took votes away from him, I think, from Carson. Had it been an off presidential year, I think Carson would have won.

JC: Well I'll shift gears a little bit here and get more towards strategies for self-determination and nation building. Indigenous self-determination is often touted as a key strategy for regenerating our communities. And I'm thinking with Cherokees that notion of *Gadugi*, of building key aspects of community, our clans, regenerating our ceremonies, et cetera. What do you think or how do you view self-determination as a strategy, and what does that entail for the Cherokee Nation and maybe other indigenous nations around the country?

CS: If you look at strategy as trying to figure out where you're going to go and your principles as how you're going to get there, you can really boil things down to very simple perspectives. If you're out in the middle of someplace and you try to figure out where you need to go, your fundamental first question is, Where have I been? That gives me a sense of my bearings. So I think in developing a long-term vision and strategy as far as self-determination and self-government, the first thing we have to do is ask, Where have we been? We did try to do that through a forty-hour history lesson required for all of our staff. We needed that historical perspective. It teaches you some historical lessons. And from that you can begin to figure out where you want to go . . . the future. It helps you know the information to articulate where you want to go in the future. And I think it's probably universal. Our vision for the future is that you want to increase quality of life. How you do that, and what that means, is really pretty broad. So then the second thing is to try and figure out or develop a consensus or have a solution around determination of where you want to go in the future, in the long, long term. And then it starts boiling down to strategy of how you get to that point. Strategy and tactics will change over time, but I think the ultimate vision is fairly constant. For us in the Cherokee Nation, our hundred-year vision is pretty much what we had a hundred years ago when it was first immortalized by Senator Dawes in 1887, in which he said he held an investigation in the Cherokee Nation and found that each family owned its own home. There was not a pauper in the whole nation, and the tribe owed not a dollar. He also went on to say that the fallacy of our system is that apparently there's no selfishness, which is at the root of civilization, and until we would agree to give up the lands being held in common to be held individually, we would make minimal progress because there was no carrot to make our home any better than that of our neighbors. So, going on that then, a hundred years ago, a hundred and twenty years ago, we had a rich cultural identity, a strong tribal government, and economic self-reliance. So basically that's the vision we have for a hundred years from now. And the strategy becomes how to methodically structure your work and your resources to get there.

JC: That's a challenge. What do you think, given that those strategies that we have that are fairly broad that are available to us, what are some of the biggest hurdles, or obstacles maybe, to achieving some of those goals of self-sufficiency today?

CS: The more you're in this office, it's not money, it's not resources; it comes down to a very simple thing of leadership and people who really believe in a long-term vision and are willing to work at it. Perhaps it's . . . there's so many competing interests, you know—consumerism, materialism, social pressures, and such— that many times people, our people, don't realize the great opportunities we have to rebuild the Cherokee Nation and how it really benefits them and their families. We get trapped in entitlement mentalities and social service mentalities and methamphetamine problems and alcohol problems, and I really do think the biggest challenge is challenging and developing leadership. Now, that leadership comes . . . folks that exercise and promote basic Cherokee attributes. And when you have those attributes, not only the individual but also the Cherokee community develops a positive quality of life.

JC: With that sort of regeneration of leadership, are we talking about revitalizing clan systems and some of the informal aspects?

CS: So a clan system can be a ceremonial system, but it's not going to be a practical system anymore. It's actually been lost for probably a hundred years. By which I mean the majority of folks don't know what their clan is. The ones that do know what their clan is don't have the same expectations of duties to their fellow clansmen. The concept that we're going to build around now, the overall idea of community and general place community but also the community of interests, 'cause Cherokees here will ask you first where you're from then who your family is. And you'll actually see people will coalesce around the community whether it's Vinita, Greasy, or Lawrence. I think it's the community system will ultimately strengthen the tribe.

JC: [Laughing] Or even Westville [where JC's family is from]?

CS: Yeah, very seriously. It's the community of interests that will help with things like softball leagues. . . . Family reunions is a community of interest, sometimes they're also a place community, but the organization of those kind of things, that is what's going to make the tribes survive.

JC: I'll shift to talking about relationships with the state of Oklahoma a little bit. A lot of my research and the book that I'm writing talks about how these relationships have changed or shifted somewhat. In other ways, it looks a lot like the 1830s with the advent of states' rights, and of course we know that preceded removal and all sorts of other hostile policies. So, trying to make sense of this so-called new federalism, and increased, as I see it, involvement of the state, how much attention do you think that Oklahoma state governments pay to what the Cherokee Nation thinks when setting policies that affect Native peoples in the state?

CS: Ten years ago, I would have said "marginal." But in the last ten years you see an increasing interest in the tribes. Basically, our survival depends upon public sentiment and public goodwill. We have the opportunity, we have a number of colleges graduating hundreds of folks in public relations because it's getting our story out and molding public opinion that is so critical to our survival. I'll say this about state relationships: over the last few years, what we've been preaching is beginning to resonate in that we're an asset for Oklahoma, and we bring $7.8 billion of economic impact to Oklahoma. Even five, six, or seven years ago, people running for office would have been Cherokee Nation. We had successful public administration guys and we back candidates now, and candidates will come to us and want our support, which is important. In politics it's not power, it's the appearance of power, so we've become a political player. We've helped the governor get a couple of initiatives going, most of them things we wanted done. We draw heat from far right reactionary self-interest groups like One Nation, which means that you've got some stroke if somebody's picking on you, you must be a player. Like that, I see this relationship with the state developing positively because once they see us as an asset, they're ready to negotiate and commit again, try to find mutual ways of benefit to have integrative solutions. But that can only continue as long as state actors, state politicians and the general public, think we have some stroke, and if we're making money from casinos, then people think we have stroke.

JC: And does it benefit Cherokees and other nations to have Native peoples in state policymaking positions? Have you seen a lot of Native people running for office, for example, in the state legislature and in other forms of office at the state level?

CS: While I think there's out of a hundred members of the Oklahoma House, eleven are tribal members. So we're 10 percent. But actually, it's higher in Oklahoma than perhaps in other places. Just because somebody is a citizen of the Cherokee Nation or some other tribe doesn't necessarily mean their interest lies with us. In fact, our gaming initiatives last time, two or three tribal members in the legislature voted against us even though we requested their support. What you have to ascertain is not whether they're tribal members, but do they recognize, appreciate, support, and advocate for tribal interests. Some non-Indians do a much better job at that than some tribal citizens do. And that's one of the values of getting involved in a campaign. We do, also, voter guides, so we send out letters to every candidate and we get their position, and in politics if you publish your position, well, you're pretty much locked into it, and that's been very helpful. Out in northeastern Oklahoma, the state representatives and senators, I'd say that 75 percent of them are very supportive of the Cherokee Nation.

JC: Well that sort of relates to my follow-up of that question. You mentioned gaming. It seems that some issues, especially if they relate to economic development, like gaming, even taxation and tobacco sales seem to be more contentious with the state, while other issues maybe resource management, cross-deputization, and things like that seem to have maybe a longer history of cooperation and work with the state. Have you found that in Oklahoma? Does it vary by issue in terms of cooperation or ability to negotiate?

CS: The biggest issue, the things you look for in an issue, is who your friends are, who could be your friends, and who's not going to be your friends. And basically you try to find ways to make friends, create communities of interest, rather than bring people into conflict. For example, our gaming deal, we found a way to get horsemen and track owners as part of the deal and they became our friends and we had a very successful state question passed. Contrary to that, we have a tobacco compact with the governor's office, poorly written, after being hammered by basically QuikTrip convenience stores because they were competitors for the market of tobacco sales. So that's been an extreme difficulty, and so to have successful relationships with the state, we really have to look at the constituents that drive state policy if we can find an integrative solution with them. Gaming we did, law enforcement we have lot of things, but we haven't been able to do that with tobacco. I think it's presently because the most vocal convenience store chain is a family-owned chain who is very antagonistic, and it's got enough money to hire a very antagonistic lobbyist. If you had someone in the industry who was more reasonable, we would have been able to develop a win-win situation. Sometimes it's how well and how early you can create allies.

JC: This sort of relates to my next question: Some indigenous nations claim that the recent move or the recent, I'd say, proliferation of a tribal-state compact system, especially relating to gaming, has ultimately infringed on their sovereign rights, while others claim it has strengthened their sovereign control over their homelands. You answered that a little bit, but what are some of your thoughts based on your experiences?

CS: I've heard the whole thing that you give away your sovereignty, and I think that's very short-sighted and shallow because there's two questions when you sit down and negotiate with the state: One is by this simple act of sitting down at the table, you're exercising your sovereignty. Now if you want to go bury your head in the sand and say the state's bad all the time and the federal government's bad all the time, that's not exercising your sovereignty, that's just hiding. The second question in dealing with the state or federal government is knowing that the tending of that is an exercise of sovereignty, then you go to next year and there's a deal or a compact and it's a good one. And a good compact is like a good business deal—both people benefit. If just one side benefits, whether it's the state or the tribe, it's not going to be a good deal because it won't last. So that's just a cost-benefit integrative kind of solution deal. Sometimes you can make it work; sometimes you can't. I think compacts are a very good way to try to control your destinies rather than letting the court or letting hostile federal policy do it.

JC: A related question: With the growth of Indian casinos around the country after IGRA in 1988 and now with the opening of the new Cherokee casino in Tulsa, and several before, how do you think general public perceptions of Native peoples has changed? Or, do you think that's led to a change in perceptions?

CS: It may begin to polarize public perception. Those who are against us, it really aggravates them that we're, quote, "getting away with something." Those who are friendly to us think that this is a pretty good deal for the Indians and it's helping Oklahoma. It's the people in the middle that you really have to begin to worry about. And those we try to show what gaming does for the entire community: creating jobs, creating economic stimulation, they're very clean operations, professionally run, high accountability, that it's an entertainment exercise rather than gambling. If we can try to promote that kind of image, those in the middle, it's easier for them to come over and support positive perception of the tribes.

JC: Have you seen any particular images emerge? I know we sort of joked during the Cherokee history course—someone in our class recounted the story of a person who became a Cherokee Nation citizen and she asked if she could have her new truck, thinking that all Cherokee citizens received new trucks every year. Have you seen any particular images emerge around this mentality?

CS: I see an excuse for those of our citizens who are still locked into an entitlement mentality, and they'll come to the tribe and ask, "What can you do for me? Give me this. Give me that." Then they see a successful gaming operation, and it sort of aggravates

them more 'cause they'll come to me and say, "If you can afford
to build all these casinos, how come you can't afford to give me
money or give me these services?" That would be perhaps the
downside to it. It is interesting, though, that with the general
population, when we succeed, whether it's in sports or gaming,
and I compare this to athletics, any time we succeed, it creates
some animosity, some jealousy, and some envy. I would much
rather be the subject of envy by non-Indian schools or the non-
Indian public or the non-Indian business community than be
patronized by them and subject to paternalism. Some expression of irritation from the general public is also an expression
that, you know, these guys are players and we can't patronize
them any more—which is pretty positive.

JC: You've already alluded to this, but some policy analysts have
basically said that when dealing with state governments, indigenous nations have two choices: they can cooperate or they
can litigate. Do you think it's this black and white, or do you
think there's more to it than that? And can you explain some
of the reasoning?

CS: I think it probably is that simple. It's litigation . . . it's negotiation or litigation. The third thing is legislation. Legislation is
probably the worst option. If you get something in the U.S.
Congress in today's present climate, you should expect something
bad to happen. So, if you can negotiate a decent deal, that's
certainly preferable. If you can't negotiate a decent deal, you
hope you can provide litigation. Going to court is like rolling
dice—you never know what's going to happen. Probably the
worst scenario is hostile legislation, either by the state or by the
feds, because it diminishes your ability to litigate; it takes away
your leverage, and very little legislation is coming to you.

JC: We're almost through; I just have two more questions.

CS: Sure, this is great.

JC: Yeah, I'm enjoying this. What are some future conflicts that you
see that might emerge in tribal-state relations, and how do you
think these conflicts can be overcome?

CS: The biggest one for the next twenty years will be water rights.
Certainly, if we were smart, we would begin to lay out the process
of how to resolve the conflict—it's going to be a major conflict.
So, if we can develop a process to resolve the conflict, we'll

have more leverage for resolving it in our favor and avoiding a head-on collision. So water rights are an issue. There's other issues that are not conflicts, but they are major challenges. Revitalization of our languages is a critical one, the challenges of leadership, the challenges of overcoming entitlement mentalities, the challenges of personal self-determination. You don't hear any more parents and aunts and uncles grabbing kids by the neck, by the back of the neck, and telling them to get their education and straighten up; we've lost that. There are some of the challenges, and I'm sure that meeting those challenges will bring conflicts both internally and externally.

JC: With the language revitalization, what are some of the ways that you see to sort of take that next step? We have a lot of people who have taken the history course now; what are some of the ways that we can maybe work towards revitalizing language? I know there are a lot of immersion schools; it seems to be one good option.

CS: Immersion schools work; there's no question about it. But we have to have just not two grades; we have to have five of them. We need a whole bunch of schools, and we're talking about tens of millions of dollars of support. There are twenty thousand Cherokee kids in immersion schools. I think we've found the solution; it just costs money. There has to be a demand by the people for that. When they put their kids in and support them and such. We're at the threshold of seeing if we can sustain that kind of interesting energy.

JC: My last question here: You said on previous occasions, gaming probably won't be such a strong generator of economic development for indigenous nations five, ten, or fifteen years from now. What are some of the legacies that you see from gaming, but maybe more importantly, what are some of the other ways that Cherokee Nation and other nations can begin or continue to promote self-sufficiency beyond gaming?

CS: The gaming operation gives us a window to develop capacity, business capacity, business capital, and credit right now. And if we don't take advantage of that in the next five to ten years, we lose a phenomenal opportunity to diversify, to create the kind of economy for the Cherokee Nation that can sustain itself and create an attraction to keep our young folks here. In the last two years, our gaming operations not only made us money; it's made a bunch of jobs and developed some expertise in customer service, cultural tourism. It's given us the ability to draw some world-class business leaders that are Cherokee, and they're drawn because they've retired from something else, and we can pay them a little bit, and you get resources that they can access, you know, "I can make something happen here." It's a pretty exciting time. It's something I didn't anticipate happening. It was a great surprise that good business leaders were attracted to the challenge of creating a diverse economy and economic proposal for the Cherokee Nation as soon as we had some resources to work with.

JC: Well, that's all I have. I don't know if you have any questions for me, or if you'd wanted to say anything else . . .

CS: I'm not sure, but any more questions you might have, or any time you want to call up, I'd be delighted to do so.

JC: *Wado.*

Interview with Brad Carson

The following is a full transcription of an interview with Brad Carson, Tsalagi citizen and former U.S. Representative, July 13, 2005.

Jeff Corntassel: I'll start by focusing the first set of questions on the 2004 election. The first question I had was that until 2004, the Cherokee Nation had an official policy that they would not contribute to a candidate or even endorse a candidate for federal or state elections. Why is it, do you think, that they made an exception to this policy to support you during the 2004 Senate race?

Brad Carson: I think there were two reasons, one general, and one more specific. Generally, the tribe appreciates the need to get involved in politics more. All across the country, and this is especially true in Oklahoma, the tribes are increasingly politically active, giving money to candidates, mobilizing their tribal membership on behalf of candidates who support Indian sovereignty. So I think the Cherokees were a bit late to that game but realized how important the game was. And second, you had a situation where a Cherokee tribal member who had represented the heart of the Cherokee Nation and worked closely with the tribal leaders in pursuing policies that would help the Cherokees, at least in Oklahoma, was running against someone who had represented the same area but had been a bitter enemy of everything that the tribe desired and was a critic of tribal sovereignty and was someone who disputed the kind of historic rights and privileges granted to Native Americans. And so I think it was the combination of those two things that led the Cherokees to make the unprecedented move, but I'm sure it won't be the last time to get involved in a big federal campaign.

JC: And just for the sake of the interview, that person was Tom Coburn.

BC: That person was Tom Coburn, right, who had represented north-east Oklahoma, the Cherokee heartland for six years.

JC: Well, that leads into my next question of how did the Cherokee Nation support you during your run for the U.S. Senate?

BC: Well the Cherokees gave financial support, but even more importantly, they gave their moral support and helped mobilize tribal members. What the Cherokees did was go out and tell the nearly one hundred thousand Cherokees who live in Oklahoma that one candidate was very good on their issues and one candidate was very bad on those issues. And, that was really their biggest support. The Cherokees control a lot of votes, and I appreciate their financial support, and I'm very grateful for it. I think their real help probably lay in mobilizing a lot of voters.

JC: And did you see a similar type of support from other Native peoples throughout Oklahoma?

BC: Yes, I had great support from Native peoples across Oklahoma and, indeed, across the nation. People knew where Tom Coburn's record was on this issue and many other issues that were anathema to Indian Country. And so, most were very, very supportive; the Choctaws were very supportive, the Chickasaws, some of the smaller tribes in Oklahoma, but the Cherokees, because I was a tribal member I think, especially. I live in Cherokee country myself. I think they certainly did more than any other tribe.

JC: You sort of alluded to this, but what were some of the key issues that influenced Cherokee involvement in the 2004 election?

BC: Well, Tom Coburn had not been a friend to the Cherokee Nation when he served in Congress, and during the course of the campaign, he did everything from question tribal sovereignty to assert when he was campaigning in western Oklahoma that the bulk of the Cherokees weren't even really Indians. So, it was those kinds of inflammatory comments that really caused the Cherokee Nation to take umbrage and to get so very involved in the campaign.

JC: Yeah, I remember reading his statement of calling Cherokee treaties "primitive agreements."

BC: Exactly, that was one among many comments, and in there he would say things that "this is the average Cherokee with only one two-hundred-and-fiftieth percent Native American." He said a lot of thing that had no basis in fact and were intended really to poke a finger in the eye of the Cherokee people.

JC: Did issues like this relating to, basically, the well-being of indigenous peoples in Oklahoma and elsewhere, were these raised during the election, and how did these issues have an impact on the election outcome?

BC: Well, they were raised very prominently. There were several media stories written about them among the Native American press, the *Native American Times,* the *Cherokee Phoenix,* the others, carried stories about them. There were lots of things in the electronic media about Coburn's comments. And so the notion that Coburn was anti-Indian was widely broadcast. I think it did play a big role in the campaign, not enough to defeat him, but it was enough to make him run far behind George Bush, who was their party's standard-bearer in the '04 elections.

JC: Sort of a related question in terms of support; the Centre for Responsive Politics shows that you are among the highest recipients of monetary contributions from Indigenous nations during the 2004 elections, with $126,000 of support. How did this, you talked about the voting support, how did this solid support, monetary support, from other indigenous nations impact your ability to run a good campaign?

BC: It was essential to running a good campaign. I raised a lot of money, as did Coburn, for this race; it was one of the most high profile senate campaigns in the country. And it would have been impossible without the financial support of lots of people, but especially Native Americans. I had worked closely with the entire Indian community across the land during my four years in Congress, and of course had the support of all the local leaders. The tribes saw Tom Coburn as someone who would be like Slade Gorton was when he was at the U.S. Senate, someone who represented the large population of Native Americans but was indeed the chief antagonist of Indian interests, and this led to a lot of support from Native Americans all across the land.

JC: I know even Slade Gordon prompted all sorts of reactions during the 2000 election, like the First Americans Education Project, to mobilize against him. Did you see similar organizations rising up, Native organizations?

BC: Fewer Native organizations than outside of the tribal structure than perhaps you saw when Slade Gordon was in office. Basically the tribes here in Oklahoma made a heroic effort to educate their own members—at various town halls, through publications, at the various national holidays—these kinds of things is where most of the Indian political activity was done.

JC: What kind of support, if any, did Coburn receive from indigenous nations?

BC: He didn't receive much at all. You're always going to find kind of "curmudgeons," who because a particular leader is for you, they are automatically against you, and there were a few people like that who fell behind Coburn. There was a moment in the campaign where he tried to hold a press conference brandishing his kind of tribal support, and basically he fell flat on his face. It was a couple of tribal leaders, people who weren't really endorsing him but wanted to stand next to him, and most had some kind of grievance with one of the larger tribes, perhaps with the Cherokee Nation. And there were some people like that who thought I might be an advocate for one particular tribe over another, but by and large he had no support from any kind of mainstream Indian leader at all.

JC: We've talked a little about the comments he's made about the Cherokee Nation. What kinds of other perceptions or images of Cherokees or even other indigenous peoples did Coburn evoke during his campaign?

BC: Largely, Coburn went out and showed himself to be insensitive at best, and inflammatory at worst, about the frictions that exist between Native Americans in Oklahoma and the larger population. These are issues that are politically sensitive, more so now that the tribes have gone into gaming and begun to assert their sovereign rights. And what Coburn did was ally himself with those people—groups like One Nation, which is a local Oklahoma group formed to roll back tribal sovereignty—and try to take advantage of their fundraising capacity, their access to media, and things like that. So, that was really what Coburn's strategy was in the campaign.

JC: Did they officially endorse him as a candidate?

BC: They did not officially endorse him, but most of the people who were highly involved in One Nation were strong Coburn supporters.

JC: Do you think these images, or these tactics that Coburn used, were effective on impacting the election outcome?

BC: No, I don't think they were particularly effective; I think the attacks on Native Americans hurt him severely in the course of the campaign. It's a state where George Bush got 66 percent of the vote, Bush won every county; there was a Republican tidal wave. And despite that tidal wave, Coburn won just over 50 percent of the vote, running thirteen points behind George Bush. And so I think his attacks on Indian Country hurt him—not enough to defeat him in such a landslide Republican year, but enough to make it more of a struggle for him than it should have been.

JC: So if it hadn't been a presidential election year, the outcome may have been different?

BC: You never can say. The counter-factual is interesting to contemplate, but it's impossible really to say. Oklahoma is a very Republican state, but there's no question that George Bush's coattails did help Tom Coburn quite a bit.

JC: The next set of questions, I wanted to talk more about strategies for Cherokee Nation, and now with your new position, this idea of self-determination is often mentioned as a key strategy for regenerating Tsalagi notions of *Gadugi,* or community, and from your perspective, what does self-determination entail for Cherokee people?

BC: I think self-determination means autonomy: the right to make decisions as you see fit about your own welfare, not hampered by outside sources. So, I think what the Cherokees need to do—and they are increasingly doing this and tribes all across the United States are doing this too—is taking their destiny in their own hands, not relying on the beneficence of the government or hope as a strategy, but rather saying, "Look, we have sound economic development policies in place; we're willing to pursue them; we're willing to leverage our right to game in many instances into more sustainable comparative advantage" in the hopes that they can take control of their own destiny and not have the fate that has been theirs for two hundred years continue for another two hundred years.

JC: What are some impediments to pursuing that self-determination, or that autonomy, that you see today?

BC: I think there are several impediments. First, you have a growing backlash against Indian nations. As tribes have become more prosperous, as they have begun to assert their rights, you have the inevitable reaction to that. So all across the land you have political tensions between state governments, between municipal governments, between city and state elites, and tribal governments, so I think that's going to be a continuing issue. I think the second matter is that tribes, at least most tribes, do not live in highly . . . not around urban areas. Their population is widely dispersed, poverty is chronic, educational attainment is relatively low, and as we try to pursue sustainable businesses outside of gaming, it's a great challenge in getting the right personnel in place, getting the workforce trained, and convincing businesses that this is a place that they should set up shop.

JC: And do you think that the fact that more and more Native people are running for office, elected office, whether it's at the senate level or whether it's at the state legislature level, do you think that's going to help overcome these impediments, or do you think that's just one small piece of the picture?

BC: I think it's an important piece of the picture. I think having people who understand issues affecting Indian country and who are sympathetic to Indian causes is extremely important. You know, that's the challenge you find in politics is that these issues are extremely complicated. Indian law is, frankly, a mess; it's understanding the overlapping jurisdictional issues. It requires a high level of expertise. So having people in office who understand these matters and are sympathetic to Indian development is something that I think is going to be essential in the next few years.

JC: Given your vast experience in elected office as a representative, how much attention do you feel that Oklahoma pays to what the Cherokee Nation thinks when they're setting policies?

BC: I think that they are increasingly paying attention to what the
      Cherokee Nation thinks and what the other Indian nations of
      the state think. Fifteen years ago, twenty years ago, very few
      people would have made it one of their first trips to meet with
      tribal leaders. Today, if you run for office, Democrat or Repub-
      lican, tribal leaders are among the very first people you call
      and talk to about your campaign. And in my mind, in the next
      ten to twenty years, you'll see Indian leaders being the very first
      people you talk to about your campaign. So, I think more and
      more people are paying attention to what the tribes have to say,
      and more and more people recognize that the tribes bring a
      lot of money to the state, and as we think about the future of
      Oklahoma, it's difficult to envision a prosperous future without
      significant tribal involvement.

JC: And do you find the same trend with the federal government,
      or has that federal government attention been there primarily
      as a government-to-government relationship?

BC: I think the federal government will always have, of course, the
      government-to-government relationship, the trust responsibility,
      paying attention to Indian issues only when it has to. In Okla-
      homa, because of the large Indian population, the fact that
      three-quarters of the state is historical Indian Country, these
      issues are much more salient than they would be in the United
      States Congress. But as these political pressures mount in states,
      you see it also reflected in Congress, so during my four years
      there, there were several battles that affected tribal sovereignty,
      about gaming questions, things like that, and I'm sure those
      battles will only intensify over the next few years.

JC: Was gaming probably the most prominent issue, or did you see
      some other issues that are coming up in mainly the state or
      feds attention?

BC: Gaming is always the issue that, if not at the forefront, is just
      around the corner. We have a lot of people who for moral reasons
      are opposed to gaming, other people who resent the tribal exemp-
      tions from otherwise generally applicable laws. So you have a
      lot of people who are out front opposed to Indian gaming. At
      the same time, the question of putting land into trust became
      much more controversial, not per se, but because many legislators

saw that was put into trust as the first step toward a gaming operation. And then you have the whole issue of tribal recognition, where you have more and more tribes spending lots of money; there's a professional apparatus today that exists around tribal recognition and tribes trying to go outside the BIA and have congressional recognition of their tribe, and this too is seen as largely driven my gaming interests, and there is no doubt that in some instances gaming interests have paid for that very expensive process: hiring historians and anthropologists. And so gaming is the issue that is always, if not out front, lurking quietly behind most of the other controversies surrounding Indian issues.

JC: I agree. I found that when I was working with a lot of Virginia Indian nations out east, and they had no desire to open up casinos or have any relation to gaming, but they were seeking federal recognition, and they were immediately tagged by the governor as wanting a casino, and that was enough for him to stop any endorsement of their federal recognition bid. So definitely that's the way I see things panning out. Some indigenous nations have claimed that the tribal-state compacting system infringes on their sovereignty, while others claim that it strengthens their sovereign or autonomous control over their Native land. What are some of your thoughts based on your experience while in office on this?

BC: I have met a few Indian leaders who thought the tribal compacting process was an infringement of their sovereignty, but most of the Oklahoma leaders seem to have made their peace with that. I don't really know how to evaluate the arguments. My hope is that we can avoid a pitched battle between state governments and Indian nations by recognizing that, in the end, their interests are quite common and not distinct. So the compacting process seems to me to be a reasonable compromise between state interests and tribal nations and a way of keeping the peace as opposed to litigating these matters in a way that one doesn't know how they'll be decided and could even be deleterious to the state or the Indian interests irrevocably. So in that sense, I do appreciate how the passage of the Indian Gaming Regulatory Act has ushered in this new era, and without doubt states are increasingly aggressive in trying to assert their authority over Indian nations. Part of that is the inevitable result of Indian success, that states are going to want a piece of the action; states are concerned with what tribes are doing in a way that when tribes were poor and desperate, states had no interest in doing.

JC: That sort of leads into the next question on perception of Native peoples, and you've touched on this already, but how do you see perceptions of Native peoples changing since the growth of, or the advent of, or really the huge increase of native run casinos after IGRA in 1988, and really since the development of Cherokee Nation casinos in Oklahoma?

BC: I think that, on one hand, more and more people are eager to be recognized as tribal citizens, and you see membership rolls swelling as a result and people claiming their ancestry and being very proud of it. And it's allowed the tribes at the same time with this new revenue source to build upon their great history. You know, Chad Smith of the Cherokee Nation is trying to resurrect the Cherokee language, for example, trying to educate people about the great history of the Cherokee Nation, and this is all made possible because of their business success. At the same time, there are lots of people who are on the outside of Indian Country who I do think have a perception that Indian nations are perhaps doing business with people who are slightly—if not fully—disreputable, maybe taking advantage of them, that the tribes are taking advantage of loopholes that exist in the law to benefit themselves but at the detriment of the larger society around them. So, I think you have this strange situation where lots of people are more proud than they've ever been before to be Native American, but you also have a greater resentment than has ever existed before.

JC: Some policy analysts have contended that when working with state governments, indigenous nations have two choices: they can either cooperate or they can litigate. Do you agree with this assessment, and can you maybe explain that a little bit?

BC: I suppose in any dilemma, you have two choices: you can try to create a peace treaty or you can declare all out war, or maybe there's a third alternative where you just kind of allow cold war to exist. I think it's been the perception, and probably rightly perceived, that litigation was extraordinarily dangerous to every party. For example, take the burning question of water rights in Oklahoma. This came to the forefront three or four years ago when cities like Dallas, Texas, were growing rapidly and they were hungry for water, there were great water sources in Oklahoma, and there was the idea that we would sell them some of our water. This contract would be for a billion dollars or more over the next century. And there was the question of who owned this water, and the state government claimed it. Other people saw it as kind of a common resource, something that everyone in the state owned. Others said just the people of the region owned. And, of course, the tribe said it is our water; this was our land to being with. Now, we could have litigated that issue; it would have been probably among the most complicated issues in United States history, with thousands of land owners involved and governments involved, and in the end we might have had a decision, either that the tribes own it all or that the tribes own nothing. Either outcome was dangerous for the litigants: the state would have been in a difficult position if the tribes had won; the tribes would have been in a difficult position if the state had won. And so they were able to reach a compromise and just sort of table the issue. But that story can be told in nearly all of these various matters. You can litigate it all—it's a high stakes game—and if you win you're definitely in the catbird's seat, but if you lose, well, you could be worse off than if you try to have a negotiated settlement. And so, I think rightly most people perceive a negotiated settlement as kind of the best option.

JC: This is my final question, and you've talked about water rights as one possible conflict. What are some other future conflicts that might emerge in indigenous-state relations, and how do you see resolving some of these conflicts, or challenges if you will?

BC: Well, I think the conflicts are all going to spring from the very notion of sovereignty itself. For example, if the Cherokee Nation, or the Choctaws, or the Chickasaws, the Seminoles, any of the thirty-nine federally recognized tribes that make their home in Oklahoma, are they states within states, or are they have a slightly different status? And that plays out in everything from water rights to environmental rules; that is a growing dispute all across the country. Do tribes have the right to set their own water and air standards? Do tribes have the right to issue their own hunting licenses? Their own fishing licenses? Do they have the right to regulate oil and gas drilling, which is something that is an important part of the Oklahoma economy? In Oklahoma, because of the many tribal actors, it is in some ways a state that has within it thirty-nine kind of "duty free" zones, where generally applicable sales taxes are either less or not present at all. How does this affect the ability of the government to raise revenues to fund programs like public education or transportation? These are all tremendous challenges. I hope the way that we can recognize them, to try to deal with them, is to have cooler heads prevail and the notion that in the end, it's in the state's interest for Indian tribes to do well, just as there is in the interests of Indian tribes for the state to do well, because Indian people are citizens of both the state of Oklahoma and a particular tribe, and citizens of the United States, too. And in the end, the interests are aligned, and so for the state they should be looking at Indian nations as a way to promote economic development, promote educational attainment, and encourage tribes to do that but place policies that will do that. At the other hand, tribes need to recognize that the state is very important, and if they undercut the state's ability to promote important policies, they are only hurting themselves and kind of fomenting that backlash that is already developing. And so that's my hope, that we can kind of get people together, and say look, sovereignty doesn't mean we're going to be at odds with the state, it merely means we have this right. And in fact we think that state policies are good for us; we can adopt state standards on clean air, clean water; we can be silent on many issues, but we don't have to litigate it, but in a practical matter, we can all be happy. I think that's quite possible. It sometimes seems a bit of a distant plan to reach.

JC: Excellent. Is there anything we haven't touched on or covered, whether it's the election of 2004 or other issues you'd like to address?

BC: No, I don't think so. I think you've pretty comprehensively covered these issues.

JC: *Wado,* thank you, Brad.

BC: My pleasure.

Indigenous Government Survey, 2000

1. Has your tribe endorsed (tribe supported or tribal leader asked tribal members to vote for) a candidate in this year's **PRIMARY** election? This includes Federal, State, and Local elections.

____ YES.   Candidate(s) and Office(s) _____

____ NO

2. Has your tribe endorsed (tribe supported or tribal leader asked tribal members to vote for) a candidate in this year's **GENERAL** election? This includes Federal, State, and Local elections.

____ YES.   Candidate(s) and Office(s) _____

____ NO

3. Has your tribe endorsed candidates in previous elections? This includes federal, state, and local elections.

____ YES.   Candidate(s) and Office(s) _____

____ NO

4. Why has your tribe chosen to support certain candidates over others? Please number your choices in order of importance.

____ Membership in the Tribe.

____ Issue Positions. What issues were important in this year's election? _____

____ Political Party of the Candidate.

____ Other.   Please Explain. _____

5. In this year's PRIMARY election has your tribe supported candidates in any of the following ways:

FINANCIAL (Donating money to candidate(s)/Holding fundraisers)

_____ Yes. Candidate(s) and Office(s) _____

_____ No.

GOTV (Get out the vote efforts for a candidate or party)

_____ Yes. Candidate(s) and Office(s) _____

_____ No.

VOLUNTEER to work for a candidate

_____ Yes. Candidate(s) and Office(s) _____

_____ No.

OTHER way your tribe has supported candidate (Please explain.)

_____

_____

6. In this year's GENERAL election has your tribe supported candidates in any of the following ways:

FINANCIAL (Donating money to candidate(s)/Holding fundraisers)

_____ Yes. Candidate(s) and Office(s) _____

_____ No.

GOTV (Get out the vote efforts for a candidate or party)

_____ Yes. Candidate(s) and Office(s) _____

_____ No.

VOLUNTEER to work for a candidate

_____ Yes. Candidate(s) and Office(s) _____

_____ No.

OTHER way your tribe has supported candidate (Please explain.)

_____

_____

7. Some tribal governments feel that they influence the outcome of federal, state, and local elections, while others feel they do not have much of an influence on these elections. Which of the following describes the feeling of your tribal government?

_____ Our tribe has a good deal of influence on election outcomes.

_____ Our tribe has some influence on election outcomes.

_____ Our tribe has little influence on election outcomes.

_____ Our tribe has no influence on election outcomes.

8. How much attention do you feel the following governments pay to what your tribal government thinks when it makes policy affecting American Indians?

Federal government   _____ a good deal

                                        _____ some

                                        _____ not much

                                        _____ none

State government   _____ a good deal

                                        _____ some

                                        _____ not much

                                        _____ none

Local government   _____ a good deal

                                        _____ some

                                        _____ not much

                                        _____ none

9. Some tribes have become involved in federal, state, or local elections because of important issues. Please describe all of the issues that influence your decision to participate in this year's general election.

_____ Tribal cultural preservation. _____

_____ Economic development. _____

_____ Political sovereignty/autonomy. _____

10. Please rank the importance of each office to your tribe. Number your responses from 1 to 10, with 1 being the most important and 10 being the least important.

_____ County commissioner/supervisor

_____ Local Mayor

_____ U.S. Senator

_____ U.S. House of Representatives

_____ State attorney general

_____ State senator

_____ State House/General Assembly member

_____ President of the United States

_____ Governor of the state

_____ Other (please specify) _____

11. Has your tribe negotiated a compact with the government of your state?

_____ YES.
_____ NO.

A. If your tribe has previously negotiated a state compact, what was/were the area(s) addressed in the compact? (e.g., gaming, child welfare, health care, law enforcement, taxation, etc.)

_____

_____

12. Some tribes claim that the recent move to a tribal-state compacting system has infringed on their sovereignty, while others claim it has strengthened their sovereign control over Indian land. Based on your experience do you feel that tribal sovereignty on your reservation has:

_____ Been strengthened a great deal (specify which area(s)
_____)
_____ Been strengthened some (specify which area(s)
_____)
_____ Remained the same
_____ Decreased some (specify which area(s)
_____)
_____ Decreased a great deal (specify which area(s)
_____)
_____ Other. Please explain.

_____

If you would like the results of the survey sent to you please check below.

_____ Please send the survey results to me.
_____ I do not want the survey results.

Notes

PREFACE

1. Snipp, *American Indians*, 5.

2. Nagel, *American Indian Ethnic Renewal*, xii–xiii.

3. See Elazar, *Exploring Federalism*. For the history of the tensions between indigenous nations, states, and the federal government and the development of a model of "trifederalism," see Tebben, "American Trifederalism."

4. Deloria, "Self-Determination," 26.

5. Bush, "Remarks to the UNITY," 1483.

6. Alfred, *Peace, Power, Righteousness*, 59.

7. Ibid., 56.

8. Holm, Pearson, and Chavis, "Peoplehood."

9. Alfred and Corntassel, "Being Indigenous," 610; Thomas cited from "Tap-Roots of Peoplehood," 29.

10. See, e.g., Wilkins, *American Indian Sovereignty*; Wilkins and Lomawaima, *Uneven Ground*; Deloria and Lytle, *American Indians*; Deloria and Wilkins, *Tribes, Treaties*; and Wilkinson, *American Indians*.

CHAPTER 1

1. For a complete listing of the 562 federally recognized tribes in the United States (314 have reservations), see Indians.org, "American Indian Resource Directory." For a current listing of approximately 245 federally nonrecognized tribes by state, see "U.S. Federally Non-Recognized Indian Tribes—Index by State," http://www.kstrom.net/isk/maps/tribesnonrec.html (accessed May 8, 2007).

2. The Navajo (Diné) Nation operates on daylight savings time during the summer months (April–October) and returns to mountain standard time for the remainder of the year. Incidentally, the Hopi Nation, which is geographically encircled by the Diné Reservation, operates on mountain standard time for the entire year.

3. See *Worcestor v. Georgia*, 31 U.S. (6 Pet.) 515 (1832), which states, "The treaties, subsisting between the United States and the Cherokees, acknowledge their right as a sovereign nation to govern themselves and all persons who have settled within their territory, free from any right of legislative interference by the several states composing the United States of America." See also the federal case *Native American Church v. Navajo Tribal Council*, 272 F.2d 131 (1959): "But as declared in the decisions hereinbefore discussed, Indian tribes are not states. They have a status higher than that of states. They are subordinate and dependent nations possessed of all powers as such only to the extent that they have expressly been required to surrender them by the superior sovereign, the United States."

4. Spilde, "Rich Indian Racism," 5.

5. Spilde, "Acts of Sovereignty," 129.

6. Other aspects of stereotyping relating to phenotype and blood quantum also influence the perception of "authenticity" among indigenous peoples today. As political scientist Renée Cramer points out, "Many will also argue that high rates of intermarriage or out-migration seem to affect a group's chances for recognition in disproportionate ways. . . . Some tribal leaders told me that 'black blood' has been treated as a contaminant of pure 'Indian blood,' and that 'white blood,' thought problematic for recognition, has been viewed with less suspicion." Cramer, *Cash, Color, and Colonialism*, 60. For an in-depth analysis on the linkages between blood/phenotype and recognition, see Cramer's book.

7. Indianz.com. "Mankiller Says Perception a Threat to Sovereignty," June 16, 2005, http://indianz.com/News/2005/008785.asp (accessed July 1, 2005).

8. For examples see Bays and Fouberg, *Tribes and the States;* Mason, *Indian Gaming;* Henson and Taylor, "Native America"; Hicks and Dossett, "Principled Devolution"; Cornell and Taylor, "Sovereignty"; Tebben, "American Trifederalism"; Wilkins and Lomawaima, *Uneven Ground;* McCulloch, "Politics of Indian Gaming"; and Wilkinson, *American Indians.*

9. Despite intentions to continue the surveys of indigenous nation leaders, the funding for this project ended in 2001. Consequently, surveys for the 2002 and 2004 elections were not conducted.

10. Niezen, *Origins of Indigenism*, 171.

11. Hicks and Dossett, "Principled Devolution," 5.

12. *Indian Country Today*, "As Texas Goes, What for Indian Country?" August 23, 2002.

13. On January 3, 2006, Abramoff pleaded guilty in Washington to three federal felonies: conspiracy, fraud, and tax evasion. Abramoff and his former business partner Scanlon, who also pleaded guilty to fraud, admitted they conspired to defraud indigenous nations in Louisiana, Michigan, Mississippi, New Mexico, and Texas, who paid Abramoff and the companies he controlled roughly $55 million. Abramoff secretly took more than $21 million for himself. As of this writing, Abramoff has begun serving a sentence of five years and ten months at a minimum security prison camp in Cumberland, Maryland, for defrauding banks of $23 million in his purchase of a Florida casino cruise line. However, he has yet to be sentenced for his fraudulent activities regarding indigenous nations.

14. Schmidt, "Insiders Worked Both Sides of Gaming Issue," *Washington Post*, September 26, 2004.

15. Ibid.

16. See, e.g., Weston, *Native Americans in the News;* Coward, *Newspaper Indian.*

17. Berkhofer, *White Man's Indian*, 113.

18. Williams, *American Indian*, 326.

19. *Johnson v. McIntosh*, 21 U.S. 543, 5 L.Ed. 681, 8 Wheat, 543, p. 591.

20. For more in-depth treatments of the history of indigenous policy, see, e.g., Nabakov, *Native American Testimony;* Prucha, *Great Father;* Debo, *History of the Indians.*

21. See, e.g., Coward, *Newspaper Indian;* Debo, *And Still.*

22. Holm "Indian Lobbyists."

23. Nabakov, *Native American Testimony*, 233.

24. Debo, *And Still.*

25. Deloria, *Indian Reorganization Act.*

26. Weston, *Native Americans in the News*, 60.

27. Ibid., 87.

28. According to Vine Deloria, Jr., and Clifford Lytle, two major Indian nations, the Klamaths of Oregon and the Menominees of Wisconsin, and a number of other smaller bands and California *rancherias* were terminated. The larger Indian nations with treaty-based sovereignty were left nearly untouched. *American Indians*, 18–19.

29. Baylor, "Media Framing," 244.

30. Weston, *Native Americans in the News*, 134.

31. Reagan, "American Indian Policy."

32. Wilkins, "Reconsidering," 481. As Wilkins points out, there are "three limited exceptions in the federal statutes that authorize tribal-state compacts explicitly: Public Law 280 (67 St. 588), which permits flexible transfer of authority to the states and retrocession of jurisdiction to the federal government; the Indian Child Welfare Act of 1978 (92 St. 3069), which provides broad authority for compacts respecting the care and custody of Indian

children, and Class III (casino) gambling operations under the Indian Gaming Regulatory Act of 1988 (102 St. 2467)." "Reconsidering," 481.

33. Spilde, "Acts of Sovereignty," 144.

34. Wilkins, "Tribal-State Affairs," 55–57. The twelve territories were Colorado, Idaho, Iowa, Kansas, Montana, Nebraska, North Dakota, Oklahoma, Oregon, Washington, Wisconsin, and Wyoming.

35. Debo, *History of the Indians,* 122. Tsalagis (Cherokees) dubbed President Jackson "Chickensnake" because he "charmed" the Cherokees the way a snake charms a chicken.

36. Fixico, *Termination and Relocation,* 98.

37. American Indian Policy Center, "Threats to Tribal Sovereignty."

38. Ibid.

39. For the purposes of this research, a compact is defined as a "negotiated agreement between two autonomous entities that resolves questions of overlapping jurisdictional responsibility." Getches, "Negotiated Sovereignty," 120–21.

40. See, e.g., Elazar, *American Federalism;* Bowman and Kearney, *Resurgence of the States;* Conlan, *New Federalism;* Greve, *Real Federalism.*

41. Cornell and Taylor, "Sovereignty." See also Henson and Taylor, "Native America," another report from the Harvard Project on American Indian Economic Development.

42. American Indian Policy Center, "Threats to Tribal Sovereignty."

43. Gross, *Contemporary Federal Policy,* 112–13.

44. Bays and Fouberg, *Tribes and the States,* xiv.

45. Randy Noka (first councilmember of the Narragansett Nation), interview, Misquamicut, Rhode Island, August 10, 2001.

46. *Providence (R.I.) Journal-Bulletin,* "Casino Group to Inaugurate Statewide Campaign," October 26, 2000.

47. Michael Mello, "Narragansetts, in Casino Battle, Say They Carry On Ancestors' Fight," Associated Press, August 21, 2000.

48. Noka interview.

49. Save Our State, "Here Are Just a Few of the Many Reasons to Vote No on Question 1," http://www.saveourstate.com/thefacts.html (accessed November 16, 2006).

50. Ray Henry, "West Warwick Casino Cast as Rhode Island's Budget Savior, Villain," *Indian Country Today,* August 25, 2006, http://www.indiancountry.com/content.cfm?id=1096413544 (accessed November 16, 2006).

51. *Washington Post,* "Rhode Island Elections," November 7, 2006, http://www.washingtonpost.com/wp-srv/politics/elections/2006/ri.html (accessed November 16, 2006).

52. Scott Mayerowitz, "Despite the Casino Vote, Gambling Will Grow," *Providence (R.I.) Journal,* November 9, 2006, http://www.projo.com/news/

casino/content/casino9_11-09-06_JF2P1JI.3faab14.html (accessed November 16, 2006).

53. State of Maine, "Referendum Election Tabulations," November 4, 2003, http://www.Maine.gov/sos/ced/elec/2003n/gen03.sum.htm (accessed August 30, 2003).

54. Wilkins and Lomawaima, *Uneven Ground,* 187.

55. "Tribes and States," 2.

56. Steinman, "American Federalism."

57. Benny Smith (elder and director of counseling services at Haskell Indian Nations University), telephone interview, March 5, 2003.

58. Of these respondents, 52 percent indicated that their nation has negotiated an indigenous nation–state compact or runs a casino. *Indian Country Today,* "Attacks on Tribal Sovereignty: American Indian Opinion Leaders Respond," October 18, 2000.

59. Ibid.

60. *Indian Country Today,* "Anti-Indian Sovereignty Movement and Its Politicians," February 22, 2002, http://www.indiancountry.com/content. cfm?id=1014391922 (accessed August 27, 2004).

61. Lindsay, "Who We Are."

CHAPTER 2

1. For educational examples, see King and Springwood, *Team Spirits;* Connolly, "What's in a Name?"; Pewewardy, "Deculturalization"; Harjo, "Chief Offenders"; and Ganje, "Native American Stereotypes." For governmental policymaking examples, see Spilde, "Acts of Sovereignty"; Williams, *American Indian;* Williams, "Documents of Barbarism"; Berkhofer, *White Man's Indian.*

2. Schneider and Ingram, *Policy Design;* Schneider and Ingram, "Social Constructions."

3. U.S. General Accounting Office, *Indian Issues,* 32–34.

4. For full text of IGRA, visit the National Indian Gaming Commission's website: http://www.nigc.gov/LawsRegulations/IndianGaming Regulatory Act/tabid/605/Default.aspx (accessed May 15, 2007).

5. Wannamaker, "Let the Games Begin"; National Indian Gaming Resource Library, "Indian Gaming Facts," http://www.indiangaming.org/ library/indian-gaming-facts/index.shtml (accessed September 1, 2004).

6. Mark Fogarty, "Casino Analysis Still in Its Infancy," *Indian Country Today,* December 22, 2003, http://www.indiancountry.com/content.cfm?id= 1072109566 (accessed July 1, 2005).

7. Jeff Corntassel, "American Indians' Tribal Sovereignty Is under Siege," *Roanoke (Va.) Times,* September 28, 1997.

8. The final report of the National Gambling Impact Study Commission, a $5 million study, is a good example of how skewed statistics promote an inaccurate view of indigenous gaming wealth. Commission members visited only one indigenous gaming site, the Pequot's Foxwoods Resort Casino in Connecticut, the most lucrative casino in the world. Spilde, "Rich Indian Racism," 5.

9. Sara Phillips, "Dicey Future for Northwest Casinos," *High Country News*, December 22, 1997, http://www.hcn.org/servlets/hcn.Article?article _id=3872 (accessed September 29, 2005).

10. Schneider and Ingram, *Policy Design*, 106.

11. Ibid., 107.

12. While Schneider and Ingram's social constructions model includes "deviant" as one of four categories, this book uses "militant" in its place to more accurately reflect the socially constructed images of Native peoples.

13. Bartlett and Steele, "Playing the Political Slots," 38–39.

14. For other examples see Susan Schmidt, "A Jackpot from Indian Gaming Tribes," *Washington Post*, February 22, 2004; Nick Jeffreys, "Gambling Pays Off Big for Native Americans," *National Examiner*, April 8, 2003; Fred Dickey, "Who's Watching the Casinos? Indian Gaming Is Transforming California into the World's Gambling Mecca. Does Anyone in Sacramento Care?" *Los Angeles Times Magazine*, February 16, 2003, 12–15, 32–33; Micah Morrison, "Big Chief Patakai," *Wall Street Journal*, March 1, 2002.

15. *The Simpsons*, "Missionary: Impossible."

16. Joe Mathews, "Arnold Schwazenegger Ad Watch," *Los Angeles Times*, September 24, 2003. Other groups, such as Stand Up for California (http://www.standupca.org), also ran ads presenting all indigenous nations in California as rich and unscrupulous.

17. Schneider and Ingram, *Policy Design*, 107.

18. Some of the analysis of Fort McDowell Yavapai Nation's conflict with Governor Symington is based on Corntassel, "Deadliest Enemies."

19. Elizabeth Manning, "Gambling: A Tribe Hits the Jackpot," *High Country News*, April 1, 1996, http://www.hcn.org/servlets/hcn.Article?article _id=1738 (accessed July 12, 2003).

20. Bob Burns, "Fort McDowell Marks Sovereignty Day," *Fountain Hills (Ariz.) Times*, May 21, 1997, http://www.fhtimes.com/times/1997archives/ 5-21-97/sovereign.html (accessed July 1, 2005).

21. The actions of Fort McDowell citizens were commemorated with a monument unveiled in 1997. The granite monument depicts two dump trucks blocking a roadway with the words "Remembering May 12, 1992." May 12 is now officially recognized as Sovereignty Day at Fort McDowell and is celebrated each year with a five-mile march from the community recreation center to the expanded casino.

22. *Arizona Republic,* "Gaming Timeline," September 29, 2002, http://www.azcentral.com/ (accessed July 12, 2003).

23. This was a result of the governors interpretation that he need not negotiate gaming compacts following the Ninth Circuit Courts ruling in *Rumsey Indian Rancheria v. Wilson,* 41 F.3d 421, 427 (1994). The court found that the state of California need not negotiate gaming compacts with indigenous governments for games not authorized under state law. Applying the same logic to Arizona, Governor Symington refused to negotiate compacts with indigenous nations that did not already have them. This placed five indigenous nations in the position of not having negotiated compacts and facing the likelihood that the governor would not negotiate a gaming compact in the future.

24. Paul Davis, "A Modern Chief," *Providence (R.I.) Sunday Journal,* August 1, 2004.

25. U.S. Court of Appeals for the First Circuit, May 24, 2006 *Narragansett Indian Tribe v. State of Rhode Island,* no. 04-1155, pp. 3–4, http://www.ca1.uscourts.gov/pdf.opinions/04-1155EB-01A.pdf (accessed November 16, 2006).

26. Ibid., 13.

27. Ibid., 66.

28. Pam Belluck, "Tribe Loses Suit on Tax-Free Tobacco," *New York Times,* December 30, 2003; Indianz.com, "R.I. Escalates Fight Over Tribal Smoke Shop," July 15, 2003, http://indianz.com/News/show.asp?ID=2003/07/15/raid (accessed September 1, 2005).

29. While there are eight state-recognized Indian nations in Virginia, the six currently seeking federal recognition through the Thomasina E. Jordan Federal Recognition Act of 2001 (HR 2345) are the Chickahominy Nation, Eastern Chickahominy Nation, Monacan Nation, Nansemond Nation, Rappahannock Nation, and Upper Mattaponi Nation. The Mattaponi and Pamunkey nations have decided not to pursue this avenue of federal recognition.

30. See the Monacan Nation's website for a full history and details of upcoming events: http://www.monacannation.com.

31. For over two hundred Indian nations seeking to strengthen their communities through federal protections and programs, there are only three ways to obtain federal recognition, and each one is costly and time-consuming: litigation, petitioning the Branch of Acknowledgement and Research (BAR), and through an act of Congress. Litigation is probably the least used method because it is extremely costly and runs the risk of being overturned by a higher court.

A more common method is to petition the BAR, which is housed in the Bureau of Indian Affairs, and meet seven criteria set out by the Department of Interior. Petitioning Indian nations must establish that (1) they have been identified as an Indian entity since 1900; (2) they have functioned as a community since first contact with Europeans; (3) they have a historical maintenance of their political authority; (4) they have requirements for tribal citizenship; (5) they have a current governing body; (6) their membership is not made up of citizens from other federally recognized tribes; and (7) they have not have been terminated by the federal government during the 1950s and 1960s.

The third method for achieving federal recognition is through an act of Congress. Several Indian nations, such as the Lumbee and Houma, have attempted to achieve legislative acknowledgment but failed due to the intervention of competing interests. However, as an alternative to the lengthier BAR process, Indian nations are increasingly likely to pursue legislative avenues of recognition.

Whether through the BAR or congressional legislation, federal recognition is a costly enterprise—it is not unusual for Indian nations to spend $300,000 or more to prepare and lobby for their petition. For peoples who have historically been culturally and economically marginalized, such an expense is a tremendous resource drain on the community. For more on the politics of the federal recognition process, see Cramer, *Cash, Color, and Colonialism.*

32. Cook, "Monacan Indian Nation," 106.

33. Using the forced federalism survey questions (see appendix G), we contacted eighteen non-federally recognized indigenous nations in southeastern states in the United States (Alabama, Georgia, North Carolina, South Carolina, Tennessee, and Virginia,) during the 1998 election cycle. Representatives from seven of the eighteen nations contacted responded to my survey, which was a 39 percent response rate. This survey was taken mainly to see if the political activities of non-federally recognized indigenous nations differed greatly from those of federally recognized indigenous nations. Predictably, the rates of political participation among non-federally recognized indigenous nations were lower (especially endorsements, financial support, etc.) than those of federally recognized indigenous nations. However, the rates for getting out the vote among non-federally recognized indigenous nations responding to the survey (29 percent) were only slightly lower than those same voting efforts by federally recognized indigenous nations surveyed (38–40 percent). Due to the responding indigenous nations' desire to maintain their anonymity, we have chosen not to disclose the names of the seven nations who responded to the 1998 survey.

34. Cook, "Monacan Indian Nation," 110.

35. Spencer Hsu, "Possibility of Indian Casinos Splits Va.," *Washington Post,* September 17, 2000.

36. For more on the challenges facing the eight state-recognized Indian nations of Virginia today, see Corntassel and Tilley, "Virginia's Indian Nations."

37. James Jefferson, "Arkansas Panel Rejects State Recognition." *Indian Country Today*, November 1, 2005, http://www.indiancountry.com/content.cfm?id=1096411818 (accessed December 1, 2005).

38. Schneider and Ingram, *Policy Design*, 123; Schneider and Ingram, "Social Constructions," 341.

39. Center for Responsive Politics, "Indian Gaming."

40. Jim Adams, "Pequot Nation Flooded with Charity Requests," *Indian Country Today*, March 18, 2003, http://www.indiancountry.com/?1047999961 (accessed September 1, 2004).

41. Blumenthal, Formal Opinion, 2.

42. Ibid., 3.

43. Ryan, "Municipal and State Impact," 553–57.

44. Donald Trump, testimony before the Senate Select Committee on Indian Affairs, March 18, 1992.

45. In 2003 the BIA granted federal recognition to the Eastern Pequot Tribal Nation, which effectively combined two groups of Pequots (Paucatucks and Eastern Pequots) who had initially filed separate petitions for federal recognition. The Paucatucks have expressed the desire to open a casino and resort on their homelands once federal recognition has been conferred.

46. Benedict, *Without Reservation*, 100.

47. Connecticut Alliance against Casino Expansion, "About Us."

48. Schneider and Ingram, *Policy Design*, 119.

49. Ibid., 120.

50. James May, "Gov. Schwarzenegger Announces Compact Deals with Five Tribes," *Indian Country Today*, June 22, 2004, http://www.indiancountry.com/content.cfm?id=1087922755 (accessed September 1, 2004).

51. Kay Humphrey, "Will Compact Ban Dilute Influence?" *Indian Country Today*, June 27, 2001, http://www.indiancountry.com/content.cfm?id=1823 (accessed September 1, 2004).

52. Eleven indigenous nations operate eighteen casinos in Minnesota, and their compacts with the state, which were negotiated fifteen years ago, have no expiration date. The $350 million amount proposed by Pawlenty was considered to be 20–25 percent of the after-expenses revenue bet annually in Minnesota but was not an accurate revenue estimate. David Melmer, "Minnesota Tribes Asked to Pay for Tax Shortfall," *Indian Country Today*, October 29, 2004, http://www.indiancountry.com/content.cfm?id=1096409779 (accessed February 28, 2006).

53. *Indian Country Today,* "In Minnesota as Elsewhere, Standing Up to Governors Is a Good Idea," May 19, 2005, http://www.indiancountry.com/content.cfm?id=1096410947 (accessed February 28, 2006).

54. Pawlenty, "State of the State Address."

55. Schneider and Ingram, *Policy Design,* 126.

56. Ibid., 93–95.

57. Fanon, *Wretched of the Earth,* 210.

58. See, e.g., Edelman, *Symbolic Uses of Politics.*

59. Schneider and Ingram, *Policy Design,* 95.

60. Ibid.

61. National Governors' Association, *Policy Positions, 1986–87,* 114.

62. Ibid.

63. National Governors' Association, *Policy Positions, 1987–88,* 46.

64. National Governors' Association, *Policy Positions, 1990–91,* 1.

65. "EC-1 Indian Gaming" was initially adopted during the winter 1993 meeting but became effective from 1995 to 1997. National Governors' Association, *Policy Positions, 1996,* 9.

66. National Governors' Association, *Policy Positions, July 1996,* 151.

67. Ibid., 34.

68. Ibid.

69. Ibid., 122.

70. National Governors' Association, *Policy Positions, 2000,* 2.

71. Scheppach to Babbit, October 14, 1999. Copy in author's possession.

72. See "EDC-6. The Role of States, the Federal Government, and Indian Tribal Governments with Respect to Indian Gaming and Other Economic Issues Policy," National Governors' Association, *Policy Positions, 2005,* 1–3.

73. Ibid.

74. Ibid.

75. Ibid., 1.

76. Ibid., 4.

77. State Legislation Database on Native American Issues, National Conference on State Legislatures, http://www.ncsl.org/orpgrams/esnr/statetribal.cfm (accessed September 1, 2004).

78. Ibid.

79. Steinman, "American Federalism," 103.

80. Ibid.

81. Ibid.

82. *Tribal Observer,* "Zogby International Conducts Follow-up Poll for the Tribe," December 1, 2001, http://www.sagchip.org/tribalobserver/article.asp?article=90 (accessed November 16, 2006). Commissioned by the Saginaw Chippewa Nation, the December 2001 poll was a follow-up to a July 2000 Zogby poll of 1,500 registered voters nationwide and yielded similar

findings. In the December 2001 Zogby poll, 1,530 registered voters were interviewed nationwide, and the margin of error for the survey was +/- 2.6 percent.

83. Nadasdy, "Transcending the Debate over the Ecologically Noble Indian," 312.

84. For an excellent historical and contemporary analysis of indigenous water use and settlement agreements, see McCool, *Native Waters.*

85. Nadasdy, "Transcending the Debate," 322.

CHAPTER 3

1. Wilkins, "Inquiry," 733.

2. For more historical details on these diplomatic missions, see Viola, *Diplomats in Buckskins;* Williams, *Linking Arms Together;* and Deloria and DeMallie, *Documents of Diplomacy.*

3. Deloria and Wilkins, *Tribes, Treaties,* 16.

4. Ibid.

5. Deloria and DeMallie, *Documents of Diplomacy,* 249–52.

6. Ibid., 681–83.

7. Viola, *Diplomats in Buckskins,* 20.

8. Ibid., 104.

9. Campisi, "Meaning in the Reverse."

10. Viola, *Diplomats in Buckskins,* 24.

11. Ibid.

12. Ibid.

13. Ibid., 28.

14. Ibid., 147.

15. Holm, "Indian Lobbyists."

16. Ibid.

17. Ibid.

18. Cherokee Nation Washington Office, "Mission," http://www.cnwo.org/ (accessed November 16, 2006).

19. Qtd. in Wilkins, "Inquiry," 735.

20. Alfred, "Why Play," 1. The Mohawk Nation is split by the U.S.-Canadian border. However, Mohawks disregard these illegally imposed borders and generally cross their traditional homelands at will.

21. Jeff Heinrich, "Kahnawake: An Election-Free Zone," *Montreal Gazette,* January 15, 2006, http://www.canada.com/montrealgazette/news/insight/story.html?id=01881abd-15a4-4729-ba8b-d91ba0f98a32 (accessed January 31, 2006).

22. Ibid.

23. Ibid.

24. *Indian Country Today,* "2000 Election: American Indian Opinion Leaders Cast Vote," September 27, 2000.

25. Ibid.

26. Duffy, "Attitudinal Study," 7.

27. For a good discussion of the process of co-optation, see Lacy, "Political Relations."

28. Little Bear, "Should Natives Vote?"

29. Lacy, "Political Relations," 83.

30. Alfred, *Peace, Power, Righteousness,* 74.

31. Lacy, "Political Relations," 91, 93.

32. Russ Lehman, telephone interview, Blacksburg, Virginia, March 2, 2001.

33. Native campaign donations have predominantly gone to Democrats in the past, but this trend has been changing somewhat lately. In 1992, 81 percent of all indigenous nations' campaign donations to political parties went to Democrats. During the 2006 election, 62 percent of all indigenous campaign donations went to Democrats. This further demonstrates that indigenous nations tend to provide support according to issues of importance to them, rather than solely basing donations on party affiliation. For more monetary figures, see Center for Responsive Politics, "Indian Gaming."

34. Barsh, "Indian Policy," 55.

35. Ibid., 66.

36. Data taken from research database at Center for Public Integrity, "Lobby Watch," http://www.publicintegrity.org/lobby/ (accessed February 28, 2006).

37. Ibid.

38. Ibid.

39. McCool, "Indian Voting," 105–33.

40. H. Peterson, "Political Participation," 125. Besides Peterson's work, there are a limited number of studies in this area: LaVelle, "Strengthening Tribal Sovereignty"; Porter, "Demise of the Ongwehoweh"; Corntassel and Witmer, "Tribal Government Support"; G. Peterson, "Native American Turnout"; McCool, "Indian Voting"; Ritt, "Social and Political Views"; Steiner, *New Indians.*

41. John M. Broder, "Tribes Now Ready to Deal with Their New Governor," *New York Times,* November 9, 2003.

42. Native Vote, http://www.nativevote.org. This organization is gearing up for a "Native Vote 2008" campaign to register new Indian voters.

43. Porter, "Demise of the Ongwehoweh," 153.

44. Ibid., 110.

45. Ibid., 154.

46. Ibid., 170.

47. LaVelle, "Strengthening Tribal Sovereignty," 559.

48. Ibid., 555.

49. For a detailed state-by-state breakdown of the indigenous 2004 vote, see First American Education Project, "Native Vote 2004," http://www. nativevote.org.

50. Indigenous nations contributed $130,193 and $126,300, respectively, to Free's U.S. House of Representatives bid and Carson's U.S. Senate campaign.

51. For a full transcript of Coburn's comments, see the Cherokee Nation's website: http://www.cherokee.org/NewsArchives/ announcements/ 2004-Coburn-Altus.asp.

52. Chad "Corntassel" Smith, interview by Jeff Corntassel, July 1, 2005. See appendix E for a full transcription of the interview.

53. Ibid.

54. For more on INDN's List, visit their website: http://www.indnslist. org/.

55. Brian Daffron, "INDN's List Celebrates Success after First Election Cycle's Results Come In," *Indian Country Today,* November 17, 2006, http: //www.indiancountry.com/content.cfm?id=1096414032 (accessed November 17, 2006).

56. Cornell, *Return of the Native,* 183.

57. Ibid., 173–81.

58. Johnson, Nagel, and Champagne, *American Indian Activism;* Nagel, *American Indian Ethnic Renewal;* Stern, *Loud Hawk;* Matthiessen, *In the Spirit of Crazy Horse;* Deloria, *Behind the Trail;* Deloria, *We Talk, You Listen;* Deloria, *Custer Died for Your Sins.*

59. Corntassel and Witmer, "Tribal Government Support," 513.

60. For more details about the Harvard Project on American Indian Economic Development, see their website: http://www.ksg.harvard.edu/ hpaied/. For more on the inception of the nation-building model, see Cornell and Kalt, *Reloading the Dice.*

61. Cornell, Jorgensen, Kalt, and Spilde, *Seizing the Future,* 4–5.

62. European Stability Initiative, "Helsinki Moment." See also, Center for Economic and Social Justice, "A New Model of Nation-Building for Citizens of Iraq," http://www.cesj.org/thirdway/paradigmpapers/iraq-nation building.htm (accessed November 1, 2006).

63. Nagel, *American Indian Ethnic Renewal,* 122–29.

64. Ibid., 123.

65. Gross, *Contemporary Federal Policy,* 94.

66. Ibid., 108.

67. Mason, *Indian Gaming,* 242.

68. Ibid., 45.

69. Wilkins, "Inquiry," 734.

70. Tarow, *Power in Movement,* 2.

71. Ibid., 5.
72. Tully, "Struggles of Indigenous Peoples," 39.
73. Hechter, "Internal Colonialism Revisited," 185–86.
74. Wilkins, "Modernization," 405.
75. Ibid.

CHAPTER 4

1. Corntassel and Witmer, "Tribal Government Support."
2. Corntassel and Witmer, "Battlelines of Sovereignty."
3. Taylor sent an eight-question survey to 245 presidents or chiefs of federally recognized indigenous nations and had a 23 percent response rate. For more details of his survey results, see Taylor, *States and Their Indian Citizens*, 254–55.
4. Corntassel and Witmer, "Tribal Government Support," 518–19.
5. Responses in the "other" category included, in 2000, "things that personally pertain to the tribe's issues," "non-Indians supporting Indian policies and sovereignty," "political contributions were given to both parties in the names of certain candidates," "recognition of tribal interests," "negative or positive outlook/comments re: Indian issues," "we support those that are sensitive to tribal issues," "local politics promises to tribes about presidential government-to-government relationship," and "nuclear waste"; in 1998, "qualifications of a candidate are critical," "we ask only that our peoples vote be counted," "member of another tribe ran for Congress," "candidates' stance on Indian issues," "his stand on gaming," "support for tribal issues, relates to tribal people well," and "DHHS, Division of Cost Allocation, berates and penalizes us for anything which might even appear to involve politics and threatens to take our funding"; in 1996, "Native American candidate," "the other candidate was anti-Indian," and "candidate's past support of Indian nation"; and in 1994, "knowledge of Indian issues," "experience and track record," "marginal support of Indian issues," "Indian policies," and "voting is left to each individual."
6. Answers to question 4, "What issues were important in this year's election?" included, in 2000, "support for Indian sovereignty" (4 responses), "support for Indian issues" (4 responses), "IHS water rights," and "land into trust"; in 1998, "support for Indian sovereignty" (14 responses), "gaming" (14 responses), "education" (3 responses), "environment" (2 responses), "taxes" (2 responses), "support of tribal legislation/government" (2 responses), "treaty rights," "economy," "fishing," "forestry," "English-only initiative," "wolf snare ban," "support for tribal programs," "support for Native American programs," "Native friendly," "Indian equity," and "to beat [political candidate's

name omitted]"; in 1996, "support for Indian sovereignty" (13 responses), "gaming" (9 responses), "budget cuts" (6 responses), "any issue dealing with Native Americans" (3 responses), "welfare reform" (3 responses), "treaty rights" (2 responses), "education/student assistance" (2 responses), "jobs," "environment, "land claim settlement/excise tax," "mining moratorium," "health funding," "water and land issues," "the assault on Indian tribes by the Republican-controlled Congress," "advocate for better services and relationship with tribal government," "our land restoration," and "the fiduciary responsibility of the U.S. government to Indians"; and in 1994, "gaming" (14 responses), "good understanding of Indian issues/government-to-government relationship" (4 responses), "support for Indian sovereignty" (3 responses), "taxation" (3 responses), "environment" (2 responses), "health care" (2 responses), "treaty rights" (2 responses), "natural resources (2)," "economic development," "tribal compacts," "funding for small tribes," "supports tribe in cultural preservation efforts," housing," "education," "mining," "law enforcement," "economy," and "child support."

7. Mark Flatten, "What Indian Money Buys," *East Valley Tribune* (Phoenix, Ariz.), October 22, 2006, http://www.eastvalleytribune.com/index.php?sty= 77175 (accessed November 16, 2006).

8. Responses in the "other" category included, in 2000, "encouraged members to vote (2 responses)," "sponsored meetings," and "employee education"; in 1998, "asked community to support," "with moral support and advice when requested," "sponsored press conference," "information to voters on candidates' position and record," "voter registration/specific issue support (lottery)," "letter writing campaign," "spoke to groups," "meet the candidates forum," "by word of mouth," and "media (newspapers, radio, and literature sheets)"; in 1996, "receptions, rallies, billboards on tribal lands, etc.," "let them post signs on reservation," "by support letter," "held candidate forums in community," "National Indian Unity PAC," "letters of support, newsletter articles," "political forums," "distributed leaflets about candidates' positions or issues reflecting the tribe," "asking other tribes to support candidates," "flyers and signs," "visible at all Democratic rallies," and "candidates visiting local communities on the reservation"; and in 1994, "posters, meeting, questions to candidates on tribal issues and concerns," "circulated nomination petitions, invited candidates to meet the people, taken candidates on tours of reservations and facilities, attended their fund-raisers," "we allowed candidate to use our phones for phone banks," "by inviting them to appear at tribal functions," "provided issue papers on various topics to primary candidates for governor," "helped with having fundraisers," "candidate made an appearance for tribal support and chairman urged tribal members to support candidate—candidate won election," "supported tribal member running for governor," and "radio station used to back candidates."

9. Jack McNeel, "Native Vote Is Big in Montana," *Indian Country Today,* November 17, 2006, http://www.indiancountry.com/content.cfm?id=1096414040 (accessed November 17, 2006).

10. The two other explanatory variables were held constant at their mean—2.568 for state attitude and .566 for compact with state.

11. David Melmer, "High Voter Turnout Credited with Senator Pressler's Defeat," *Indian Country Today,* November 25, 1996.

12. U.S. Census figures used to determine percent of the county that were indigenous. U.S. Bureau of the Census, "Social and Economic Characteristics."

13. Election results are available at the South Dakota secretary of state webpage: http://www.state.sd.us/sos/sos.htm. See also David Melmer, "Candidates Supporting Indian Issues Are Elected: Educating the New Congress Is Prioritized," *Indian Country Today,* November 25, 1996.

14. The Arizona Republic, "Gaming Timeline."

15. This was a result of the governors interpretation that he need not negotiate gaming compacts following the Ninth Circuit Courts ruling in *Rumsey Indian Rancheria v. Wilson,* 41 F.3d 421, 427 (9th Cir. 1994). The court found that the state of California need not negotiate gaming compacts with indigenous governments for games not authorized under state law. Applying the same logic to Arizona, Governor Symington refused to negotiate compacts with indigenous nations that did not already have them. This placed five indigenous nations in the position of not having negotiated compacts and facing the likelihood that the governor would not negotiate a gaming compact in the future.

16. Mark Engler, "Voters Pass Prop 201," *Navajo Times,* November 7, 1996. See also Stan Bindell, "Native Americans Can Fight Back by Voting," *Navajo Times,* November 7, 1996.

17. The indigenous population in Apache County in 1999 was 53,251, or 77.7 percent of the population. In Coconino County the number was 34,359, or 30 percent of the population. U.S. Bureau of the Census, "American Indian Population."

18. Information on voting in Coconino and Apache County was obtained from each county's election office. The documents are the official election canvass for the corresponding year.

19. McCool, "Voting Patterns."

20. Tom Wanamaker, "Maine Casino Plans Go Up in Flames," *Indian Country Today,* November 14, 2003, http://www.indiancountry.com/content.cfm?id=1068836967> (accessed February 28, 2006).

21. Jim Adams, "Secret of Indian Casinos: Everyone Wins," *Indian Country Today,* December 13, 2002, http://www.indiancountry.com/?1039788606 (accessed September 1, 2004).

22. Little Bear, "Should Natives Vote?"

CHAPTER 5

1. Alfred, *Wasáse*, 242–43.

2. For more details on treaty operations and applications under international law, see Van Dervort, *International Law*, 375–21; Shaw, *International Law*, 632–73.

3. Corntassel, "Deadliest Enemies."

4. United Nations Commission on Human Rights, *Study on Treaties*, 19.

5. Alfred, "Deconstructing the Treaty Process."

6. Ibid., 41.

7. Tully, "Struggles of Indigenous Peoples," 50. For more on the basic differences between U.S. and Canadian indigenous policies, see Brock, "Finding Answers."

8. Tsosie, "Negotiating Economic Survival," 52n157.

9. Wilkins, "Reconsidering."

10. Getches, "Negotiated Sovereignty," 120–21.

11. Ibid., 924.

12. United Nations Commission on Human Rights, *Study on Treaties*, 42.

13. One clear exception to this is the Mashantucket Pequots, whose gaming rights are held in perpetuity through publication in the Federal Register as "federal procedures" under the dictates of IGRA (see details in chapter 2).

14. Gibb, "Intergovernmental Compacts," 922.

15. For an overview of the provisions of IGRA, see Getches, Wilkinson, and Williams, *Federal Indian Law*, chapter 9, "Reservation Economic Development."

16. For additional examples of indigenous-state gaming compacts, see National Congress of American Indians, "Gaming Compacts," http://www.ncai. org/Gaming_Compacts.103.0.html (accessed September 1, 2004).

17. Efforts to bypass litigation have not always been effective. E.g., the Supreme Court ruled in *Seminole Tribe of Florida v. Florida*, 517 U.S. 44 (1996) that the provision in IGRA allowing indigenous nations to sue if a state does not negotiate in good faith was not valid, as states were protected from suit by the eleventh amendment to the U.S. Constitution. See also Getches, Wilkinson, and Williams, *Federal Indian Law*, for an overview of additional cases.

18. Tsosie, "Negotiating Economic Survival," 52n157.

19. Trosper, "Economic Policy."

20. Qtd. in Steve Wideman, "Gaming Revenue Transforms Life for Oneida Tribe," *Appleton (Wis.) Post-Crescent*, July 8, 2005, http://www. wisinfo. com/postcrescent/news/oneida2005/update_21743786.shtml (accessed February 28, 2006).

21. Qtd. in ibid.

22. Qtd. in ibid.

23. Ibid.

24. Qtd. in ibid.

25. *California v. Cabazon Band of Mission Indians,* 48 U.S. 202.

26. *Oklahoma Tax Commission v. Citizen Band of Potawatomi,* 489 U.S. 505 (1991).

27. *Oklahoma Tax Commission v. Chickasaw Nation,* 115 S. Ct. 2214 (1995).

28. Washington State also had gaming measures on the ballot in 1995 and 1996. They failed in large part because they lacked support from all but a few indigenous nations and were not viewed as a credible alternative to gaming compacts already in force.

29. For an indigenous-state compact list, see National Congress of American Indians, "Gaming Compacts," http://www.ncai.org/Gaming_Compacts.103.0.html (accessed September 1, 2004).

30. Lombardi, "Long Road Traveled."

31. Ibid.

32. For tribal information for those with approved tribal-state compacts as of July 6, 2000, see U.S. Department of the Interior, Bureau of Indian Affairs, "Tribal-State Compact List."

33. James May, "Gov. Schwarzenegger Announces Compact Deals with Five Tribes," *Indian Country Today,* June 22, 2004, http://www.indiancountry.com/content.cfm?id=1087922755 (accessed September 1, 2004).

34. Cafferty, "Gambling across State Lines."

35. The information available for a number of states is incomplete or preliminary in the report, making these results suggestive. Campaign financing data for federal officials shows a similar trend with increases to federal elected officials clearly increasing throughout the 1990s from $0 in 1990 to nearly $3 million in 2000. Center for Responsive Politics website, http://www.opensecrets.org/.

36. Center for Responsive Politics, "Indian Gaming."

37. Mason, *Indian Gaming.*

38. From National Conference of State Legislatures, "Native American Legislators (2007)," http://www.ncsl.org/programs/statetribe/2007triblg.htm (accessed July 2, 2007). The data for 2002 and 2005 was not available through the National Conference of State Legislatures. Thanks to Jeanne Kaufmann for providing this information.

39. For more on INDN's List, visit their website: http://www. indnslist. org/.

40. Tsosie, "Negotiating Economic Survival," 52n157.

CHAPTER 6

1. Indianz.com, "Mankiller Says Perception a Threat to Sovereignty," June 16, 2005, http://indianz.com/News/2005/008785.asp (accessed July 1, 2005).

2. Spilde, "Acts of Sovereignty," 129.

3. Tsosie, "Negotiating Economic Survival," 52n157.

4. Pommersheim clarifies that sovereignty accords would "involve no waiver or abridgement of any rights by either side." See Pommersheim, "Tribal-State Relations," 268–70.

5. Ibid., 269.

6. See the Indianz.com website for more details: http://www.indianz.com/.

7. Qtd. in Niezen, *Origins of Indigenism*, 171.

8. American Indian Policy Center, "Threats to Tribal Sovereignty."

9. Government of the Netherlands, *Petition*, 3. Based on the actions of Canada and Great Britain, Deskaheh was denied a hearing at the League of Nations. However, several states at the time were supportive of his petition: Estonia, the Netherlands, Ireland, Panama, Japan, and Persia. Niezen, *Origins of Indigenism*, 35.

10. Taiaiake Alfred and Jeff Corntassel, "A Decade of Rhetoric for Indigenous Peoples," *Indian Country Today*, May 11, 2004, http://www. indiancountry.com/content.cfm?id=1084285271 (accessed August 30, 2004).

11. Ibid.

12. Commission on Security and Cooperation in Europe, *Fulfilling Our Promises*, 164.

13. For more on this, see Ross, *Returning to the Teachings;* Porter, "Strengthening Tribal Sovereignty."

14. American Indian Policy Center, "Threats to Tribal Sovereignty."

15. Benny Smith (elder and director of counseling services at Haskell Indian Nations University), telephone interview, March 5, 2003.

16. Russ Lehman (managing director of the First Americans Education Project), telephone interview, Blacksburg, Virginia, March 2, 2001.

17. Belluck, "States Moving to End Tribes' Tax-Free Sales," *New York Times*, September 28, 2003, A2.

18. Smith, *Conquest*, 137.

19. Deloria and DeMallie, *Documents of Diplomacy*, 681.

20. See, e.g., Williams, *Linking Arms Together.*

21. Corntassel, "Partnership in Action?"

22. Alfred, *Wasáse*, 242–43.

23. See Corntassel and Holm, *Power of Peoplehood.*

Bibliography

COURT CASES

California v. Cabazon Band of Mission Indians. 48 U.S. 202 (1987).

Johnson v. M'Intosh. 21 U.S. 543, 5 L.Ed. 681, 8 Wheat. 543 (1823).

Narragansett Indian Tribe v. State of Rhode Island. U.S. Court of Appeals for the 1st Circuit. No. 04-1155 (2006).

Native American Church v. Navajo Tribal Council. 272 F.2d 131 (1959).

Oklahoma Tax Commission v. Citizen Band of Potawatomi. 489 U.S. 505 (1991).

Oklahoma Tax Commission v. Chickasaw Nation. 115 S. Ct. 2214 (1995).

Rumsey Indian Rancheria v. Wilson. 41 F.3d 421, 427 (9th Cir. 1994).

Seminole Tribe of Florida v. Florida. 517 U.S. 44 (1996).

Worcestor v. Georgia. 31 U.S. (6 Pet.) 515 (1832).

BOOKS AND ARTICLES

Adams, Jim. "Mixed Referenda Debunk Casino Backlash Claim." *Indian Country Today,* November 5, 2004. *http://www.indiancountry.com/content. cfm?id=1096409815* (accessed February 28, 2006).

Alfred, Taiaiake. "Deconstructing the British Columbia Treaty Process." *Balayi: Culture, Law, and Colonialism* 3 (2001): 37–66.

———. *Peace, Power, Righteousness: An Indigenous Manifesto.* Ontario: Oxford University Press, 1999.

———. *Wasáse: Indigenous Pathways of Action and Freedom.* Ontario: Broadview Press, 2005.

———. "Why Play the White Man's Game?" *Wind Speaker* 17, no. 4 (October 1, 1999).

Alfred, Taiaiake, and Jeff Corntassel. "Being Indigenous: Resurgences against Contemporary Colonialism." *Government and Opposition: An International Journal of Comparative Politics* 40, no. 4 (2005): 597–614.

Allen, W. Ron. "Gorton's Lost Crusade." *Native Americas* 17, no. 3 (2000): 32–33.

American Indian Policy Center. "Threats to Tribal Sovereignty." 1998. *http: //www.airpi.org/research/sovthreat.html* (accessed August 31, 2004).

Barsh, Russel Lawrence. "Indian Policy at the Beginning of the 1990s: The Trivialization of Struggle." In *American Indian Policy*, ed. Lyman H. Letgers and Fremont J. Lyden, 55–70. Westport, Conn.: Greenwood Press, 1994.

Bartlett, Donald L., and James B. Steele. "Playing the Political Slots: Part Two: How Indian Casino Interests Have Learned the Art of Buying Influence in Washington." *Time* 160, no. 26 (December 23, 2002): 38–47.

Baylor, Timothy. "Media Framing of Movement Protest: The Case of American Indian Protest." *Social Science Journal* 33, no. 3 (1996): 241–55.

Bays, Bray A., and Erin Hogan Fouberg. *The Tribes and the States: Geographies of Intergovernmental Interaction.* Boulder: Rowman and Littlefield, 2002.

Benedict, Jeff. *Without Reservation: How a Controversial Indian Tribe Rose to Power and Built the World's Largest Casino.* New York: HarperCollins, 2001.

Berkhofer, Robert F., Jr. *The White Man's Indian.* New York: Vintage Books, 1979.

Blumenthal, Richard. Formal Opinions 1993-2004, Attorney General of Connecticut. February 11, 1993. *http://www.ct.gov/ag/cwp/view.asp?A= 1770&Q=281384* (accessed May 7, 2007).

Bowman, Ann, and Richard C. Kearney. *The Resurgence of the States.* Englewood Cliffs, N.J.: Prentice-Hall, 1986.

Brock, Kathy. "Finding Answers in Difference: Canadian and Aboriginal Policy Compared." In *Canada and the United States: Differences that Count*, ed. David M. Thomas, 2nd ed., 338–58. Peterborough, Ont.: Broadview Press, 2000.

Bush, George W. "Remarks to the UNITY: Journalists of Color Convention and a Question-and-Answer Session." Presidential Documents Online, August 6, 2004. *http://frwebgate.access.gpo.gov/cgi-bin/getdoc.cgi?dbname= 2004_presidential_documents&docid=pd09au04_txt-22* (accessed August 30, 2004).

Cafferty, Heather. "Gambling across State Lines." The National Institute on Money in State Politics, June 23, 1999. *www.followthemoney.org/issues/ gamble.html* (accessed November 1, 2000).

Campisi, Jack. "Meaning in the Reverse: Indian Peace Medals." *Cross Paths* (Winter 2003–2004). *http://www.pequotmuseum.org/Home/CrossPaths/ Cross PathsWinter20034/MeaningintheReverseIndianPeaceMedals.htm* (accessed November 16, 2006).

Center for Responsive Politics. "Indian Gaming: Top Contributors to Federal Candidates and Parties." 2000–2006. *http://www.opensecrets.org/ industries/ contrib.asp?Ind=G6550&cycle=2006* (accessed November 16, 2006).

Commission on Security and Cooperation in Europe. *Fulfilling Our Promises: The United States and the Helsinki Final Act: A Status Report.* Washington, D.C.: Commission on Security and Cooperation in Europe, 1979.

Conlan, Timothy. *From New Federalism to Devolution: Twenty-Five Years of Intergovernmental Reform.* Washington, D.C.: Brookings Institution Press, 1998.

Connecticut Alliance against Casino Expansion. "About Us." 2002. *http://www.connecticutalliance.org/about.asp* (accessed September 1, 2004).

Connolly, Mark R. "What's in a Name? A Historical Look at Native American–Related Nicknames and Symbols at Three U.S. Universities." *Journal of Higher Education* 71, no. 5 (2000): 515–47.

Cook, Sam. "The Monacan Indian Nation: Asserting Tribal Sovereignty in the Absence of Federal Recognition." *Wicazo Sa Review* 2 (Fall 2002): 91–116.

Cornell, Stephen. *The Return of the Native: American Indian Political Resurgence.* New York: Oxford University Press, 1988.

Cornell, Stephen, Miriam Jorgensen, Joseph P. Kalt, and Katherine Spilde. *Seizing the Future: Why Some Native Nations Do and Others Don't.* Joint Occasional Papers on Native Affairs, no. 2005-01. The Harvard Project on American Indian Economic Development, 2005. *http://www.jopna.net/pubs/jopna_2005-01_Seizing.pdf* (accessed July 1, 2005).

Cornell, Stephen, and Joseph P. Kalt. *Reloading the Dice: Improving the Chances for Economic Development on American Indian Reservations.* Joint Occasional Papers on Native Affairs, no. 2003-02. The Harvard Project on American Indian Economic Development, 2003. *http://www.jopna.net/pubs/jopna_2003-02_Dice.pdf* (accessed July 1, 2005).

Cornell, Stephen, and Jonathan Taylor. "Sovereignty, Devolution, and the Future of Tribal-State Relations." National Congress of American Indians Mid-Year Session, June 26, 2000.

Corntassel, Jeff. "'Deadliest Enemies' or Partners in the 'Utmost Good Faith': Conflict Resolution Strategies for Indian Nation/State Disputes in an Era of Forced Federalism." *Ayaangwaamizin: International Journal of Indigenous Philosophy* 3, no. 1 (2003): 141–67.

———. "New Battlelines of Sovereignty for American Indians: Negotiating Tribal/State Compacts in an Era of Forced Federalism." *International Review on the Rights of Indigenous Peoples* 2, no. 2 (2001): 11–22.

———. "Partnership in Action? Indigenous Political Mobilization and Co-optation during the First UN Indigenous Decade (1995–2004)." *Human Rights Quarterly* 29 (February 2007): 137–66.

Corntassel, Jeff, and Tom Holm. *The Power of Peoplehood: Contemporary Indigenous Community-Building.* Austin: University of Texas Press, forthcoming.

Corntassel, Jeff, and Tomas Hopkins Primeau. "Indigenous 'Sovereignty' and International Law: Revised Strategies for Pursuing 'Self-Determination.'" *Human Rights Quarterly* 17, no. 2 (1995): 343–65.

Corntassel, Jeff, and Reeva G. Tilley. "Virginia's Indian Nations: Policy Issues and Solutions for Future Generations." *Virginia Issues and Answers: A Public Policy Forum* 8, no. 2 (Spring 2002): 16–21.

Corntassel, Jeff, and Richard Witmer. "American Indian Tribal Government Support of Office-Seekers: Findings from the 1994 Election." *Social Science Journal* 34, no. 4 (1997): 511–25.

———. "Battlelines of Sovereignty: Forced Federalism and American Indian Mobilization in the 1990s." Paper delivered at the annual meeting of the American Political Science Association, Washington, D.C., August 30–September 3, 2000.

Coward, John M. *The Newspaper Indian: Native American Identity in the Press, 1820–90.* Urbana: University of Illinois Press, 1999.

Cramer, Renée. *Cash, Color, and Colonialism: The Politics of Tribal Acknowledgement.* Norman: University of Oklahoma Press, 2005.

Debo, Angie. *And Still the Waters Run.* Norman: University of Oklahoma Press, 1984.

———. *A History of the Indians of the United States.* Norman: University of Oklahoma Press, 1970.

Deloria, Vine, Jr. *Behind the Trail of Broken Treaties.* 2nd ed. Austin: University of Texas Press, 1985.

———. *Custer Died for Your Sins.* New York: McMillen, 1969.

———. *The Indian Reorganization Act: Congresses and Bills.* Norman: University of Oklahoma Press, 2002.

———. "Self-Determination and the Concept of Sovereignty." In *Economic Development in American Indian Reservations,* ed. Roxanne Dunbar-Ortiz and Larry Emerson, 22–28. Albuquerque: University of New Mexico Press, 1979.

———. *We Talk, You Listen: New Tribes, New Turf.* New York: McMillen, 1970.

Deloria, Vine, Jr., and Raymond J. DeMallie. *Documents of American Indian Diplomacy: Treaties, Agreements, and Conventions, 1775–1979.* Norman: University of Oklahoma Press, 1999.

Deloria, Vine, Jr., and Clifford Lytle. *American Indians, American Justice.* Austin: University of Texas Press, 1983.

———. *The Nations Within: The Past and Future of American Indian Sovereignty.* Austin: University of Texas Press, 1984.

Deloria, Vine, Jr., and David E. Wilkins. *Tribes, Treaties, and Constitutional Tribulations.* Austin: University of Texas Press, 1999.

Duffy, Diane. "An Attitudinal Study of Native American Patriotism." Paper presented at the annual meeting of the International Society for Political Psychology, Krakow, Poland, July 22, 1997.

Edelman, Murray. *The Symbolic Uses of Politics.* Urbana: University of Illinois Press, 1964.

Elazar, Daniel J. *American Federalism: A View from the States*. New York: Harper and Row, 1984.

———. *Exploring Federalism*. Tuscaloosa: University of Alabama Press, 1986.

European Stability Initiative. "The Helsinki Moment—European Member State Building in the Balkans." February 1, 2005. *http://www.esiweb.org/pdf/esi_document_id_65.pdf* (accessed February 1, 2006).

Fanon, Frantz. *The Wretched of the Earth*. New York: Grove Press, 1963.

First American Education Project. "Native Vote 2004: A National Survey and Analysis of Efforts to Increase the Native Vote in 2004 and the Results Achieved." 2004. *http://www.ccp.org/resources/libraryresearch/vote-2.attachment/302246/Native%20Votes%20Report%202004.pdf* (accessed February 28, 2006)

Fixico, Donald L. *Termination and Relocation: Federal Indian Policy, 1945–1960*. Albuquerque: University of New Mexico Press, 1986.

Foreman, Grant. *Indian Removal*. Norman: University of Oklahoma Press, 1972.

Ganje, Lucy. "Native American Stereotypes." In *Images That Injure*, ed. Paul M. Lester, 41–46. Westport: Praeger, 1996.

Getches, David. "Negotiated Sovereignty: Intergovernmental Agreements with American Indian Tribes as Models for Expanding First Nations Self-Government." *Review of Consitutional Studies* (1993): 120–21.

Getches, David, Charles Wilkinson, and Robert Williams, Jr. *Federal Indian Law*. 4th ed. St. Paul, Minn.: West Publishing, 1998.

Gibb, Dennis. "Intergovernmental Compacts in Native American Law: Models for Expanded Usage." *Harvard Law Review* 112 (1999): 922–39.

Government of the Netherlands. *Petition to the League of Nations from the Six Nations of the Grand River*. C.500, VII. August 7, 1923.

Greve, Michael S. *Real Federalism: Why It Matters, How It Could Happen*. Washington, D.C.: AEI Press, 1999.

Grogan, Susan E. "Justice Paradigms and Practice: The Piegan Nation Sentencing Circle." *Legal Studies Forum* 23, nos. 1 and 2 (1999): 155–75.

Gross, Emma. *Contemporary Federal Policy toward American Indians*. New York: Greenwood Press, 1989.

Hall, Anthony. *The American Empire and the Fourth World: The Bowl with One Spoon, Part One*. Kingston, Ont.: McGill-Queen's University Press, 2003.

Harjo, Suzan Shown. "Chief Offenders." *Native Peoples* (Summer 1999): 34–37.

Hechter, Michael. "Internal Colonialism Revisited." In *New Nationalisms in the Developed West*, ed. Edward A. Tiryakian and Ronald Rogowski, 18–26. Boston: Allen and Unwin, 1985.

Hechter, Michael, and Margaret Levi. "Ethno-Regional Movements in the West." In *Nationalism*, ed. John Hutchinson and Anthony D. Smith, 184–95. New York: Oxford University Press, 1994.

Henson, Eric, and Jonathan B. Taylor. "Native America at the New Millennium." The Harvard Project on American Indian Economic Development,

2002. *http://www.ksg.harvard.edu/hpaied/pubs/pub_004.htm* (accessed August 30, 2004).

Hicks, Sarah, and John Dossett. "Principled Devolution: Protecting Tribal Self-Determination in an Era of Growing State Power." NCAI Working Paper, September 19, 2000. *http://www.legis.state.wi.us/lc/committees/study/ STR/files/feb_conf_devolution.pdf* (accessed August 30, 2004).

Holm, Tom. "Indian Lobbyists: Cherokee Opposition to the Allotment of Tribal Lands." *American Indian Quarterly* 5, no. 2 (1979): 115–34.

Holm, Tom, J. Diane Pearson, and Ben Chavis. "Peoplehood: A Model for American Indian Sovereignty in Education." *Wicazo Sa Review* 18, no. 1 (Spring 2003): 7–24.

Indians.org. "American Indian Resource Directory." *http://www.indians.org/ Resource/FedTribes99/fedtribes99.html* (accessed February 1, 2006).

Johansen, Bruce E. "The New Terminators: The Anti-Indian Movement Resurfaces." *Native Americas* 17, no. 3 (2000): 43–53.

Johnson, Lyndon B. "Special Message to the Congress on the Problems on the American Indian: The Forgotten American." *The American Presidency Project*, March 6, 1968. *http://www.presidency.ucsb.edu/ws/index. php?pid=28709&st=Indian&st1* (accessed July 1, 2005).

Johnson, Troy R., Joane Nagel, and Duane Champagne. *American Indian Activism: Alcatraz to the Longest Walk*. Urbana: University of Illinois Press, 1997.

Jones, Dorothy V. "British Colonial Indian Treaties." In *Handbook of North American Indians: Volume 4, History of Indian-White Relations*, ed. William C. Sturtevant and Wilcomb E. Washburn, 185–94. Washington, D.C.: Smithsonian Institution, 1988.

———. *License for Empire*. Chicago: University of Chicago Press, 1982.

King, C. Richard, and Charles Fruehling Springwood. *Team Spirits: The Native American Mascots Controversy*. Lincoln: University of Nebraska Press, 2001.

Lacy, Michael G. "The United States and American Indians: Political Relations." In *American Indian Policy in the Twentieth Century*, ed. Vine Deloria, Jr., 83–104. Norman: University of Oklahoma Press, 1985.

LaVelle, John P. "Strengthening Tribal Sovereignty through Indian Participation in American Politics: A Reply to Professor Porter." *The Kansas Journal of Law and Public Policy* 10, no. 3 (2001): 533–80.

Library of Congress. "Historical Caricature of the Cherokee Nation." 1886. *http://hdl.loc.gov/loc.pnp/cph.3b36104* (accessed September 1, 2004).

Lindsay, Barbara. "Who We Are." One Nation United. *http://www.onenationok. com/index.php?menu=1* (accessed August 27, 2004).

Little Bear, Leroy. "Should Natives Vote?" Roundtable discussion at Aboriginal Awareness Week, University of Victoria, Victoria, British Columbia, February 23, 2005.

Lombardi, Michael. "Long Road Traveled I, II, and III." Nations Indian Gaming Association. *http://www.cniga.com/facts/History_of_CA_Gaming _Part_2.pdf* (accessed December 17, 2000).

Mason, W. Dale. *Indian Gaming: Tribal Sovereignty and American Politics.* Norman: University of Oklahoma Press, 2000.

Matthiessen, Peter. *In the Spirit of Crazy Horse.* New York: Viking, 1991.

McCool, Daniel. "Indian Voting." In *American Indian Policy in the Twentieth Century,* ed. Vine Deloria, Jr., 105–33. Norman: University of Oklahoma Press, 1985.

———. *Native Waters: Contemporary Indian Water Settlements and the Second Treaty Era.* Tucson: University of Arizona Press, 2002.

———. "Voting Patterns of American Indians in Arizona." *The Social Science Journal* 19, no. 3 (1982): 101–13.

McCulloch, Anne Merline. "The Politics of Indian Gaming: Tribe/State Relations and American Federalism." *Publius: The Journal of Federalism* 24, no. 3 (Summer 1994): 99–112.

Michel, Karen Lincoln. "Fielding New Clout: Indian Power and Party Politics." *Native Americas* 15, no. 3 (1998): 3–21.

Nabakov, Peter. *Native American Testimony: A Chronicle of Indian-White Relations from Prophecy to the Present, 1492–1992.* New York: Penguin, 1992.

Nadasdy, Paul. "Transcending the Debate over the Ecologically Noble Indian: Indigenous Peoples and Environmentalism." *Ethnohistory* 52, no. 2 (2005): 291–331.

Nagel, Joane. *American Indian Ethnic Renewal: Red Power and the Resurgence of Identity and Culture.* New York: Oxford University Press, 1996.

Nast, Thomas. "Give the Natives a Chance, Mr. Carl: The Cheapest and Quickest Way of Civilizing Them." *Harpers Weekly* 24, no. 1211 (March 13, 1880): 173.

National Governor's Association. *Policy Positions.* Washington, D.C.: Hall of States, 1987–2000.

Niezen, Ronald. *The Origins of Indigenism.* Berkeley: University of California Press, 2003.

Nixon, Richard. "President Nixon: Special Message on Indian Affairs." *Public Papers of the President of the United States.* Office of the Federal Register, July 8, 1970, 566.

O'Brien, Sharon. *American Indian Tribal Governments.* Norman: University of Oklahoma Press, 1989.

Pawlenty, Tim. "The State of the State Address." January 18, 2005. *http:// www.governor.state.mn.us/documents/2005StateoftheState.pdf* (accessed February 28, 2006).

Peterson, Geoff. "Native American Turnout in the 1990 and 1992 Elections." *American Indian Quarterly* 21, no. 2 (1997): 321–31.

Peterson, Helen. "American Indian Political Participation." *Annals of the Academy of Political and Social Science* 31 (1957): 116–26.

Pewewardy, Cornel. "The Deculturalization of Indigenous Mascots in U.S. Sports Culture." *The Educational Forum* 63 (1999): 342–47.

Pommersheim, Frank. "Tribal-State Relations: Hope for the Future?" *South Dakota Law Review* 36 (1991): 268–70.

Porter, Robert B. "The Demise of the Ongwehoweh and the Rise of the Native Americans: Redressing the Genocidal Act of Forcing American Citizenship upon Indigenous Peoples." *Harvard Black Letter Law Journal* 15 (1999): 108–83.

———. "Strengthening Tribal Sovereignty through Peacemaking: How the Anglo-American Legal Tradition Destroys Indigenous Societies." *Red Ink* 5, no. 2 (1997): 54–60.

Prucha, Francis. *The Great Father: The United States Government and the American Indians.* Lincoln: University of Nebraska Press, 1984.

Reagan, Ronald. "American Indian Policy." *Public Papers of the President of the United States.* Office of the Federal Register, January 24, 1983, *http://www.reagan.utexas.edu/resource/speeches/1983/12483b.htm* (accessed September 1, 2004).

Ritt, Leonard G. "Some Social and Political Views of American Indians." *Ethnicity* 6 (1979): 45–72.

Ross, Rupert. *Returning to the Teachings: Exploring Aboriginal Justice.* Toronto: Penguin Books, 1996.

Ryan, Kevin. "Municipal and State Impact of Gaming." *New England Law Review* 38 (April 25, 2003): 553–57.

Schneider, Anne, and Helen Ingram. *Policy Design for Democracy.* Lawrence: University Press of Kansas, 1997.

———. "Social Constructions of Target Populations: Implications for Politics and Policy." *American Political Science Review* 87, no. 2 (1993): 334–46.

Shaw, Malcolm N. *International Law.* 4th ed. Cambridge: Cambridge University Press, 1997.

The Simpsons. "Missionary: Impossible," episode 241, first aired February 20, 2000 by Fox. Directed by Steven Dean Moore and written by Ron Hauge.

Smith, Andrea. *Conquest: Sexual Violence and American Indian Genocide.* Boston: South End Press, 2005.

Snipp, C. Matthew. *American Indians: The First of This Land.* New York: Russell Sage Foundation, 1989.

Spilde, Katherine Ann. "Acts of Sovereignty, Acts of Identity: Negotiating Interdependence through Tribal Government Gaming on the White Earth Indian Reservation." PhD diss. University of California, Santa Cruz, 1998.

———. "Rich Indian Racism: Direct Attack on Tribal Sovereignty." *Hocak Worak: A Publication of the Ho-Chunk Nation.* (1999): 5.

State of Maine Government Homepage (November 4, 2003). "Referendum Election Tabulations." 4 November 2003, <*www.Maine.gov/sos/cec/elec/ 2003n/gen03.sum.htm*> (30 August 2003).

Steiner, Stan. *The New Indians.* New York: Dell Publishing Co., Inc., 1968.

Steinman, Erich. "American Federalism and Intergovernmental Innovation in State-Tribal Relations." *Publius: The Journal of Federalism* 34, no. 2 (2004): 95–115.

Stern, K. S. *Loud Hawk: The United States versus the American Indian Movement.* Norman: University of Oklahoma Press, 1994.

Swift, Jonathan. *Gulliver's Travels and Other Works.* London: George Routledge and Sons, 1906.

Taliman, Valerie. "Native Nations and the Politics of 2000: Platforms for Indian Country." *Native Americas* 17, no. 3 (2000): 10–17.

Tarrow, Sidney. *Power in Movement: Social Movements and Contentious Politics.* 2nd ed. Cambridge: Cambridge University Press, 1998.

Taylor, Theodore. *The States and Their Indian Citizens.* Washington, D.C.: U.S. Department of the Interior, 1971.

Tebben, Carol. "An American Trifederalism Based upon the Constitutional Status of Tribal Nations." *Journal of Constitutional Law* 5, no. 2 (2003): 318–56.

Thomas, Robert K. "The Tap-Roots of Peoplehood." In *Getting to the Heart of the Matter: Collected Letters and Papers,* ed. Daphne J. Anderson, 25–32. Vancouver: Native Ministries Consortium, 1990.

"Tribes and States." *Honor Digest* (October/November 1999): 2.

Trosper, Ron. "Traditional American Indian Economic Policy." In *Contemporary Native American Political Issues,* ed. Troy R. Johnson, 135–62. Walnut Creek, Calif.: Altamira Press, 2000.

Tsosie, Rebecca. "Negotiating Economic Survival: The Consent Principal and Tribal-State Compacts under the Indian Gaming Regulatory Act." *Arizona State Law Journal* 29 (Spring 1997): 25–96.

Tully, James. "The Struggles of Indigenous Peoples for and of Freedom." In *Political Theory and the Rights of Indigenous Peoples,* ed. Duncan Ivison, Paul Patton, and Will Sanders, 36–59. Cambridge: Cambridge University Press, 2000.

United Nations Commission on Human Rights. *Study on Treaties, Agreements, and Other Constructive Arrangements between States and Indigenous Populations: Final Report by Miguel Alfonso Martinez, Special Rapporteur.* E/CN. 4/Sub.2/1999/20, 1999.

University of Arizona. *Indians and Arizona's Future.* Tucson: Arizona Academy, 1979.

U.S. Bureau of the Census. "American Indian Population by County." Population Estimates Program, Population Division, 2000. *http://www.census.*

gov/population/estimates/county/rank/aiea-r.txt (accessed December 12, 2000)

———. "Selected Social and Economic Characteristics for the 25 Largest American Indian Tribes: 1990." August 1995. *http://www.census.gov/population/socdemo/race/indian/ailang2.txt* (accessed February 1, 2005).

U.S. Congress. Senate. Select Committee on Indian Affairs. *Proposed Changes to the Indian Gaming Regulatory Act: Hearings of the Committee on Indian Affairs.* 102nd Cong., March 18, 1992.

U.S. Department of the Interior. Bureau of Indian Affairs. "Tribal-State Compact List." http://govinfo.library.unt.edu/ngisc/reports/a8.pdf (accessed January 1, 2001).

U.S. General Accounting Office. *Indian Issues: Improvements Needed in Tribal Recognition Process* (November 2001): 32–34.

Van Dervort, Thomas R. *International Law and Organization.* 4th ed. Thousand Oaks: Sage Publications, 1997.

Viola, Herman J. *Diplomats in Buckskins.* South Carolina: Rivilo Books, 1995.

Washburn, Wilcomb. *The American Indian and the United States: A Documentary History.* NY: Random House, 1973.

Weston, Mary Ann. *Native Americans in the News: Images of Indians in the Twentieth Century Press.* Westport: Greenwood Press, 1996.

Wilkins, David E. *American Indian Politics and the American Political System.* Lanham, Md.: Rowman and Littlefield, 2002.

———. *American Indian Sovereignty and the U.S. Supreme Court: The Masking of Justice.* Austin: University of Texas Press, 1997.

———. "An Inquiry into Indigenous Political Participation: Implications for Tribal Sovereignty." *The Kansas Journal of Law and Public Policy* 9, no. 4 (2000): 732–51.

———. "Modernization, Colonialism, Dependency: How Appropriate Are These Models for Providing an Explanation of North American Indian 'Underdevelopment'?" *Ethnic and Racial Studies* 16, no. 3 (1993): 390–419.

———. "Reconsidering the Tribal-State Compact Process." *Policy Studies Journal* 22, no. 3 (1994): 474–88.

———. "Tribal-State Affairs: American States as Disclaiming Sovereigns." *Publius* 28, no. 4 (1998): 55–81.

———. "The U.S. Supreme Court's Explication of 'Federal Plenary Power.'" *American Indian Quarterly* 18, no. 3 (1994): 349–68.

Wilkins, David E., and K. Tsianina Lomawaima. *Uneven Ground: American Indian Sovereignty and Federal Law.* Norman: University of Oklahoma Press, 2001.

Wilkinson, Charles F. *American Indians, Time, and the Law: Native Societies in a Modern Constitutional Democracy.* New Haven: Yale University Press, 1987.

Williams, Robert A., Jr. *The American Indian in Western Legal Thought.* New York: Oxford University Press, 1990.

————. "Documents of Barbarism: The Contemporary Legacy of European Racism and Colonialism in the Narrative Traditions of Federal Indian Law." *Arizona Law Review* 31 (1989): 237–78.

————. *Linking Arms Together: American Indian Treaty Visions of Law and Peace, 1600-1800.* Oxford University Press, 1997.

Index

CPSIA information can be obtained at www.ICGtesting.com
Printed in the USA
LVOW08s2205031115

461022LV00001B/137/P